ISLAMIC VALUES AND WORLD VIEW

Khomeyni on Man, the State and International Politics, Volume XIII

Farhang Rajaee

With a Preface by

Kenneth W. Thompson

UNIVERSITY PRESS OF AMERICA

LANHAM • NEW YORK • LONDON

4720 Boston Way
Lanham, MD 20706

3 Henrietta Street
London WC2E 8LU England

Printed in the United States of America

Library of Congress Cataloging in Publication Data

Rajaee, Farhang, 1952–
Islamic values and world view.

(American values projected abroad ; v. 13)
Bibliography: p.
1. Khomeini, Ruholla. 2. Muslims–Iran –
Biography. 3. Shì ah–Iran. I. Title. II. Series.
JX1417.A74 1982 vol. 13 303.4'8273s 83–19832
[BP80.K494] [320.5'5]
ISBN 0–8191–3578–X (alk. paper)
ISBN 0–8191–3579–8 (pbk. : alk. paper)

All University Press of America books are produced on acid-free paper which exceeds the minimum standards set by the National Historical Publications and Records Commission.

Rosalind Gwynne
Charlottesville, 1986

AMERICAN VALUES PROJECTED ABROAD

A SERIES FUNDED BY THE EXXON EDUCATION FOUNDATION

FOUNDATIONS OF AMERICAN VALUES

Vol. I Western Heritage and American Values: Law, Theology and History
By Alberto Coll
Vol. II Political Traditions and Contemporary Problems
Edited by Kenneth W. Thompson
Vol. III Institutions for Projecting American Values Abroad
Edited by Kenneth W. Thompson
Vol. IV Essays on Lincoln's Faith and Politics
By Hans J. Morgenthau and David Hein
Vol. V The Predicament of Human Rights: The Carter and Reagan Policies
By Nicolai N. Petro
Vol. VI Writing History and Making Policy: The Cold War, Vietnam, and Revisionism
By Richard A. Melanson
Vol. VII American Diplomatic Traditions and Values: The Founders
Edited by Norman Graebner
Vol. VIII American Diplomatic Traditions and Values: 1840-1940
Edited by Norman Graebner
Vol. IX American Diplomatic Traditions and Values: The Post War Era
Edited by Kenneth W. Thompson

AMERICAN VALUES VIEWED THROUGH OTHER CULTURES

Vol. X The Elements of International Strategy: A Primer for the Nuclear Age
By Louis J. Halle
Vol. XI Nationalism and Internationalism: European and American Perspectives
By Erich Hula
Vol. XII The Search for Values in Diplomacy: The Life and Works of Stephen Kertesz in Europe and America
Edited by Kenneth W. Thompson
Vol. XIII Islamic Values and World View: Khomeyni on Man, the State and International Politics
By Farhang Rajaee
Vol. XIV African and American Values: Liberia and West Africa
By Katherine Harris

CONTENTS

ACKNOWLEDGMENTS

Without the unceasing encouragement and constructive criticism of Kenneth W. Thompson, this volume would not have been possible. I am indebted to a number of my colleagues and friends who read the draft of this book and made useful comments for its improvement. Professors Muhammad R. Ghanoonparvar, William Millward, Richard Barnett and Mr. David Clinton read the whole manuscript and gave me valuable suggestions. Professors R. K. Ramazani and Abdulaziz Sachedina and Messrs. Faraj Saghri, Joseph Devaney and Brian Klunk kindly read the manuscript or its various chapters when it was being written as a dissertation and made suggestions. Numerous other friends and colleagues in Iran and in the United States gave me helpful advices during various stages in the project. My father in Iran acted as research assistant "in the field" for me. Mrs. Margaret M. O'Bryant, Miss V. Irene Norvelle and Mr. Martin Davis from Alderman Library provided generous assistance. Mrs. Shirley Kingsbury of the White Burkett Miller Center for Public Affairs provided much needed assistance with typing. The author's work was facilitated by grants from the White Burkett Miller Center at the University of Virginia and the Institute for the Study of World Politics in New York.

On the System of Transliteration, Dates, etc.

For the sake of precision, Arabic and Persian words have been transliterated according to two different systems. The Arabic words are transliterated according to the system used by the Library of Congress (see Cataloging Service, Bulletin 118/summer 1976). Arabic definite article (*al*) has been preserved before all words even those which begin with a sun letter, hence Jamal al-Din instead of Jamal ad-Din.

Persian words are transliterated according to the system developed by Nasser Sharify (see Nasser Sharify. *Cataloging of Persian Works*. Chicago: American Library Association, 1959).

All the dates throughout the text have been given only according to the Christian calendar. The notes and the bibliography, however, give both the Islamic and the Christian calendar dates for those sources which have been published in Persian or Arabic languages. If the year of the publication of the book is in Islamic lunar calendar it has been marked by a capital Q.

Translation of the Qur'ānic verses are from Marmaduke Pickthall *The Glorious Koran* (Albany: State University of New York Press, 1976) unless otherwise indicated.

A few words should be said about Ayat-Allah Khomeyni's titles. Since his return to Iran from exile, Khomeyni has been given many titles: *Ayat-Allāh al-'Oẓmā'* (the grand Ayat-Allah); Imām; *Na'eb al-Imām* (the deputy of the Imam); *Rahbar 'aẓīm al-sha'n* (the high statured leader); *Rahbar Enqelāb* (the leader of the Revolution); *za'īm al-shī'a* (the leader of Shī'ism); and etc. He is more known, however, as Imam Khomeyni.

Since the title Imām within the Shī'ī thought is used exclusively for the twelve infallibles (see chapter II), to avoid confusion in the discussion, this title is not being used. For simplicity either only the general title Ayat-Allah has been used or none at all.

PREFACE

The highly respected American theologian and political philosopher, Reinhold Niebuhr, having presented his own views on morality and politics, characteristically turned to an audience of students and scholars from other countries and cultures and asked: "Is there any relationship between what I have said and the prevailing concepts and ideas in your lands?" In contrast with some western thinkers, Niebuhr was conscious of the rich diversity of political ideas and practices around the world even as he sought to discover certain universals. He was as prepared to learn as he was to teach and he knew that values were related to the culture and societies of which they were a part.

Dr. Farhang Rajaee in his remarkable study of Islamic values has answered the challenge Professor Niebuhr laid down. He has traced with consummate analytical skill and profound scholarship the origins and development of Khomeyni's worldview of man, the state and international politics. It would be difficult to match the clarity of thought, depth of scholarship and intellectual power of his study. What is demonstrated is that Khomeyni's ideas are not readily understood through simply imposing on them the framework of western or American thinkers. It is essential to go to the heart of the religious and political views of Khomeyni and this is Rajaee's lasting contribution.

Farhang Rajaee is possessed of that rarest of all scholarly qualities: philosophical imagination. In what must be seen as a landmark study of the religion and politics of an Islamic leader, Dr. Rajaee has helped us to see what we had only dimly perceived in the West. He has helped us understand the leader of the Iranian Revolution. But his study has a far wider and more universal value. With unique restraint, Rajaee brings his readers into touch with an important body of thought otherwise denied them. Dr. Rajaee's volume is likely to remain for years to come the classic study of Khomeyni's thought and it also provides an open door to the understanding of Islamic values. Without that understanding, it is impossible for Americans in particular to foresee the patterns of relations and interactions between their values and those of another great world culture.

Kenneth W. Thompson

CHAPTER I
PRELIMINARY DISCUSSION AND INTRODUCTION

The disagreements that occur between the visionary and the scholar are caused by their failure to understand each other's language, for each has his own distinctive way of expressing things. . . . The philosophers, for example, have their own language and terminology: so do the mystics, the theologian jurisconsults, and even the poets.

Ayat-Allah Khomeyni

The Qur'ān assures the Muslims that they "are the best community that hath been raised up for mankind." (III:110). From the dawn of Islam, Muslims have differed as to what the "best community" should be comprised of and what it should be like; no one ideal has ever prevailed among Muslims. However, the hope that such a community will be realized has continuously persisted among Muslims. They have periodically renewed this hope and endeavored to live holy lives, both as individuals and as a community. One of the most recent manifestations of this vision is associated with Ayat-Allah Khomeyni whose effort to draw up a political program for Muslims in the twentieth century has baffled many people.

His emergence as the leader of the revolution in Iran (1977–79) and subsequently as the most powerful man in post-revolutionary Iran made Ayat-Allah Khomeyni a significant international figure but little has been written concerning his general world view or his political values and moral vision, which have influenced the formation of the domestic and foreign policies of the new Iran.[1] Ayat-Allah Khomeyni's concept of guardianship of the theologian jurisconsult (*Velāyat-e Faqīh*) has become the foundation stone for the structure of the Islamic Republic of Iran.[2] His motto, "Neither the East nor the West," a Qur'anic phrase, (XXIV:35), has become the basis for the foreign policy of the Islamic Republic.

Yet these ideas represent only parts of Khomeyni's complicated *weltanschauung*. This inquiry is intended to provide a systematic treatment of that world view, its origins and background. What sets this work apart from others which have been written on Khomeyni is that it treats his work in their totality. Since the early days of the revolution, most works on Khomeyni are either strongly weighted on the side of praising or condemning him, or are otherwise factually distorted. Generally speaking, studies of Khomeyni have concentrated on an analysis of the Ayat-Allah himself, either portraying him as a holy man or as a power-hungry despot.

Princeton's professor of international law, Richard Falk, for example, while observing that the difficulty of dealing with the new Iran is that unfamiliarity and ignorance dominate the world's understanding of Khomeyni, regards him as a trustworthy person and a hope for the future.

> . . . [T]he depiction of him as fanatical, reactionary and the bearer of crude prejudices seems certainly and happily false. . . . Iran may yet provide us with a desperately-needed model of humane governance for a third-world country.[3]

Interestingly, Falk's understanding of Khomeyni arises not from his understanding of the Ayat-Allah's philosophy but from his familiarity with the Ayat-Allah's entourage:

> One of Washington's problems in formulating a position toward Khomeyni's movement may be its relative ignorance of the Ayatollah's philosophy of Shi'ite Moslem doctrine generally. . . . The entourage around Khomeyni, in fact, has had considerable involvement in human rights activities and is committed to a struggle against all forms of oppression.[4]

Ironically, a member of the same entourage to which Professor Falk refers for this analysis recently described Khomeyni as a despot saying that "Khomeyni is as much a Muslim as Jim Jones was a Christian."[5]

Rubin Carlesen, a Canadian author who has written extensively on the revolution in Iran, claims that the purpose of his visit with Khomeyni in Tehran was "to scrutinize" him and evaluate the Ayat-Allah for himself. He presents another romanticized portrait of Khomeyni.

> He was a flowing mass of light that penetrated into the consciousness of each person in the hall. . . . Imam Khomeini was . . . that singular reality which could expand my consciousness, purify my heart, clarify my brain, and leave in his wake the sense of an undiminishable grace. . . .[6]

Certainly it is very important to determine a person's moral character; but that in itself does not reveal much about the person as a political thinker and expecially as a political leader. The perception of "goodness" in a leader is often too highly subjective and it emphasizes his presumed intention rather than the complexity of his ideas or the consequences of his actions.

Of course, there are others who voice viewpoints at opposite extreme on the spectrum. In this category, the most comprehensive depiction of Khomeyni is that of the psychopolitics interpreter, Bruce Mazlish, in his analysis of "The Hidden Khomeini."[7] Mazlish begins his argument with an attack: "This Ayatollah who denies any ambition hides a man—a revolutionary ascetic with grandiose traits that would tempt a clinician to label him a classic narcissist."[8] He then proceeds to assemble all the pertinent evidence in support of this thesis. Following a rather distorted presentation of the political history of the past half-century in Iran, and a romanticized, at times even erroneous version of Khomeyni's life, Mazlish concludes that Khomeyni:

> . . . alternates between a sense of himself as a grandiose and [a] humiliated figure. On one side, we have the Khomeini who shares in the total perfection of Islam. . . . On the other side, we have the Khomeini who feels inferior to a West that can put a man on the moon. . . . These traits—the alternating but overlapping senses of grandiosity and humiliation—fit the classic definition of a narcissistic personality.[9]

By far the most distorted picture of Khomeyni is that put forward by *Time* magazine in its presentation of him as 1980 "Man of the Year." Endorsing the experts' simplified characterization of Khomeyni as "arrogant and pious, stubborn and vengeful, humorless and inflexible and ascetic and power-hungry," the article concludes:

> But from discussions with former students, talks with Western scholars who have visited Khomeini, profiles prepared by Western intelligence analysts, and the speeches and interviews he has given during the years on the world stage, it is possible to gain some insight into the Ayatollah's thinking. First and foremost, all sources agree, he is an Islamic mystic who believes that God tells him directly how to apply the principles of the Koran and the Shari'a (Islamic law) to life and politics.[10]

It is true that Ayat-Allah Khomeyni is preoccupied with mysticism, but it is false to suggest that he claims to have any direct contact with God. Such a claim, according to Khomeyni himself, would constitute blasphemy. Only those individuals who have "cosmic guardianship" (*velāyat-e takvīnī*), Khomeyni says, can claim to have direct connection with God.[11] That viceregency is reserved only for the Prophet and the Imams.

Neither the "holy man" nor "narcissist-mystic" images will help us to understand Khomeyni's political ideas. The problem lies in the fact that few writers treat him as a political thinker. Those who do have so far failed to undertake a systematic study of the major aspects of his political thought. Some have concentrated mainly on one issue—namely his anti-monarchical view—while others have only concentrated on one of his works.[12]

This treatise attempts a systematic overall textual examination of all of Ayat-Allah Khomeyni's works whether directly related to politics or not. The object of this method is to ascertain the deliberate intention of this important Muslim thinker rather than seeking an explanation of his works as the product of his psychological or the social conditions under which he worked. Thus, this study concentrates on what Khomeyni says and what he means by what he says, viewed in the context of his overall philosophy. This has meant a close examination not only of his numerous sermons, messages decrees, declarations, and pronouncements, but also of his books on theology, morality, Qur'ānic exegesis, and Islamic government. Although most of Khomeyni's work appears to deal with religious issues and not directly with political ideas, this is no reason to overlook the religious writings. Politics in Islam is not an independent field of inquiry, separated from religious matters; religion is considered to embrace all aspects of life—the political realm included. Khomeyni's thoughts on theology, philosophy and mysticism are all of interest in this study insofar as they bear directly upon the explication of his world view.

The approach taken here is to try to look at Khomeyni's views as he sees them himself. "The philosophers, for example," writes Khomeyni, "have their own language and terminology; so do the mystics. The theologian jurisconsults and even the poets."[13] Therefore this author has tried to begin with those crucial questions and issues on which Khomeyni's vision centers and also with the images, metaphors and language that he employs. To state it differently, this author has tried to describe and analyze Khomeyni's political vision in his own terms. The attempt has been to make this inquiry an interior analysis of that vision without losing sight of objectivity in the process.

Ayat-Allah Khomeyni's major concern seems to be the creation of "the good man." Unlike the Muslim philosophers and mystics, who see this process as basically a personal and individual one, Khomeyni thinks the training of "the good man" is possible through the establishment of a political society ruled by the *faqīh* (pl. *fuqahā*). This belief gives meaning and significance to Khomeyni's total vision. To unravel the complexity of this vision the following question will be addressed throughout this study. How does Khomeyni view man? Why does he think the creation of the good men is possible and how? How does he define politics, government and the state? What makes his approach to these pertinent issues so special which in his view results in the formation of the virtuous polity?

Khomeyni's "good man" and his "virtuous" polity has to deal with the rest of humanity, who may not yet have been converted. Thus another question is how does Khomeyni's political society deal with other parts of the world, that is, what are his views on international relations? If his view differs from the existing approach to international politics how does he deal with it? Does he intend to transform it and how? What are his views on such pertinent issues as war and peace?

To treat these questions, the present volume has been organized in the following manner. Chapter two, "From the Imām to the Faqīh," sketches the evolution of political thought in Shī'ī Islam as expounded by the major Shī'ī thinkers. The chapter attempts to show that, while Khomeyni's political ideas reaffirms the basic tenets of Islamic political thought in particular Shī'ī political theory, they also modify it by insisting on the rule of the *faqīh* as the ideal rule. Considering that Khomeyni is a *faqīh*, the development of Shī'ī political thought will be examined in the works of important *fuqahā*. The discussion concentrates on those aspects of Shī'ī political thought which concern the power of the *fuqahā* in their role as leaders of the community and acting sovereigns. The central thrust of Khomeyni's doctrine rests on the notion of the guardianship of the *faqīh*. The chapter describes the main foundations of this doctrine in Khomeyni's thought, the roots of which go back to (a) the Shī'ī view of authority, in particular, the theory of *Imāmate* in the early history of Islam and (b) to the dispute between the *Usūlī* and *Akhbārī* approach to jurisprudence in the eighteenth century. The *Usūlī* leaders, who believed in the importance of independent reasoning (*ijtihād*) in legal ruling, achieved ascendancy over the *Akhbārīs*, who emphasized literal implementation of and close conformity to the Prophet's and the Imams' words and deeds. Although the dispute concentrated on juridical issues, it had far-reaching political implications. The victory of the *Usūlī* view over that of the *Akhbārī* granted a greater prerogative to the Shī'ī *'ulamā*. Later, the evolution of the *'ulamā's* power attained momentum both in theory and in practice. Some *fuqahā* elaborated on the notion that the *'ulamā* are the rightful heirs of the Prophet and the Imams, therfore maintaining that they are the persons qualified to manage the affairs of the Muslims. Others, who were politically opposed to the central government of that time due to the injustices it committed, generated more respect and honor for the *'ulamā*.

Although the *'ulamā* suffered great political setbacks during the reign of the Pahlavis, Ayat-Allah Khomeyni revitalized the *Usūlī* view and, indeed, carried it one step further: the *'ulamā*, Khomeyni maintains, are the legitimate acting sovereigns in the absence of the Imam. He has put this theory into practice insofar as he has strengthened the role of the

Shī'ī *'ulamā* in politics, and insofar as he has become the most active protagonist in the political process in Iran.

Chapter three presents a brief biography of Ayat-Allah Khomeyni. The discussion mainly focuses on Khomeyni's educational background, in order to show the lasting effect the subject areas to which he was exposed have had on his outlook. Ethics, for example, was his favorite topic both as a student and a teacher. The discussion also points out the important social and political events in which Khomeyni participated.

Having introduced Khomeyni, both by locating his ideas within the context of Shī'ī Islamic thought and by giving a biographical account of his development as a thinker, the study will proceed in chapter four to present Khomeyni's view of the nature of man and his purpose on earth. Certainly one's view of the nature of man inevitably influences one's wider outlook on life. Such is even more the case with Khomeyni, in whose world view the main actors are man and God. As a Shī'a and a student of Sufism and gnosticism (*'erfān*), Ayat-Allah Khomeyni seems to have a paradoxical view of man. On the one hand, he sees man as a beast whose desires, pride, anger and lust know no limits, and on the other hand, he believes that man is essentially good and hence can be educated to piety and goodness. Indeed, Khomeyni's political philosophy is colored by this latter optimistic belief in man's goodness. It is man's prime purpose in life, Khomeyni maintains, to elevate himself to the highest possible spiritual stature. Man can achieve this through his personal efforts and with a helping hand which will guide and direct him along "the right path." This helping hand is provided for man by Islam, whose perfect and final universal program regulates every aspect of human mundane and spiritual conduct on earth.

Chapter five shows how this universal program is realized according to Khomeyni. It examines Khomeyni's views of politics, government and the state. According to him, politics in general means "managing the affairs of the country."[14] Since for Khomeyni the affairs of the country should be regulated by the *Sharī'a*, "politics" becomes synonymous with "implementing the laws of Islam." Hence, politics means individual conformity to the principles of the law, and the collective implementation of that law. Likewise, his views of government and state proceed directly from the *Sharī'a*. Two conclusions can be drawn from this fact. First, government and state are seen, in the final analysis, as the means by which the *Sharī'a* is implemented, and, by the same token, geographical territory is seen as the domain over which the *Sharī'a* rules. Second since the *Sharī'a* is considered a universal guide for humanity regardless of time and place, any reference to the merits of specific political regimes is deemed redundant, as long as the *Sharī'a* is being implemented in the community. All that is important is the presence of someone to ensure the proper implementation of the law. It is through this line of reasoning that the concept of the guardianship of the *faqīh* has become the keystone of Khomeyni's political theory.

Khomeyni's view of the state, which is also directly related to the *Sharī'a*, is completely different from the Western view. The Western concept of territorial state runs contrary to the basic tenets of Islamic society (better known as the *Umma*). The *Umma* is a society based on a shared ideology (i.e., the divine scheme) whereas the territorial state is based on temporal elements such as shared memory, language, race, or the mere choice of its members. Khomeyni dismisses the notion of territorial state and nationalism as the product of Western imperialism. He believes that the West has damaged the solidarity of the Muslim people by promoting divisive nationalism in the Muslim world. Nationalism and statism, for Khomeyni, are, in fact, obstacles to the advancement of Islam. In short, politics and government are simply the means by which the *faqīh* ensures the implementation of the *Sharī'a*, and the state is reduced to his base of operation.

Chapter six explores Khomeyni's view of international relations. Khomeyni's understanding of the relation between his own political society and other parts of the world is colored by the classical Islamic perspective according to which the world is divided into the spheres: the *Dār al-Islām*, the abode of Islam, and the *Dār al-Ḥarb*, the abode of the enemies of Islam. Khomeyni follows the same tradition but uses different terms; he speaks of the *Mostaẕ'afān* and the *Mostakbarān*, Qur'ānic words which translate as "the oppressed" and "the oppressors," respectively.[15] These two concepts, nevertheless, are broader in his usage than those used in the classical period. Khomeyni's concepts can be used to explain the relationship between two individuals, the interactions between segments of a society, or the relations between and among states. At the international level, *Mostakbarān* is used to signify the two superpowers of East and West. So long as the "oppressed" people have not prevailed in the world, the proper course of action, in Khomeyni's mind, is a policy of "neither East nor West," and following their victory, the proper policy is to implement the Islamic laws.

Like Jamal al-Din al-Afghani (1833–1889), who is considered the father of Pan-Islamism, Khomeyni hopes to promote a unified community of Muslims. There is, however, a significant difference between the two men's goals. Whereas Afghani desired political cooperation among various Islamic countries, Khomeyni strives for the complete political, ideological and cultural unity of Muslims. He seems to call for the establishment of an Islamic form of government, preferably modeled after the Islamic Republic of Iran, in each of these countries. The sixth chapter demonstrates that Ayat-Allah Khomeyni ultimately hopes for the formation of an Islamic world government which will include all the peoples of the world.

The final chapter synthesizes the concepts of Khomeyni as thinker and Khomeyni as leader. As a thinker he has shown remarkable consistency in his works throughout his public career. He has always believed that a good man can only be produced through the implementation of the Islamic law and the realization of what he conceives to be the true Islamic government. As a political leader, since the triumph of the revolutionary forces, Khomeyni has persistently worked toward realizing his theory of the guardianship of the *faqīh*. The final chapter, therefore, attempts to show how Khomeyni the leader has implemented the political ideas of Khomeyni the thinker. This chapter examines how Khomeyni the leader proved to be uncompromising when it came to the implementation of his fundamental beliefs. His concern has proved to be basically with political principles and not with political consequences.

To sum up, Khomeyni belongs to the juridical trend of Shīʿī political thought, which maintains that the proper political order is one in which Islamic law rules. Khomeyni, personally, thinks this is possible only with the establishment of the rule of the *faqīh*. This belief is treated in chapters 4, 5 and 6. Before that, it is necessary to study briefly the development of the Shīʿī juridical trend, as represented in the thought of major Shīʿī jurists.

CHAPTER II
FROM THE IMĀM TO THE *FAQĪH*

The greatest principle of all is that nobody, whether male or female, should be without a leader. Nor should the mind of anybody be habituated to letting him do anything at all on his own initiative; neither out of zeal, nor even playfully. But in war and in the midst of peace—to his leader he shall direct his eye and follow him faithfully. And even in the smallest matter he should stand under leadership. For example, he should get up, or move, or wash, or take his meals. . . only if he has been told to do so. In a word, he should teach his soul, by long habit, never to dream of acting independently, and to become utterly incapable of it.

Plato

The current political regime in Iran has its ideological underpinning in juridical Shī'ī thought which emphasizes full implementation of Islamic law as it has been preserved for fourteen centuries.[1] The fundamental tenet of Shī'ī political theory focusses on designation of the person or persons who should assume responsibility for the implementation of this law. Today the prevalent view in Iran is that of Ayat-Allah Khomeyni's which advocates a qualified *faqīh* for that role.

What makes this idea so significant is that, in the words of one Iranian scholar,

> This has come about in a moment of Iranian history when—for two main reasons—it was least expected: First, the process of modernization or Westernization, with all its aberations, set backs, and imbalances, seemed to have gone too far to allow the return to what many think of as an anachronism—that is, the sobordination of politics to religious precepts; second, although religions thinking among Iranian Shī'īs displayed an unusual vitality during the last decade of the Shah's era, it was far from reaching any consensus over the feasibility or advisability of the *faqīhs'* governing.[2]

This idea—that political aspects should be dictated by religious beliefs—is deeply ingrained in Islamic political thought. The necessity for a qualified leader to guarantee the implementation of the law originates in Shī'ī theory. To understand how the seemingly inexplicable state of affairs has come to be, it is necessary to review the development of Shī'ī thought concerning the identity and the role of the sovereign.

The fundamental goal of Islam is man's salvation both in this world and the hereafter. To realize this goal, there is an ordained scheme or path which provides guidance for man in all aspects of his life—the Islamic law. Consequently, the end of Islamic political theory is to realize this revealed path; the foundation for the decisions and actions of the Islamic state should be the Islamic law. For this reason, some scholars maintain that an Islamic state should be called not a theocracy but a "nomocracy," thereby denoting the sovereignty of the law.[3] As a corollary to this, Islamic political theory is basically concerned with the concept of authority rather than power. This distinction has its roots in the belief that authority belongs to man, whose *raison d'être* is to implement the law, but the true power belongs to the ultimate lawgiver—God. Because of this fundamental division between authority and power, Muslim thinkers generally insist on the difference between the idea of "government" (ḥukūmat), denoting sovereignty, and "guardianship" (velāyat) denoting deputyship of God.[4] In other words, government is God's and guardianship is man's whose duty it is to ensure the implementation of the law on God's behalf. Nevertheless, to say there is a difference between authority and power still leaves unanswered the question of the guardian(s)' identity.

The two major Islamic groups, the Sunnis and the Shī'īs, have addressed this question and arrived at different solutions. Based on the Prophetic saying that "my community never agrees upon error," Sunni political theory considers the Muslim community to be the holder of such authority. The Shī'ī theory, however, rejects the notion that the majority opinion is necessarily just and right. Instead, it promotes the delegation of authority to a special leader, who leads the society along the right path. This belief underlies the doctrine of *Imāmate* in Shī'ism. It also forms the basis for Khomeyni's theory of the guardianship of the *faqīh*.

The Imāms and Imāmate

The theory of *Imāmate* evolved during the first century of the Islamic calendar by the Shī'ī minority, who thought their leaders had been deprived of their legitimate rights. After the death of the Prophet (d. 632), the historical development of the newly established community furthered the development of Shī'ī political theory in two ways. First, the suppression by the Sunni majority allowed the Shī'ī scholars and their leaders (or Imams) to develop their ideology fully. Second, being in opposition to the governing Sunni majority, the Shī'ī population refused to compromise, at least in theory, with the perceived "illegitimate" Sunni establishment. The Shī'ī decried the pragmatic compromises of the Sunni, claiming that if Shī'ī leaders had assumed authority no deviation from the true path of Islam would have occurred.[5] Therefore early Islamic history is a clear example of the interaction between ideals and political necessities. As an Islamic scholar puts it:

> The conflict between the supporters and the opponents of Abu Bakr [the first successor of the Prophet in Sunni view] centered on considerations of *what is necessary under the circumstances*, and *what ought to be*. The former principle soon resulted in the establishment of a mighty and sweeping caliphate-empire. The latter principle of *what ought to be* led a group of the community, though small, to develop its own interpretation of Islamic ideals and polity.[6] (emphasis in the original).

The downfall of the Umayyad empire in the mid eighth century and the rise of the Shī'ī-sympathetic Abbasids, at least initially, provided greater possibilities, freedom, and a more favorable atmosphere for the growth of Shī'ī theories of jurisprudence and theology. A student of the sixth Shī'ī Imām, Ja'far ibn Muhammad (702-765), and of the seventh Imām, Musa ibn Ja'far Kazim (744-799), Hisham ibn Hakam, elaborated on, and gave definite shape to the theory of *Imāmate*. His elaboration "has remained the basis of the Imāmi doctrine."[7]

As defined by one of the prominent Shī'ī *fuqahā* 'Allamah Helli (d. 1325), *Imāmate* means "a universal authority in the things of religion and of the world."[8] Such authority is vested in the person of the Imām by God through the Prophet; the first Imām was appointed by the Prophet and the others selected their own successor. According to the Shī'ī belief, the Imām should have special qualities and only God, and those who have been designated by God, can judge whether a person possesses such attributes or not.[9] The person qualified to assume such a role should be "immune to sin" (ma'ṣūm) and "the most knowing" (a'lam).[10] The Shī'īs believe that their Imāms possess these qualities. These attributes are compatible with the paradoxical Shī'ī view of man. On the one hand, man is seen as God's representative on earth whose mission it is to realize God's revealed truth (the *Sharī'a*),[11] but, on the other hand, man is a wicked creature who would corrupt the earth if left on his own.[12] To control the dark and wicked side of man's existence God has extended His benevolence by appointing his representative on earth to guide the people and serve as a noble paradigm for them. They are the prophets and in particular the few infallible leaders.[13] Accordingly, since an Imām's duty is to lead humanity to salvation, he should be infallible and the most knowledgeable of all men.

This theory solved most of the important and complex problems that the Shī'ī community faced. The first and the most important issue was the position of the Imām *vis-a-vis* political realities. If they were the Imāms, the Shī'īs asked, why would they not rise up and resist oppressions and deviations? Since direct designation by the Divine meant that it was up to Him to command the Imām to rise up, until such a command is provided, the Imām—the most knowledgeable person—preserved the tenets of the creed and guided the Shī'ī community. Moreover, since acceptance or rejection of the Imāms has no bearing on his stature, this solved the problem of their acceptability by the people.

Hence, the Shī'ī minority was saved and preserved until the death of the eleventh Imām, Hassan ibn 'Ali 'Askari (845-872). Having found no particular successor to the eleventh Imām, the Shī'ī community was faced with a new crisis.[14] Aided by the favorable atmosphere, provided by the Shī'ī dynasty, the Buwayhid (932-1055),[15] the great Shī'ī thinkers resolved the dilemma with the theory of occultation, according to which the twelveth Imām is alive but has disappeared from among the Shī'īs and will reappear at the end of time.[16] "It was," as Professor Hamid Algar puts it, "Naubakhti, Abu Sahl 'Ali b. Isma'il, who took a prominent part in formulating the doctrine of *ghaybat*, the occulation of the Imām."[17] Thus, a new chapter in Shī'ī political thought began.

Theologically, the occultation of the Imām provided living proof (*ḥujja*) of God's revelation on earth.[18] Politically, it established the basis of strength for the religious intelligentsia, the *'ulamā*. No doubt the religious scholars enjoyed respect and prestige during the lifetime of the Imāms, but with the actual removal of the Imām from the scene, the power of the *'ulamā*, as the representatives of the Imām, was greatly enhanced. In the absence of the Imām, the *'ulamā* filled the vacuum by collecting the special taxes, answering judicial questions and performing civil functions such as marriage ceremonies and so on.

The 'Ulamā's Deputyship

The theory of representation of the Imām or, as it is known, deputyship (*n̄iyābat*), was therefore established. According to it the occultation or the disappearance of the Imām had two phases, the shorter occultation (*al-ghaybat al-qaṣīra*) and the complete occultation (*al-ghaybat al-tāmma*). During the first phase, which began in 873–74, four prominent jurists were in direct contact with the Imām, and were known as special deputies (*nuvvab-e khās*).[19] The second phase began with the death of the last special deputy (940–41). Since then, the *'ulamā* have claimed to be the deputies of the Imām. According to Shī'ī thought, those individuals who "master the religious sciences and are able to grasp the religious rulings better than anyone else" are deputies of the Imām.[20] *To put it simply, anyone who successfully finished the Islamic religious schools could claim to be the Imām's representative.* Technically, such persons are known as general deputies (*nuvvab-e 'ām*) and, generally, the *mujtahids* (those who practice independent reasoning in their rulings). Concerning the role of the general deputies in solving Muslims' problems pertaining to personal and religious duties, no disagreement existed among the *'ulamā* themselves and no objection was expressed by a practicing Muslim. It was on the *'ulamā's* role in public and political affairs (that is as the acting sovereign—which was considered exclusively the province of the Imām) that the disagreement arose.

Such an issue, however, was rarely raised because, for most of its history, Shī'īsm has been the creed of the minority under the actual rule of the Sunni majority. Moreover, the doctrine of occultation explicitly left the political domain to the Imām. The establishment of the Safavid empire in Iran (1501–1722) gave significance and substance to the appropriate role of the *'ulamā*. Whatever their motives, the Safavids made Shī'īsm the official religion of their empire thereby creating the first Shī'ī state. Claiming descent from the seventh Imām, the founders defined the aim of the new empire as the upholding and the guarding of Twelver Shī'īsm.[21] To that end they encouraged and, in fact, enforced the influx of Shī'ī scholars from the traditional Shī'ī centers in the Arab world.[22] The enthusiasm of Safavid kings for Shī'īsm drove into the background the traditional Shī'ī political theory—the notion that, it was exclusively the Imām's right to engage in political affairs. Indeed, the religious group became part of the state apparatus. "The natural consequence of this," Professor Lambton writes, "was that much of the writing of the period was devoted to religious polemic and exposition of Shī'ī doctrine."[23] The modern major compilation of Shī'ī books of traditions, namely *Vāfī, Beḥār al-Anvār* and *Vasā'il al-Shī'ā*, are the product of this period.[24]

There were, however, individual *'ulamā* who rarely associated with the court. Shaykh Ahmad Ardabili (d. 1586), for example, always kept his distance. In a letter requesting pardon for a certain individual, he addressed the king with the following phrase, "the founder of the borrowed kingdom," reminding the Safavid royalty that the Imām and not he was the true king.[25]

By and large, though, no explicit organized opposition to the kings was heard, nor was a fundamental doctrinal justification worked out.[26]

The alliance of the two, the rulers and the *'ulamā*, proved fruitful for both until the fall of the Safavid empire and the occupation of their capital by the Afghans (1722).

The Usūlī/Akhbārī Dispute

The *'ulamā* suffered in several ways. They experienced political setbacks because the Shī'ī dynasty was destroyed and also because the new king, Nader Shah who drove the Afghans out and declared himself the new king (1736–47), tried to reduce Shī'ism to another school of jurisprudence (*fiqh*) in Islam.[27] They suffered ideologically because some of their fellow *'ulamā* (known as *Akhbārī*) were advocating closer conformity to the words and deeds of the Prophet and the Imāms. It was not so much traditional Shī'ī political thought that was being threatened as it was the position and the independence of the *'ulamā* themselves.

According to the *akhbārī* position, it is forbidden to follow the opinion of those *'ulamā* who claim greater exercise of their independent reasoning (*ijtihād*):

> Every believer must [. . .] follow the *akhbār* of the *Imāms*, for whose proper understanding no more than a knowledge of Arabic and the specific terminology of the Imāms is needed. If an apparent conflict between two traditions cannot be resolved by the methods prescribed by the *Imāms*, *tawakkuf*, abstention from a decision, is obligatory.[28]

Ironically such a view was welcomed by some highly regarded members of the *'ulamā* in the early seventeenth century. Notable among them were Mulla Muhammad Taqi Majlisi (d. 1659–60), Mulla Muhsin Fayz Kashani (d. 1680) and Muhammad ibn Ḥassan Ḥur 'Amoli (d. 1692–93).[29] The last two are among the major compilers of Shī'ī books of traditions in the modern period (*muta'akherīn*) in the history of Shī'ī jurisprudence.[30] Their acceptance of the *akhbārī* position may be partly explained by their concern for the tenets of Shī'ism. Friday prayer, which according to the traditional Shī'ī view, was to be performed exclusively by the Imām, was reinstated during the Safavid period. A closer observance of the Imāms' words and deeds, therefore, would cut back on ideological compromises. Consequently, by the mid-eighteenth century the *akhbārī* school was predominant in all major Shī'ī centers.[31]

As long as there existed an empire with a central government committed to the cause of Shī'ism, the *akhbārī* position indeed enhanced the power of the *'ulamā* in that it provided some mechanism for checking the power of the rulers. With the fall of that empire, and with the policy of the new dynasty to reduce Shī'ism to another school of jurisprudence in Islam, the *akhbārī* position would have carried a different implication; it would have devalued the *'ulamā* from the proper representative of the Imām and one of the sources of the law (*ijtihād*) to that of simply a transmitter of Shī'ī traditions.[32] This new crisis was resolved by Muhammad Baqir Behbahani.[33]

Behbahani's position, set forth in his tract *al-Ijtihād wa al-Akhbār*, begins with the proposition that every individual is obligated to live in accordance with the law; hence, a leader is needed to guide people and to extract their duties from the law of Islam (the *Sharī'a*).[34] He then argues that it was impossible to have access to the Prophet or to the Imāms during the occultation. It followed that a group of "skilled *fuqahā* was necessary because they were the path to reaching the legal injunctions (*al-aḥkām*).[35] Moreover, he used the division of labor as another reason for the necessity of theologian jurisconsults. "If one claims he can reach the proper injunctions without the help of a *faqīh*," he writes, "in my opinion, one is like a mother who claims she can cure her sick child without referring to a physician."[36] And, finally, he turned to Shī'ī history for support. Since they were a minority in Islam, the Shī'ī Imāms had to conceal their identity as a precautionary measure (*taqīyya*).[37] Consequently, "many of the [Shī'ī] traditions were reported by people who were practicing *taqīyya* . . . [hence] sometimes extracting the real intention and injunction of the lawgiver requires independent reasoning (*Ijtihād*)."[38] In other words, the knowledge of the Arabic language and the terminologies of the Imāms is not sufficient, as the *akhbārī* maintain; rather knowledge of the principle of jurisprudence (*usūl al-fiqh*) is a necessity. Therefore, *ijtihād* is a necessary part of religion and the *'ulamā*, who are able to practice *ijtihād*, are a necessary part of the community.

Behbahani resorted to other means in his struggle with his opponents. For example, he pronounced that the *akhbārī 'ulamā* were infidels, and successfully undermined their position.[39] It is reported that, through Behbahani's ruling (*fatvā*), the *akhbārī 'ulamā* were forced out of Karbala.[40]

As a result of this "scholastic renaissance," as one scholar puts it, the power of the *usūlī 'ulamā*—those who opposed the *akhbārī* position and who considered the principle of jurisprudence very important—was restored.[41] For his achievement Behbahani was granted the title of the renewer (*mujaddid*) of the Shī'ī creed in the beginning of the twelfth century Islamic calendar.[42]

Although the *akhbārī* vs. *usūlī* argument arose later in the mid-nineteenth century under a different name (*Shaykhī* vs. *Bālāsarī*), the *akhbārī* position essentially lost its momentum.[43] After Behbahani, most of the Shī'ī *ulamā* followed his school. Behbahani's restoration of the position of the *'ulamā*—that they could now express their opinions and exercise independent reasoning (*ijtihād*)—was elaborated on by some of his students and followers. Notable among these are Mulla Ahmad Naraqi (d. 1828–29)[44] and the peerless Shaykh Murtaza Ansari (d. 1864–65).[45] The political situation in Iran was also going through some changes as well. By the late eighteenth century, the Shīʿī state was under the rule of the Qajars (ruled 1785–1925). A split occurred among the Shīʿī thinkers in their view on the *ʿulamā*'s involvement in political affairs. Some, like Naraqi, advocated political involvement by the *ʿulamā*, and some, like Ansari, argued that there is no definite ruling on the issue.[46]

Naraqi's views of Shīʿī political thought is well expressed in his work *ʿAwa' id al-Ayyām*.[47] He begins by arguing that only the Prophet and the infallible Imāms together with those people that God, by his Prophet (Muhammad) or by the Imāms, appoints possess *wilāya* (authority and guardianship).[48] Such individuals, he says, include the righteous theologian jurisconsults (*al-fuqahā al-ʿudūl*), the parents, ancestors, legatees, husbands, masters and deputies and their authority is limited (*maqṣura*) to certain specified affairs.[49] He then concentrates on the limits of the authority of the *fuqahā*. He begins with the question: Is the guardianship of the *fuqahā*—who are the acting sovereigns (*hukām*) during the occultation of the Imām and who are the deputies of the Imām—extended to those areas which are approved (*thābita*) for the Imām?[50] By way of an answer, Naraqi distinguishes between four types of guardianship (authority): political guardianship, *wilāya al-hākim*,[51] judicial guardianship, *wilāya al-qaḍa*[52] administrative guardianship, *wilāya al-ḥudūd*[53] and guardianship of the other affairs such as the well beings of the orphans (*al-aytām*) and the insane (*al-majnūn*) as well as management of the special Shīʿī taxes which are paid to the Imāms (*al-taṣarruf fī al-amwāl al-Imām*).[54]

This discussion is concerned primarily with the role of the *ʿulamā* as the acting sovereigns during the occultation of the Imām.[55] Naraqi believed that the *ʿulamā* are the true rulers in the absence of the Imām. He drives his point home in two ways. First, he cites nineteen traditions of the Prophet or of the Imāms in support of his argument that the *ʿulamā* are the deputies of the Imāms.[56] For example, he quotes this tradition: "The ruler has authority over the people and the *faqīh* has authority over the ruler."[57] Second, he resorts to rational analogy. It is not logical, he argues, to think that, in the absence of the Imām, people should stop their social lives. Therefore, both traditions and common sense make it imperative for a person or a group to assume the necessary role of rulership, as well as guardianship of the religion and the community against deviation and corruption. The person or persons who assume this role should be familiar with the laws of Islam and be righteous in their conduct. The similarities between Naraqi in his views and line of reasoning and those of Ayat-Allah Khomeyni is striking, as we shall see in chapter five.[58]

On the basis of this belief in the authority of the *faqīh*, Naraqi took an active role in political affairs as well as in controversial issues of his time. He engaged in a polemical argument with the British missionary, Henry Martyn.[59] Furthermore while in Kashan, he used his influence and public support to exile the governor appointed by the Shah from the city because, according to *Qeṣaṣ al-'Ulamā*, the governor had been unjust.[60] When Fath 'Ali Shah (d. 1834) summoned Naraqi and questioned him about the incident Naraqi ignored the Shah and prayed loudly, in the following words: "Oh God! This unjust ruler appointed an unjust governor over the people. And when I put an end to the oppression, this oppressor reproaches me."[61]

Interestingly, one of Naraqi's students who achieved the position of the most learned and the sole source of following (*marja' al-taqlīd*), Shaykh Murtaza Ansari, deviated from his teacher's position and kept his distance from political issues.[62] Two of Ansari's works are consulted frequently and used as textbooks in religious schools—*Farā'id al-Usūl (al-Rasā'il)* on principles of jurisprudence and *al-Makāsib* on jurisprudence proper. They were first published in Tehran in 1851 and 1863 respectively. For the purpose of this study attention is turned to *al-Makāsib*.[63] In this work Ansari defines the functions of the position of the qualified theologian jurisconsult (*al-faqīh al-jāmi' al-sharāyet*), without enumerating their sources. He maintains that one must distinguish between three functions of the office: the first one deals with religious matters and relates to the practice of independent reasoning and the issuing of legal rulings (*al-iftā'*). All jurists agree that this function belongs to the *faqahā*. The second function deals with adjudication or arbitration for matters (*al-ḥukm*) concerning disputes among the Muslims. Without any objection, this institution has been entrusted to the *'ulamā*. The third function deals with political authority, namely the power to control the life and wealth of the people (*wilāya al-taṣarruf fī al-amwāl wa al-nufūs*). This function, however, is divided into two categories; either the guardian (*wali*) acts on his own discretion or he must have special permission.[64] The former means sovereignty, which in Ansari's view is the prerogative of the Prophet and his successors, the Imāms. The latter refers to functions pertaining to managing the affairs of certain groups of individuals. In other words, the *fuqahā* have the authority to exercise certain kinds of power with regard to the affairs of those Muslims who, for various reasons, are unable to administer their own affairs, such as minors, the insane, the ailing, and beneficiaries of public endowments.[65] Nor does Ansari grant legitimacy to the existing political rulers. He dismisses the idea as requiring detailed discussion.[66]

Ansari's views on politics are reflected in his actual life as he remained completely inactive in the area of political and social issues. He apparently stood in good stead with the royal court.[67] The British

Ambassador allegedly said: "Ansari is either Jesus himself or his special deputy on earth."[68] Furthermore, Ansari did not engage in the controversy over Babism.[69] According to Babi sources, Ansari attended the assembly in Kazemeyn (Iraq) held to condemn the Babis, but when he discovered the intention of the gathering he left, saying that he was not familiar with this new faith.[70] Many Iranians criticised him for not getting involved in politics. One thinker writes: "God has not given Ansari enough insight to understand why Iran is in the state of collapse and why the Iranians are suffering abasement."[71]

The Guardianship of the Faqīh in the Twentieth Century

Although Ansari did not directly engage in politics, his achievements in other areas had great political consequences. By utilizing the strength which Ansari restored to the *'ulamā* and the Shī'ī centers, his followers and students led some of the most important political movements in modern Iranian history. Notable among them are the Tobacco Protest (1891–92)[72] and the Constitutional Revolution (1905–11).[73] The establishment of Constitutional regime, however, presented a great ideological challenge to Shī'ī political thought because it introduced such alien notions as popular sovereignty. Some members of the *'ulamā*'s circle, therefore, objected to the idea of constitutionalism altogether, while others supported it. The debate about the vices and virtues of constitutionalism is identified with Shaykh Fazlullah Nuri (d. 1909)[74] and Mirza Hossein Na'ini (d. 1937).[75] Both were adamant believers in the centrality of Islam in Muslim's life and its ability to guide them along the right path. And both accepted the interpretation that the ideal government was that of the Imām. They differed, however, in their response to the challenge at hand. Na'ini and pro-constitutionalists thought that "now when the lawgiver (the Imām) is in occultation and it is not possible to implement the *Sharī'a* fully . . . there should be a consultative assembly" to take care of the nation's affairs.[76] Nuri and anti-constitutionalists did not object to the formation of an assembly but they thought it should only work within the framework of the Islamic law.[77]

Shaykh Fazlullah Nuri's views on politics can be found in a series of leaflets known as *lāyeḥa* in which he refuted constitutionalism.[78] He based his opposition on the traditional Shī'ī view that "relying on the opinion of the majority is wrong,"[79] and on the fact that Islamic law is sufficient. As he puts it: "The law for us Muslims is only Islam which, thanks to God, the exalted traditionalists and *mujtahids*, generation after generation, have taken pains to protect and keep in order."[80]

Nuri's answer to the question of implementation was that "I am not at all opposed to a consultative assembly . . . but [it must be] an assembly which is based on Islam and does not function in disagreement with

Muhammadan Laws and Twelver Shī'ī tenets."[81] He wanted what he coined as *mashrūteye mashrū'a*, constitutionalism based on the Islamic law. Since the present assembly does not meet this demand, he reasoned, the old institution, the monarchy, will be sufficient. He supported his position further by arguing that

> the function of Islam is laid upon these two (sets) of affairs; deputyship in the affairs of prophecy and kingship. Without these two, Islamic provisions would be inactive. As a matter of fact, kingship is the executive power of Islamic provisions and [is a requirement for] doing justice.[82]

As this passage suggests, Nuri implicitly accepts the monarch as the representative of the Imām in administering the laws. In theory, however, he does not. " . . . [D]uring the [greater] occultation of the Imam, peace may be upon him, [only] the Shī'ī *fuqahā* are authorized to handle the new problems (*havādeṣ*) and to control [all] the affairs."[83]

Equally adamant in his belief in the comprehensiveness of Islamic laws and creed, Na'ini had a different approach. His views are presented in his well-known work, *Tanbih al-Umma va Tanzih al-Mella*, a tract in defense of constitutionalism. The work begins with an exposition on the necessity of rulership in human society; there are two types of rulership (*esṭila*): *tamlīkīyya* (domination) and *velāyatīya* (guardianship).[84] By the first he means a type of government which has absolute and unrestricted power over the people's lives and property.[85] The second, however, is a system whose ruler is not in control but rather must perform duties in the people's interest.[86] The true Islamic rulership is a guardianship over the implementation of the affairs of the community.[87] According to Na'ini, it is the duty of Muslims to promote the establishment of the second type of rulership and to stop the growth of the first one.

How does one oppose oppressive regimes? Na'ini argues, when the Imām returns it is he who will provide the answer. In his absence, however, those remedies which will effectively stop oppression should be adopted. Since the consultative assembly seems to be a good method, and since all the *'ulamā* of Najaf have approved and in fact encouraged it, such an assembly would be the best remedy.[88] Even that is conditional on the presence of a group of righteous *mujtahids* in the assembly.[89] Thus, Na'ini believed that, during the absence of the Imām, it is a "religious duty of the *'ulamā* to possess the ruling power."[90] At the end of his book, Na'ini reveals his intention to add two chapters to the work to present the proof of and the function of the deputyship (*niyābat*) of the *fuqahā*. These chapters were never written, because, in a dream, the Imām discouraged him from such an act.[91]

Na'ini's argument enhanced the position of the constitutionalists, but the debate between Nuri and Na'ini did not resolve the tension between popular sovereignty and the divine authority of the religious leaders. The policies of the Pahlavi dynasty, which formally came to power in Iran in 1925, coupled with the quietist attitude of some religious leaders like Ayat-Allah Burujerdi (d. 1961), who became the preeminent *marja' al-taqlīd* (source of following) and nominal leader of the Shī'ī community in 1945, drove the discussion on Shī'ī political theory into obscurity.[92] In the late 1940s and early 1950s one of the major *'ulamā*, Ayat-Allah Kashani (d. 1962), both involved in politics and helped to lead the national movement for the nationalization of the oil industry, but this did not produce any major theoretical or doctrinal reconstruction of Shī'ī political thought.[93]

The 1960s proved to be the decade of Islamic ideological reconstruction. The national movement of 1950–53 which ended with a coup d'etat in August 1953, the death of Ayat-Allah Burujerdi and, most importantly, the failure of the 1963 uprising, presented a challenge to the Islamic circle in Iran.[94] The concern here is with the response of the *fuqahā* and its influence on the juridical trend of Shī'ī thought. Significant reaction came with the publication of a book of self-criticism by a member of the *'ulamā*, entitled *Rohānīyat dar Shī'a* (Religious Leaders in Shī'ism). This was soon followed by a very influential collection of essays on important issues in Shī'ī political thought, *Baḥsī dar bāreye Marja'īyat va Rohānīyat* (A Discussion on the Source of Following and the Religious Leaders.)[95] While the first was mostly negative and critical of the *'ulamā*, the second was constructive and treated fundamental issues.[86]

Roḥāniyat dar Shī'a criticized the *'ulamā* on many grounds. For the present purpose, I will mention only three. The most important problem with the *'ulamā*, the work argues, is that they are not united. Rather than pursue in harmony that which they are authorized to do, the *'ulamā* compete with one another.[97] The author asserts that concurrence and unity among the *'ulamā* would ensure unity among the people. To substantiate his assertion, the author alludes to the Tobacco Protest and its success.[98] "The obvious reason for such a victory," he writes, "was that there existed unity of opinion (*eteḥād kalamah*) among the 'ulamā."[99] The second problem concerns the *'ulamā*'s aloofness from politics. "Although government is one of the basic tenets of Islam, unfortunately some *'ulamā* do not allow either themselves or their followers to meddle with politics."[100] In their works, the book claims, the *'ulamā* rarely, if ever talk about government or about familiarising the people with political issues. Indeed, after the Imām, the *'ulamā* are the true heirs of the Prophet's authority; therefore, it is a religious duty to be involved in politics.[101] Finally, the book criticizes the curriculum and the textbooks of religious educational institutions. He finds them useless in dealing with the contemporary world. "Apparently," he argues, "the *'ulamā* think the modern sciences have no relevance to Islam."[102]

Apparently the book angered many people because the author spent much of the second volume, which was published a few years later, in answering objections to the first volume.[103] At the same time, and as a response to Burujerdi's death, the second book was published; it is suggested, in the book, that the death of Burujerdi inspired the *'ulamā* and concerned thinkers to write the articles.[104] The central theme of *Baḥsī dar Bāreye Marja'īyat va Roḥānīyat*, as the title suggests, revolves around the question of leadership in the Shī'ī community and the position of *'ulamā*. The book is significant for two reasons. First, the contributors avoided any type of political propaganda against the regime. Second, the book addresses some of the most important issues of Shī'ī political thought in a positive and constructive way. The book, as Lambton puts it, "represents, perhaps, the first attempt by a group of writers in modern times in Persia, to examine and reappraise the different aspects of a fundamental issue of the faith."[105]

The contributors mainly delineate the problems and the shortcomings of the institution of *'ulamā*, and the *'ulamā*'s responsibility and duties in society. Ayat-Allah Mutahari (d. 1979) one of the influential and powerful members of the *'ulamā* during the 1977–79 revolution, for example, addresses the difficulties of the *'ulamā*. He identifies three problems within the religious organization (*dastgāh-e roḥānīyat*). The first is related to unrestricted use of the special religious garb; anyone can buy them and, using them, can pretend to be one of the *'ulamā*.[106] The second is related to the unaccountable financial system. Since there is no central place for all the taxes to be collected, the money is not properly handled.[107] The third, which for Mutahari is the most important one, is related to the *'ulamā*'s reliance on the masses. Because our *'ulamā* greatly rely on common people for their livelihood, he argues, they are limited by them and so are not very independent; they mostly follow rather than lead.[108] His solution was that, the *'ulamā* should free themselves and try to play their traditional role, that is, leading rather than following.[109]

Mahdi Bazargan addresses the political involvement of the *'ulamā*. Believing that Islam is a comprehensive way of life, Bazargan would expect the *'ulamā* to take a leading role in society and to initiate programs in society which would benefit everyone.[110] He asserts that, in the absence of the Imām, it has always been the *'ulamā* who have provided leadership and a place of refuge (*malja'*) for the people.[111] He expects such institutions to be restored. In other words, he encourages the *'ulamā* to get involved in politics and provide leadership in the affairs of "religion and the world" and in those affairs pertaining to "theoretical as well as practical" issues.[112] It is clear to see how such an argument would lay the ground for the theory of the guardianship by the *faqīh*.

Another important issue addressed in the book is the ideological threat to Islam. Most of the contributors refer to the infiltration of Western and Communist ideologies as a dangerous challenge to Islam.[113] Bazargan, for example, saw the situation this way: "In the past, the Iranians were born Shī'a . . . and they would know nothing else. . . . Nowadays, however, things have changed. Young and old men are subject to irreligiousity and temptation from various sources."[114]

Bazargan's outcry was justified because, from the time of Stalin's death in 1953 and the de-Stalinization policies, neo-Marxism had been gaining popularity within the Islamic world.[115] Marxism and its adapted versions presented a great ideological threat to Islam. Indeed, most of the works of Muslim thinkers, in this period, are refutations of Marxism.[116] There is also evidences to suggest that this ideological challenge precipitated theorizing on the nature of Islamic government in its elaborated form. Many believed that the *Mojāhadin Khalq* organization, originally a guerilla outfit established in the mid-1960s, was propagating Marxism under the guise of Islam.[117] According to an observer, in the late 1960s, a group of concerned Muslims, notably, Hossein Bahonar (d. 1980), the third prime minister of the Islamic Republic of Iran, Muhammad Beheshti (d. 1980), Hossein Ali Montazeri the *faqīh* contemplated to become the head of the state after Khomeyni, Murtaza Mutahari (d. 1979), a prominent member of the *'ulamā* during the revolution, and Ali-Akbar Hashemi Rafsanjani, the present head of the parliament, prepared a report on the situation in Iran and sent it to Khomeyni in Najaf.[118] They informed the Ayat-Allah of the rapid progress of the Marxisms among the Muslim youth. The following comment by Khomeyni in June of 1980 suggest that the story is true. According to Khomeyni:

> When I was in Najaf they (the *Mojāhedin's* representatives) came to fool me too. Some say they stayed about twenty-five days. . . . I listened to what they had to say. They referred to the Qur'an and *Nahj al- Balāgha* [Imam Ali's sermons, saying and letters] a great deal . . . I concluded that they want to destroy us by using the Qur'an and *Nahj al-Balāgha.*[119]

The report, among other things, brought to Khomeyni's attention that the Iranian youth were of opinion that Islam had no actual political program and certainly no plan of action for fighting the perceived "corrupt" Pahlavi regime. This realization and the duty of defending Islam were the impetus which led Ayat-Allah Khomeyni to deliver a series of lectures on the nature of Islamic government in Najaf between January 21 and February 8, 1970; these lectures formed the bulk of his famous tract on *Islamic Government*. The tract reaffirms the role of the *faqīh* as the acting sovereign in the manner which Behbahani, Naraqi and Nuri had described. In addition to expounding upon this theory of politics, it calls for political revolution—the spreading of propaganda against the Pahlavi regime and preparation for the establishment of a new form of polity.[120] As to the concept of guardianship, Khomeyni reiterated the views of Behbahani insofar as he renewed Shī'ī political thought and strengthened the position of the *'ulamā*, and the views of Naraqi, insofar as he considered the *faqīh* to be the only legitimate sovereign. Ayat-Allah Khomeyni's scheme of Islamic Government will be discussed further in chapter five of the present study.

Conclusion

The notion of the guardianship of a theologian jurisconsult (*Velāyat-e Faqīh*), in the manner presented by Ayat-Allah Khomeyni is a relatively new idea within Shī'ī political thought. This notion grants far-reaching political authority to a *faqīh*; indeed, he is considered to be the sovereign. As this discussion has shown, none of the Shī'ī thinkers granted as much authority to the *'ulamā* as this new concept does. The novelty of the notion of guardianship of the *faqīh*, however, should not be mistaken for innovation. Today, there are a number of scholars, who insist on the drastic differences between Ayat-Allah Khomeyni's political ideas and those of the classical Shī'ī doctrine.[121] Such assertions, to say the least, are exaggerations. As this short review has demonstrated many prominent Shī'ī thinkers in the past maintained that, during the Imām's absence, the *fuqahā* were the rightful guardians. Khomeyni and his supporters seem to have taken the argument one step further. They argue that the political danger of the Pahlavi's policies of anti-Islam, the direct and indirect influences of foreign powers and, most important of all, the ideological challenge of neo-Marxism, made it imperative to take action. No doubt, they maintain, that the ideal rulership will only materialize when the Imam returns; but, so far as present conditions permit, one should try to implement the Islamic rulings and tenets. Therefore, they conclude, in the absence of the Imam, the rule of someone who is familiar with the Islamic law and is righteous is second best.

The notion of the guardianship of the *faqīh* seems to be a logical progression in the evolution of the Shī'ī political thought. Like the views of thinkers such as Nawbakhti (d. 937–38), who helped to formulate the theory of occultation, and Behbahani (d. 1793–94), who strengthened the position of the *'ulamā* and the *usūlī* school of jurisprudence, Ayat-Allah Khomeyni's views will greatly influence Shī'ī political theory for a long time to come. Before examining Khomeyni's fundamental political ideas, the question to consider is, who is Ayat-Allah Khomeyni?

CHAPTER III
THE LIFE OF AN 'ĀLIM: A POLITICAL BIOGRAPHY OF KHOMEYNI

We have a tradition (hadith): The people are dead except the 'ulamā. The 'ulamā are dead except those who practice their knowledge.

Aqa Najafi

Sayyed Ruhollah Mustafafi[1] better known as Ayat-Allah Ruhollah Musavi Khomeyni, was born on August 28, 1902, the sixth and the last child in a religious family in Khomeyn, a small town about two hundred miles southwest of Tehran.[2] His father, a prominent religious leader in that city, was murdered six months after Ruhollah was born. The young Ruhollah began his education by studying Persian and Arabic languages and literature until 1919 with his older brother Murtaza Pasandidah. He then moved to Arak, a neighboring city with a good reputation as an Islamic educational center, to study with Haj Sheykh 'Abd al-Karim Ha'iri Yazdi (1859–1937). Khomeyni followed his teacher to Qum when the latter transferred the whole school to that city in 1921. He there finished his formal education and by 1937 had become a prominent religious scholar.[3] As one biographer puts it: "By the time Ayat-Allah Ha'iri died [1937] Imām Khomeyni had already attained sound independent juridical knowledge and had become one of the distinguished *mujtahids* and a religious genius."[4]

From Ha'iri 's death until the establishment of the Islamic Republic of Iran in February 1979, Khomeyni's public life can be divided into two periods: The first began immediately following Ha'iri 's death and continued until the 1960s during which he was, for the most part, a scholar. The second began in the early 1960s with his political protest against the policies of the government, which resulted in his exile until 1979, when he returned victoriously to Iran as the political leader of that country.

The First Phase: A Teacher and a Scholar

From early in his life, Khomeyni has been concerned with two major issues: the training of people to become good human beings and the preservation of Islam. For him, the two are directly related. The first stems from his belief in man's capabilities to educate himself to perfection and goodness. Perhaps this is the reason, even at a time when philosophical studies were not looked upon favorably in the traditional schools, that Khomeyni was so preoccupied with them. One scholar suggests that Khomeyni was not considered to be an *'ālim* (pl. *'ulamā*) of high stature because of this preoccupation with philosophy:

> An additional reason for his somewhat lower status may have been that he had taught philosophy, and as such, he was one of the few to do so. Philosophy had long since been regarded with misgivings among the basically conservative teachers of the *madrasahs*.[5]

Khomeyni's second concern—the preservation of Islam—stems from his belief that it is Islam which helps man to reach perfection. In his first book, *Meṣbāḥ al-Hedāyeh* (the Light of Guidance), ca. 1929/1930, Khomeyni clearly elaborates these notions:[6]

> Each creature, according to its capability, posesses an intrinsic deputyship. [the representation of God on earth]. Such a deputyship is found in all things [that God has created]—in galaxies and in plants.[7]

Passages such as this one recur throughout the book. It is God, Khomeyni adds, who will show the way to man.

> You should note that the exalted God will guide you toward His presence, and through His benevolence, He will show you the divine path.[8]

Such a belief helps to explain why, as an Islamic scholar, Khomeyni began his teaching career with "intellectual" (*ma'qūl*) science (i.e. philosophy); philosophy and gnosticism held great attraction for him. He was influenced by the philosophy of motion in the thinking of Muhammad ibn Ibrahim Sadr al-Din Shirazi (d. 1640), known as Mulla Sadra or Sadr al-Muta'allehin and, through al-Farabi and other Muslim philosophers, by the thought of Plato and Aristotle.[9] Khomeyni used *Asfār*, the most significant of Mulla Sadra's works, as a textbook in his courses. According to one of his students, Khomeyni believed that "Mulla Sadra has explained the complexities of the issue of resurrection which Ibn-Sina (Avecina) was unable to enumerate."[10] The same observer claimed that Khomeyni "believes in conformity of religion, gnosticism and philosophy."[11]

The most important courses he offered were those on morality and ethics, the subjects which play an important role in Khomeyni's social and political thought. Through moral training, he argued, one can create a new person. In an essay, entitled *lega' Allah* (meeting God), he maintained that it is possible to encounter God. By knowledge and faith, and especially by faith, Khomeyni says, man can achieve closeness to God. The path to God and the search for Him, he says,

> is for man to spend his time contemplating God. He should learn the knowledge of God and His attributes from the teachers of that science. Then, through theoretical and practical ascetic life, one should make this knowledge part of oneself. Of course it will bear fruits."[12]

A corollary to this belief is his view that it is possible and practicable to form a society of good men. Consequently, his longest-running course treated ethics and morality, and it was this course that made the Iranian government suspicious. Reza Shah's police prohibited Khomeyni from offering it, but he secretly continued the course.[13] He also taught courses on jurisprudence and principles (*usūl*). In 1944 he began offering courses and seminars at the highest level (*Khārej*) of the educational system in the religious schools.[14] Most of his students during this period have been raised to prominent positions in post-revolutionary Iran. Two of them, Seyyed Ali Khamene'i and Ali-Akbar Hashemi Rafsanjani are now the president of the Islamic Republic and the head of the parliament respectively.[15]

Ayat-Allah Khomeyni did not limit himself simply to teaching. He wrote many books during this period, ranging from works on ethics, jurisprudence, and commentaries on the works of others and on works of politics.[16] The most important of Khomeyni's works from this period is his book *Kashf Asrār* (Revealing the Secret).[17] During the thirties and forties, along with the governmental policies of secularization and emphasis on the pre-Islamic heritage of Iran, a movement of reforming Shīʻism in Iran gained currency. Among others, Seyyed Ahmad Kasravi (d. 1946), a prominent lawyer and historian, began criticizing some of the Shīʻī tenets.[18] As well as in his books, Kasravi's attacks on Shīʻism and his call for its reform were publicized in his weekly magazine called *Parcham* (The Flag). One of Kasravi's symphathizers, Ali-Akbar Hakami-Zadeh, who was, ironically, from a religious family, systematically refuted most of the Shīʻī precepts in a long essay which was published as a supplement to the journal.[19] Khomeyni perceived these publications as a threat to Islam and thus wrote *Kashf Asrār* to rebut Hakami-zadeh's charges. The book is literally a line-by-line refutation of the latter's essay; the six chapters of the book—Monotheism, *Imāmate*, *'Ulamā*, Government, Law, and traditions—correspond to the six sections of Hakami-Zedehi's essay and bear the same titles. More than a mere rebuttal, however, Khomeyni's book also constitutes a harsh attack against secularism and Reza Shah's anti-*'ulamā's* policies.

The Second Phase: Involvement in Politics

Ayat-Allah Khomeyni was not visibly involved in the political life of Iran during this first phase. His role in the nationalization of the Iranian oil industry during 1951–53 is still a mystery. The literature dealing with that episode does not include any account of his activities.[20] There are two possible explanations for his inactivity. According to one view, Khomeyni's zealous approach to Islam ran contrary to Ayat-Allah Seyyed Muhammad Hossein Burujerdi's (d. 1961) aloofness from political involvement; it was the imperialists who "installed their able and skillful agents in Burujerdi's office and distracted him from social problems. . . . They were able to stop him from direct contact with the masses."[21] One observer even went so far as to ascribe to Khomeyni the reasoning that nothing could be done while Ayat-Allah Burujerdi was alive, because "Haj Ahmad [Burujerdi's special associate] was a British agent who would persuade Burujerdi to stay aloof."[22] Khomeyni, therefore, concluded that he ought to concentrate on strictly academic works. However, this view seems too conspiratorial to have been the case, because Ayat-Allah Burujerdi's abstention from politics was quite clearly a deliberate and calculated choice. That decision was publicized in 1949. According to Akhavi:

> . . . [P]olitical activism was another matter. A large conference convened to discuss this provocative issue was held in Qum in February, 1949. Ayatullah Burujirdi specifically invited some 2,000 or so members of the clergy to attend the session, held in the city's largest *madrasha*, the Fayziyah. The members adopted a firm non-interventionist position which prohibited all members of the clergy from joining parties and trafficking in policitics.[23]

It is hard to believe that the British were involved in the formulation of this position. The other possible explanation might be that Khomeyni had not at the time reached a sufficient level of public recognition to be noticed. This view seems to be closer to the actual situation.

Bourjerdi's death in early March 1961 changed the picture. Ayat-Allah Khomeyni emerged as a prominent religious leader. Presumably the government tried to influence Burujerdi's succession by sending a telegram to Najaf.

> On the death of Burujerdi the Shah sent a telegram of commiseration to Ayatullah Shaykh Muhssin al-Hakim, [d. 1970] an Arab *mujtahid* resident in Najaf, thereby intimating the desirability of his succession to Burujidi as sole *marja'*. Doubtless it was hoped to lessen the importance of Qum and prevent the emergence of a center of clerical power within Iran.[24]

Assuming this was the regime's intention, it did not foster the desirable result. Three Iranian *fuqahā* emerged as joint heirs to Burujerdi's position: Ayat-Allah Khomeyni, Ayat-Allah Muhammad Hadi Milani of Mashhad and Ayat-Allah Kazim Shari'atmadari of Qum. This marked the beginning of the second phase in Khomeyni's public life.

Ayat-Allah Khomeyni's emergence as a *marja'* coincided with the Shah's initiation of the reform policies, which had already begun with land reform.[25] By opposing some aspects of these policies, Khomeyni made his first appearance on the national political scene. Contrary to what the government later claimed, Khomeyni did not oppose land reform. His quarrel pertained to two issues within the electoral reform plan which he thought were contrary to the Islamic view. Two articles of the State and Local Council Election Bill, passed by the Council of Ministers on October 6, 1962, were objectionable to the *'ulamā*, Khomeyni included.[26] The opposition objected to Article Two of the bill for two reasons: first, it removed the requirement of believing in Islam or in any of the accepted religions in Islam (Zoroastrianism, Christianity, and Judaism) for both the candidates and the voters; second, it removed "women" from the list of those prohibited, by law, from participating in electoral process—henceforth ensuring women's franchise. They also objected Article 41 of the bill because it replaced the word "Qur'ān" from the affidavit of the elected, when assuming office with "a divine book."

Following a prolonged session, the *'ulamā* vociferously spoke out against this innovation by sending a joint telegram to the Shah:

> The State and Local Council Election Bill which considers Muslims and non-Muslims (*Kofār*) as equal and replaces the Qur'ān with 'a divine book' in the swearing ceremony is not only a setback to real progress, it is contrary to the interest of Islam, the country and the kingship. Furthermore, it is contrary to the constitution and the aspirations of the absolute majority of the people.[27]

They also sent individual telegrams to the Shah requesting the abrogation of the bill.[28] Khomeyni's telegram read:

> As it is reported in the newspapers, the government has not mentioned the belief in "Islam" as requirement for both the candidates and the voters and has ensured women's franchise in the State and Local Council Election Bill. This has raised concern among the Eminent *'ulamā* and other groups of Muslims. It is obvious . . . that the interest of the country lies in preserving the Islamic religion.[29]

The pressure was mounting. Many people got involved; telegrams flooded Tehran from around the country. Even the Shī'ī *'ulamā* residing in Najaf, Iraq, sent telegrams of condemnation to Tehran. The opposition succeeded, the government withdrew the bill a month later, and the crisis was temporarily defused.

Determined to implement its version of the reforms, the government reintroduced the bill as part of a sixpoint program, later to be known as "the White Revolution," on January 9, 1963. The people of Iran were scheduled to vote on this program in a referendum on January 26. The prime minister shrewdly declared that the program was a package and opposition to any of its principles meant opposition to all of it.[30] In this way any opposition could be condemned as retrogressive and anachronistic. Although the *'ulamā* boycotted the referendum on the grounds that the people were not given sufficient time and opportunity to ponder the issues, the reform plan was approved.[31] From the time of the apparent defeat of the opposition to the holy month of Moḥarram many clashes occurred between the opposition and the government.[32] The most notable was the attack of the Shah's police on Feyziyya school in Qum on March 23, 1963, in which one student was killed.[33] The *'ulamā* continued their opposition unostentatiously until the month of June, which coincided with Moḥarram.

Cognizant of the people's sensitivity during this month, the government took precautionary measures. It summoned some of the *'ulamā* among others and warned them against any attack on the policies of the government.[34] In a leaflet addressing the religious leaders, Khomeyni condemned the government for such a policy:

> Oh, religious preachers . . . do not be afraid of a few days of imprisonment. . . . You gentlemen should know that the present danger against Islam is no less than that of the Umayyads. The tyrannical regime with all its power cooperates with Israel[35] and her lackeys (the misguided group) [i.e. the Baha'is]. . . . You should remind people of the dangers of Israel and her lackeys.[36]

Most religious leaders delivered anti-government sermons during the first week of Moḥarram. However, Khomeyni's was the most provocative; it resulted in his arrest. Among other things, he said:

> I was informed today that a number of preachers and speakers in Tehran were taken to the offices of SAVAK [the secret police of the Shah's regime] and were threatened with punishment if they spoke on three subjects. They were not to say anything bad about the Shah, not to attack Israel, and not to say that Islam is endangered. . . . If we overlook these three matters, we have no dispute with the government.[37]

On June 4, 1963, the day after this speech, the authorities arrested Khomeyni in Qum at three o'clock in the morning. The head of SAVAK at the time accused Khomeyni of cooperating with reactionary elements against "the high interest of the country."[38] Other religious leaders were arrested in other cities as well. As the news of the arrests spread, demonstrations broke out in major cities. According to some reports more than five thousand people were killed and many more were injured.[39] Martial law was declared in Tehran on the same day. In the course of three days the opposition was put down. A few months later the government made some conciliatory gestures by freeing some of the participants of the uprising and reducing Khomeyni's detention to house arrest on July 20, 1963. Simultaneously, the government released the following statement:

> . . . [U]nderstanding has been reached between security authorities on the one side and their Eminences Khomeini, Qumi and Mahllati on the other, according to which the gentlemen will cease to interfere in political matters; and since this understanding has given full assurance that the gentlemen will not act contrary to the interest and law and order of the State, they have been transferred to private houses.[40]

The statement is significant for two reasons. First, the fact that the government took the unusual step of issuing this public statement reveals the gravity of the situation. Second, upon gaining his freedom on April 7, 1964, Khomeyni denied the existence of any *modus vivendi* between the *'ulamā* and government. In his first sermon after his relese, Khomeyni said:

> Even if they hang Khomeyni he will not compromise. . . . Now that it is appropriate, I say . . . Islam is all politics. They have not introduced Islam properly. Politics has its roots in Islam. I am not a religious leader who sits and plays with his rosary beads. I am not a Pope who only performs certain acts on Sundays.[41]

Khomeyni's outcry brought very few political consequences. The opposition had already lost momentum and the government actively carried out its reforms.

The Shah's policy of increasing Iranian military power by borrowing money from the United States opened an old wound. The government introduced a bill to the Senate on October 31, 1964 to borrow two hundred thousand dollars from the United States, and it was linked with granting legal immunity for the American technicians stationed in Iran.[42] The bill passed, but there were a considerable number of negative votes. A number of prominent political and religious leaders condemned the passage of the bill.[43] The most serious attack on the government came from Ayat-Allah Khomeyni in his sermon of October 25th, and in a subsequent leaflet on October 30, 1964. In the sermon, among other things, he said: ". . . Iran has sold itself to obtain these dollars. The government has sold our independence, reduced us to the level of a colony."[44] His language became even harsher in a leaflet, which provoked his arrest:

> "Allah will not give the disbelivers any way (of success) against the believers." [IV:141] Do the Iranian people know what has been going on in the Parliament (*Majles*) over the past few days? . . . Acting at the behest of the government, the parliament has signed the document (*sanad*) of the Iranian nation's servitude. It has accepted the status of a colony for Iran. . . . Why? Because America is the country of the Dollar and Iran needs Dollars. . . . Do the Iranian people know that the armed forces no longer have to take an oath by the holy Qur'an, that the new phrase is "by the book in which I believe?" This is the very danger to which I have repeatedly referred—a danger for the holy Qur'an, a threat to our beloved Islam, a threat to the Islamic country and to our independence.[45]

A few days later, Khomeyni was arrested for threatening the "interest of the people" and "the security, independence and territorial integrity of the state."[46] He was taken directly from Qum to Tehran's international airport and exiled to Busar in Turkey. A year later, on October 5, 1965, the Iranian regime transferred Khomeyni to Najaf in Iraq. No further significant incident is reported in Khomeyni's life until the early 1970s.

From January 20, to February 6, 1970, Ayat-Allah Khomeyni delivered twelve lectures on the theory and practice of Islamic government under the title *Velāyat-e Faqīh*.[47] He wrote another book in Arabic, *Al-Bay'*, in which he dealt with the notion of an Islamic government in a more juridical fashion.[48] In these works he opposed monarchy entirely. He writes: "Islamic government is not a form of monarchy, especially not an imperial system. . . ."[49] And "It is our duty to work toward the establishment of an Islamic government."[50] He contends that while the

Muslims have no political power they should limit their activities to "propaganda, training and preparation." This was the repeated theme in his messages during the 1970s.[51]

The publication of a short essay published with the approval of the government defaming Khomeyni in one of the daily newspapers on January 7, 1978, brought him back on to the Iranian political scene.[52] The essay provoked massive demonstrations in important cities in support of Khomeyni on the following day.[53] To stop the demonstration, government forces attacked the participants producing some casualties, particularly in Qum. Ayat-Allah Khomeyni delivered a long sermon in Najaf the following day which was distributed in Iran in the form of cassette tapes. In the sermon, Khomeyni laid complete responsibility for the bloodshed at the Shah's feet and charged that the Shah's father was a lackey of the british and the Shah himself a lackey of the Americans.[54] He then asked all groups and classes to unite and fight against the Shah and his regime.[55]

It is a custom in Irano-Islamic culture to commemorate a person's death forty days after he or she dies. Therefore, on the fortieth day after the January 8 death in the demonstration, new demonstrations broke out. The cycle repeated itself until the government imposed martial law in Tehran and seven other Iranian cities. The most serious clash occurred on September 8, 1978, when the people ignored the regulations and the army opened fire on the crowd. In a message to the Iranian people, Khomeyni asked them to continue to resist the regime and promised victory.[56] According to some reports the Iranian government requested the Iraqi government to restrict Khomeyni's political activity in the hope of controlling the situation.[57] Consequently on September 25, 1978, the Iraqi officials imposed restrictions on Khomeyni, thereby influencing him in his decision to leave Iraq. After acquiring a visa from the Kuwaiti embassy, he began his journey on October 4, 1978. Realizing that "Mr. Mustafavi" was indeed Khomeyni, the Kuwaiti officials found it politically inexpedient to let him enter their capital.[58] So Khomeyni travelled to Paris, where he launched a massive media compaign against the Shah's regime. In his first leaflet from Paris on October 7, Khomeyni forbade any compromise with the regime. He said:

> Any cooperation with the monarchy, either explicitly or implicitly, through a plan which prolongs the regime is a betrayal of Islam, of the Holy Qur'ān, of the Muslims and of the Iranian people.[59]

The struggle for power and control of Iran continued until the Shah departed from Iran.[60] Khomeyni triumphantly returned to Iran on February 1, 1979. The Shah's last appointed Prime Minister and his government withered away and Khomeyni assumed the most important political role in the new Iran—the acting sovereign and the commander-in-chief. Since his return he has siezed every opportunity to establish his vision of political order and to further the Islamization of Iranian society. The question to consider now is what is this vision? Our study turns next to this question.

CHAPTER IV
KHOMEYNI'S CONCEPT OF MAN

A good man can save a country and a bad man can destroy it.

Ayat-Allah Khomeyni

Why Begin with Man?

The American theologian, Reinhold Niebuhr, begins one of his major works with the statement that "man has always been his own most vexing problem."[1] All man's intellectual contemplation, Niebuhr continues, is an effort to explain and understand himself. Khomeyni seems to share this view and he deals with it in all his major works. It is the understanding of man, Khomeyni believes, that enables us to solve all other human problems. One can point to the following reasons for such a belief.

First, according to Khomeyni, man is the microcosm of the macrocosm, that is, the basic order of the universe. In a sermon he says, "The Almighty God has created two cosmoses; one large cosmos which is the whole universe and a small cosmos that is man."[2] If one understands man, one has understood everything. Khomeyni goes one step further. Referring to the verse of the Qur'ān which says, "And He taught Adam all the names," (II:31), Khomeyni asserts that man is the only creature to whom God has given special attention. He posits that man is the microcosm of the universe by his mere bodily existence and at the same time he is the microcosm of God by his spirit.[3] Man is therefore the key to understanding God,[4] and reforming him is the solution to all the ills of the world.[5]

Secondly, Khomeyni points to the centrality of man in the history of human activities. He believes that man has been obsessed with understanding himself because he perceives himself as the source of all human problems. "If this creature (man)," Khomeyni says, "is left on his own, he will lead the whole world into destruction."[6] On another occasion he says, "The source of all the difficulties for man, from Adam to the present and from the present to the Day of Resurrection (*rūz ḥashr*), is man himself, in particular, his love of self."[7] One might ask how this relates to social problems? Khomeyni has provided an explicit answer.

> Muslims have had difficulties from their early history. A group of men who did not allow, after the death of the Prophet, the right political order to be established [i.e. the rule of the Shī'ī Imāms] is responsible for that. Even the problems we face today are the result of the self love of these selfish men.[8]

Thirdly, Khomeyni emphasizes the understanding of man because, according to him, all prophets, philosophers, and mystics have made man the principal focus of their concerns. Note, for example, the following passage which represents a recurrent theme in his thought:

> All religions have been revealed to reorient man. Man has been the subject of all prophetic missions. All prophets from Adam[9] to the last one [the Prophet of Islam] were concerned with man. They did not think about any other thing, because the essence of all existence is man.[10]

Finally, Khomeyni is well known for his preoccupation with gnosticism (*'erfān*) and philosophy. Similar to all Muslim gnostics, Khomeyni is obsessed with the notion of perfect man (*ensān kāmel*)—a concept of paramount importance in Islamic gnosticism. It is from gnosticism that Khomeyni takes his belief in man's ability to traverse the path of perfection. In his philosophical thoughts, similar to most Muslim philosophers, he is also influenced by the Platonic tradition and views. Just as the Platonic philosophers based their political theory on the good man and aimed at educating men to become good citizens, Khomeyni's theory of politics is based on the theory of "reformed man" who conforms his life to the revealed divine law. Note for example the following passage:

> A good man can save a country whereas a bad man can destroy it. . . . Therefore it is very important that our schools, from the first grade to the university, become training and educating (*tarbīyatī*) institutions. They should become schools which train good men.[11]

It is therefore easy to see why an understanding of Khomeyni's views of human nature would be pertinent to the understanding of his political theory. Because for him man is both the problem and the solution, the point of departure of any inquiry into Khomeyni's theories of politics, society and morality must be his views of the nature of man. If, as Khomeyni believes, man is the microcosm of the mundane world as well as the microcosm of the divine, then, understanding and solving the problems in man's mundane life as well as in his spiritual life means understanding himself. Moreover, if, as Khomeyni believes, the solution to all problems is a reformed man, the key to that process is found in man himself. From whatever angle, Khomeyni's view of man is a central element of his political philosophy and one way that the mystery surrounding that philosophy can be understood.

Man's Nature

Ayat-Allah Khomeyni's philosophy is replete with antinomies or dichotomies: man vs. God, the undeveloped man (*ensān tarbīyat nashode*) vs. perfect man (*ensān kāmel*), the straight path (*rāh khodā*) vs. Satanic path (*rāh ṭāghūt*), divine politics (*sīyāsat khodā'ī*) vs. Satanic politics (*sīyāsat sheyṭānī*), manmade laws (*qavānīn ensānī*) vs. divine laws (*qavānīn elahī*) and the oppressors (*mostakbarān*) vs. the oppressed (*mostaẕ'afān*). These dichotomies are deeply rooted in his thoughts and, for the most part, evidenced by his behavior. Attributing the pertinence of these dichotomies in his philosophy to either psychological deficiencies such as xenophobia or narcissism[12], or to a desire to exhort Iranian Muslims[13], is to say the least, misleading. There are two possible sources of these beliefs. First, they may have roots in the Islamic story of creation.[14] According to the Qur'ān, when God made man out of clay, all the angels bowed down before him except Satan. God punished Satan by dismissing him from His presence. Satan said:

> My Lord: Because Thou sent me astray, I verily shall adorn the path of error for them in the earth, and shall mislead them every one, save such of them as are Thy perfectly devoted slaves. (XV:39–40).

For Khomeyni there are two poles, one attributed to God and the other attributed to the power of evil, hence the existence of the antinomies or dichotomies.

The second possible explanation is sociological. Dichotomies appear to be the inescapable lot for any system of thought which is comprehensive in nature and claims to possess the truth. As a corollary, it is natural for a devoted and professing religionist to see the world in this way.

The first dichotomy reveals itself when one considers Khomeyni's view of man. Note the following passage.

> [M]an . . . is a mystery, a mystery within mystery. All we see of man is his outward appearance, which is entirely animal and maybe even inferior to other animals. Man, however, is an animal endowed with aptitude of becoming human and attaining perfection, even absolute perfection; of becoming what is now inconceivable of him and transcending existence.[15]

This pasage points to a dichotomy in man's nature. On the one hand, man is an animal but, on the other hand, he can become a perfect being— undeveloped man (*ensān tarbīyat nashodeh*) vs. perfect man (*ensān kāmel*). This view resembles Plato's view in *The Republic*. Like Khomeyni, Plato is not happy with the existing man who is in the cave and lives in the state of in-between (*metaxy*). Only when he leaves the cave, through his spiritual conversion (*metanoia*), can he experience the good (*agathon*). Only then can he reach excellence.[16] Similarly, Khomeyni's man lives in the state of bestiality and reaches perfection only after he is guided to travel the right path.[17]

The questions which come to mind in this regard are: What are the characteristics and qualities of the undeveloped man which make him so undesirable? Why does Khomeyni believe that man can reach the highest level of excellence? And what is the route man must follow for reaching perfection? The answers to these questions make sense if the following concept is understood. According to Khomeyni man is the essence of all creation. Two principles are drawn from this. First, since God is the source of all creation, and God creates no evil, man is essentially good and strives for perfection. Second, because man has in him aspects of all creations, a variety of forces are at work within him. As Khomeyni puts it:

> Man is endowed with different dimensions. He shares some attributes with plants; similar to them man requires basic sustenance. . . . He shares certain qualities with animals; he has senses and sexual desires. He is endowed, however, with certain unique qualities which surpass other creatures. Only man possesses such qualities as the power of reasoning (*ta'aqqol), spirituality (ma'naviyat*), and the power of abstraction (*tajarrod*).[18]

Only if one understands this general picture of man does the dichotomy of undeveloped vs. perfect man make sense. The undeveloped man possesses all the undesirable qualities and lacks all the desirable ones. He has not realized the potential which distinguishes him from other creatures. If left on his own, man "understands the basic needs of food and shelter and the indulgence in sexual pleasure and nothing else."[19] Khomeyni, however, does not stop there. For him the undeveloped man is worse than animals because he possesses certain undesirable characteristics which makes him worse than other creatures.[20] The most notable of these characteristics are love of self (*nafs*), love of the world (*donya*), and the love of power.

It is not easy to explain Khomeyni's concept of the love of self, partly because of the multiple meanings of the word *nafs*. It sometimes means the self and sometimes means the soul.[21] In the Qur'ān it is used in both senses.[22] In Khomeyni's thought however, it means the lower part of the soul. He believes there are three parts of the soul: reason (*'agl*), spirit (*rūḥ*) and appetite (*nafs*). The appetite is responsible for our desire of mundane pleasure.[23] This lowest part of the soul translates as "the self," and by the love of self Khomeyni means self-centeredness. A person who loves himself (*nafs*) is very short-sighted because of his obsession with immediate gratificatin. Khomeyni warns that such a man, without knowing it, loves his worst enemy, because:

> Your self is worse than all your enemies, worse than all idols. It is, in fact, the chief of all idols, compelling you to worship it with a greater force than that of all other idols.[24]

Since the greatest cause of evil in human existence is within man himself, the problems of worldly life are caused by man himself. In short, for Khomeyni "all the disasters that afflict man derive from his love of self."[25]

The problem of the love of self is so significant that the most important holy war (*jihād*), Khomeyni thinks, is the war against the self. In a lecture delivered in late 1972 entitled "the supreme *jihād,*" he provides the following reason for considering the struggle against the self as the supreme struggle.

> The disease of arrogance and selfishness causes no pain . . . . If a person derives pleasure from a disease, and moreover, if it entails no pain, he will never seek to be cured of it.[26]

So, he persuaded his hearers that the paramount duty for a human being is to struggle against this seemingly painless disease. In fact he told them that the struggle against the love of self has priority over learning *per se,* because, with that disease in their hearts, their knowledge will become greater darkness (*ḥejāb akbar*) rather than source of illumination.[27]

The other undesirable quality of the undeveloped man is his love of the world. Khomeyni's view on this point could be summarized in a tradition (*ḥadith*) from Imām 'Ali to which he repeatedly refers: "Love of the world is the root of all sins, the path to all misfortunes, the source of all temptations and the cause of all calamities."[28] In one sense, love of the world means treating worldly endowments as ends in themselves. In another sense, it is pursuing one's worldly desires—a life of too much worldliness. As Khomeyni puts it:

> For what we mean . . . by 'world' is the aggregate of man's appetites (*nafs*) that effectively constitute his world, not the external world of nature with the sun and the moon, which are manifestations of God. It is the world in this narrow, individual sense that prevents man from drawing near to the realm of sanctity and perfection.[29]

His own life style and the exemplary one he often cites suggest that he would prefer an ascetic life to a life of indulgence in worldly pleasures. His involvement in the worldly realm of politics seems to contradict this tenet. Explanations of this apparent contradiction will be offered in the next chapter with respect to Khomenyni's view of government and politics. Generally, however, Khomeyni believes that indulgence in worldly life should be avoided because, as he puts it, "so far as the heart is lost to the world and is immersed in the love of the world, the path to reforming the heart is blocked and man is deprived of all salvation."[30] A person who has the love of world will resent God because anything that "does not pertain to this world will disgust him."[31] Moreover,

> If man does not remedy his state and detach himself from the world by ridding his heart of love for it, it is to be feared that he will surrender his soul with a heart full of resentment and hatred toward God and His *awliya* (the prophets).[32]

Not surprisingly, though, Khomeyni attributes the love of the world to man's first undesirable characteristic, namely, the love of self. As he puts it, "the root of the love of the world is also the love of self. . . . All the calamities and corruptions afflicting humanity up to now and to the end of time are rooted in the love of self in man."[33]

Another undesirable attribute of man is his lust for power. The undeveloped man for Khomeyni has an absolute lust for power.[34] This is so because man strives for absolute security. Based on the Qur'ānic verse, "verily man is rebellious," (XCVI:6), Khomeyni argues that the Pharoah was not the only person who exalted himself to the stature of God; that tendency exists in all of us.[35] He elaborates on this point in the following analogy:

> Suppose a certain individual is appointed as the mayor of a town. He will not be satisfied in his heart because he would desire the governorship of a province. If and when he is appointed as the governor he will not be satisfied because he wishes to dominate a whole country and so on.[36]

In Khomeyni's view man's desires are thus infinite (*gheyr-e motanāhī*). Man's nature is built in such a way that it creates desires and aspirations which know no limit. "As man's wealth increases, his desires increase as well; as man's power increases, his desire for more power increases with it."[37]

On this point Khomeyni's thinking seems to resemble that of certain Western political thinkers like Machiavelli, and Hobbes, or Hans Morgenthau and Reinhold Niebuhr,all of whom consider man's desire for power as a universal and permanent aspect of human nature. One scholar summarizes this issue in the term the "security/power dilemma" of human existence.[38] As man acquires more power in order to feel secure, he will feel less secure because he fears he might lose his newly acquired power and therefore strives for more power. However, the similarities between Khomeyni and these Western thinkers end here. Whereas the latter see the security/power dilemma as a permanent and universal aspect of social relations and the solution in the "ever temporary balancing of [power and] interests," and aim for the "realization of the lesser evil,"[39] Khomeyni considers this characteristic of man a disease which is merely temporary and curable.

According to Khomeyni, man can free himself from the vicious circle of the 'security/power dilemma' because of his other qualities which the world's more pessimistic thinkers ignore. It is true that man has an infinite lust for power, Khomeyni asserts, but it is also true that he has an infinite appetite for perfection. Citing this verse of the Qur'ān "surely we created man of the best stature," (XCV:4), Khomeyni supports his belief that man has divine potential which enables him to reach perfection in this world.[40] Since God made man, His creation is by essence good. At the same time man is vulnerable to the temptation of the world and those of Satan. However, it is logical to assume, Khomeyni argues, that the divine aspect of man has more power than other aspects, because the divine aspect is infinite. As he puts it:

> Man has what is "with himself" [animal aspect] and he also has what is "with God" [divine aspect]. As long as he is preoccupied with what is "with himself" he will perish but if he turns to the other aspect he will live forever.[41]

To put it simply, man has the potential to live like other creatures as an undeveloped man given to his animalistic instincts and behavior or he can choose to elevate himself and reach the stature of the divine. Khomeyni believes that by sharing the same essence as that of God, man easily can achieve that stature. As he puts it:

> Reaching perfection is the true desire of man because the nature of man is "the nature (framed) of Allah, in which He hath created man," (XXX:30). Since man's nature is by essence perfect, he will constantly search for truth and perfection even while he is after other things.[42]

Perfection for Khomeyni means an absolute attunement to the divine path. The prophets who are the living embodiment of the divine path are good examples. "If all the people in the world were prophets," Khomeyni says repeatedly, "no dispute would ever arise."[43] The problem with us, Khomeyni argues, is that we are not able to identify the path to perfection and more often than not we confuse spiritual status with worldly status. The truth is that since perfection is found only with God, we are engaged in search of God even if we think otherwise.[44]

To sum up, Khomeyni views man as a creature with various dimensions but governed by two conflicting drives: passion and desire versus the need to perfect himself spiritually. To use Plato's parable again, Khomeyni seems to suggest that man is living in the cave in the state of the in-between. While his essence drives him upward toward a life of higher quality, his desires and appetites pull him down to a life of animalistic qualities.

Man's Rights

Before considering the remedy which Ayat-Allah Khomeyni offers for man to remove himself from this uneasy situation, we should consider man's rights as Khomeyni sees them. Does man have any natural rights which might serve and guide him out of this situation? Only one of man's rights, namely, liberty, will be considered here.

Liberty is commonly perceived to be an unequivocally simple concept when in fact it is always ambiguous. The two most common meanings cited in most standard dictionaries are "state of being free from . . ." and "right or power to . . . ." The first meaning points to man's freedom from any captivity, control, imprisonment, governmental restraints or other similar limitations. The second points to his freedom to decide for himself. The two prepositions "from" and "to" lend quite different meanings to these definitions—one is negative and the other is positive. I have adopted these connotations from Isaiah Berlin's discussion of freedom. He defines the two senses of freedom as follows:

> The first of these political senses of freedom or liberty . . . , which . . . I shall call "negative" sense, is involved in the answer to the question "What is the area within which the subject—a person or group of persons—is or should be left to do or be what he is able to do or be, without interference by other persons? The second, which I shall call the "positive" sense, is involved in the answer to the question 'What, or who, is the source of control of interference that can detemine someone to do, or be, this rather than that?''[45]

According to the theory of natural law, man naturally is endowed with rights to be free from restraint and suppression (save those situations to which he consents) and at the same time he is free to practice the type of religion he chooses and to pursue the life tyle he desires. Is Khomeyni's man endowed with positive freedom or negative freedom? His man is not free from restraints because he has only two options; either he lives within the restraints and rules provided for him by God or he lives in accordance with the restraints of a non-divine order. His view is based on a very complicated argument.

According to Khomeyni, man has no natural rights because "there is no being in the world that possesses independence."[46] Man owes everything he possesses to God. As he puts it:

> Who is man to claim independence and power. Not only man, but even arch angels and exalted prophets possess no power. No one possesses anything on his own. All there is, stems from God. It is because of Him that we are victorious [in the revolution].[47]

The theory of natural rights of man rests upon the proposition that, regardless of the source, man is born independent and free. Such a preposition in Khomeyni's view is the source of all problems. Consider, for example, the following passage from Khomeyni:

> Our fundamental problem is that we know neither ourselves nor God, and we believe neither in ourselves nor in God. That is to say, *we do not believe that we are nothing [on our own] and that everything is from Him.*[48] (emphasis added).

Man, therefore, by nature is dependent on some source for guidance. This, in turn, means that, for Khomeyni, total dependency on God is the proper state. Man depends either on God or on other than God (*gheyr-khodā*), because, says Khomeyni, "humanity has two poles—one in this world and the other in absolute submission to God (*'Abd-Allah*)."[49]

Khomeyni's view of liberty is very much in harmony with classical Islamic views on this issue. According to most Muslim thinkers, the idea of natural rights of man represents an "infringement upon the omnipotence of God."[50] Three basic Islamic definitions of liberty offered by an *'ālim* (pl. *'Ulamā*), a mystic, and a philosopher show the similarities between Khomeyni's view and the general Islamic view. According to Al-Isfaheni (ca. 1110) there are two kinds of freedom, "the one referring to the person who is not subject to any authority, and the other to the person who is not dominated by such ugly qualities as greed and the desire for worldly possessions."[51] Both these connotations fall within Berlin's category of "negative" freedom.

The mystics seem to have both meanings in mind when they define freedom to mean "complete relief of the mind from attachment to anything but God."[52] This definition considers freedom both in its negative sense—that is, freedom "from" other-than-God and its positive sense—that is, freedom "to" submit. The philosopher mystic Ibn-Arabi (d. 1240) saw absolute submission to God as ultimate freedom. According to him "freedom means that man is a slave only to God, so that he is free from everything except God, and freedom is true slavery (*'ubūdīya*) with God as the master."[53] The similarity between these definitions and Khomeyni's understanding of freedom is striking. For Khomeyni, as previously mentioned, the ultimate freedom is absolute submission to the divine to the point that "whatever man looks at, he will see as God."[54]

It is true that man possesses no independence or freedom but he does enjoy a limited "right to choose" (*ekhtīyār*) which is generally translated as free will. To Khomeyni, "the exalted God has created man with the right to choose between the right path and the wrong one."[55] [This position is very much in conformity with the Shī'ī position on the dilemma of free will and predestination. A tradition attributed to the sixth Shī'ī Imām says, "There is neither consent nor compulsion (in life), but something between these two conditions."[56]] Professor Rosenthal has captured the essence of the Islamic view of liberty in the following passage:

> As they [Muslim thinkers] saw it, there can be no freedom from the divine presence, either in this life or in the hereafter, unless that presence is rejected. Such rejection, however, would mean the most terrible slavery and lead to the most painful prison of all, Hell and damnation.[57]

The essence of tthe Islamic view of liberty may also be seen in the following story narrated by Rosenthal about a mystic "who asked for freedom from the service of God, from his status of slave with respect to God. The freedom granted was insanity."[58]

The passage and the story both illustrate two important issues. On the one hand, they point to man's limited right of either accepting or rejecting the revealed plan and, on the other hand, they point to the inevitability of only two paths for man. Khomeyni holds with both points.

Man's Two Paths

Indeed another dichotomy in Khomeyni's thought is based on this argument: there is either the right path or the wrong one with no middle road. The first or the correct path leads to God and the second is the path to doom and damnation which leads to *ṭāghūt,* a term adopted from a verse of the Qur'ān meaning false deity.[59] The term basically means the same thing as *Sheyṭān* (Satan) which has been used throughout Islamic history.[60] The Iranian revolutionaries gave up *Sheyṭān* and adopted *ṭāghūt*. They define this term both religiously and politically as those forces who oppose Islam as well as those who oppose the revolutionary ideals. Khomeyni uses *ṭāghūt* in this broad sense also. As he puts it:

> There are only two paths for humanity; either servitude to God or servitude to *ṭaghūt*. If man freed himself from others

> and submitted to God's servitude (*ubudīyat*) . . . all that such a person does will be considered proper.[61]

This belief is very significant because the distinction between the right path and the wrong one serves as a fundamental premise in Khomeyni's political thought: any political order which helps man follow the right path is an accepted one and any political order which distracts man from it is not an accepted order.

The true end of life and *raison d'être* of man's existence is to follow the right path. "Man," Khomeyni writes, "follows the same path as those of other creatures until they all reach the state of bestiality. From here on there are only two paths which man alone will take with the power of his free will. One is the path to salvation which is that of God and the 'straight path' (I:6) and the other is the path of oppression which is that of Satan."[62] The straight path is what Khomenyni is mostly concerned with. On many occasions, he has elaborated what he means by the straight path. "The straight path," he says, "begins with clot ['Read: In the name of thy Lord who createth, createth man from a clot,' XCVI:1–2] and extends as far as the divine."[63]

If a man walks this path then he will become what Khomeyni refers to as a perfect man. A perfect man is a mature being who employs all the dimensions of his soul in God's service. "Such a man," Khomeyni says, "will become divine in his higher dimension that is his rational faculty, in his middle dimension that is his imagination, and in his lower dimension that is his practical life."[64] Moreover, he adds, such a mature person will be the symbol of "the divine scripture. He will be the key to understanding God . . . [because] every manifestation of him will be a sign of God."[65]

Although man fails to reach this stage on his own, he is naturally driven toward it, Khomeyni says, because it is only in such a stage that man will find peace of mind. "Absolute perfection, " Khomeyni says, "is when man does not pay attention to . . . the world of material goods, to status, to governing . . . and becomes the manifestation of this Qur'ānic verse "Ah! Thou soul at peace' (LXXXIX:27)."[66] Where does man find such a refuge? Can he achieve it by his own potential? To the first question Khomeyni answers:

> The refuge which will protect man from all opposing forces in his mind is nothing but God. It means constant remembrance of God; 'Verily in the remembrance of Allah do hearts find rest,' (XIII:28). All those men who have experienced the divine and took refuge with Him are in peace and the rest of humanity are the followers of *ṭāghūt* and therefore have no refuge.[67]

The answer to the second question—can man find the path on his own?—is an important key to understanding Khomeyni's political theory. Man possesses all necessary tools, Khomeyni argues, but without the divine assistance he does not have the power of distinguishing between the two paths. "Man needs," Khomeyni says, "a helping hand from the world of the unseen to reach him and lead him out. It is precisely for this purpose, to lead man out of his idol temple [self and the world], that all the prophets have been sent and all the heavenly books revealed."[68]

Why is man unable to do it on his own? This can be explained by another dichotomy in Khomeyni's thought. Ideologies, or schools of thought, (*makāteb*) are either divine (*khodā'ī*) or man-made (*ensānī*). According to Khomeyni there are two main problems with man-made ideologies. First, they are not able to satisfy man's spiritual needs. Man has a spiritual dimension or some divine potential in him that acquires perfection through connection with the divine. "Man does not have," Khomeyni says, "direct access to the divine. He can only relate to the Divine through Revelation."[69] Therefore, any man-made ideology neglects one important dimension of man—his need for direct access to God—and hence is deficient as a way of looking at the world and as a guide to practical actions. Moreover,

> the result of a careful and comprehensive analysis of the ideologies presented by nondivine thinkers can be summarized as follows: "None of them are *free from negligences and excesses* and have not been able to ease the burning desires of man for worldly gains."[70] (emphasis added).

The "negligences and excesses" of man-made ideologies, if they are put to practice, will cause confusion and corruption. Even if they do not cause corruption, they only satisfy the mundane aspect of man's desires. "Man-made laws," Khomeyni writes, "invite man to a worldly life and ignore the eternal life of the spirit. Such laws inflict unlimited damage and cause grave harm to man. Moreover, since man lives two lives, one here and the other hereafter, he needs provisions for both lives; man-made laws fail to provide provisions for man's higher life."[71] Khomeyni's solution seems to be clear by now. "The only remedy," Khomeyni says "which can stop man from treachery and crime is religion."[72]

The necessity of divine intervention becomes the foundation for Khomeyni's "right" political order; for Khomeyni any divinely inspired political order by definition is the right one. Man has access to this political order, Khomeyni believes, because of God's benevolence and justice, and because God shows us this right order by revelation through His prophets.[73] As Khomeyni says:

> The exalted and benevolent God favored the people by sending the prophets, so that they show the path to the people. All the teachings of the prophets are for showing the people the path . . . . If man is left on his own he dies like an animal, but if he follows the prophets he will perfect his essence.[74]

Universality is built into this passage. It is an all-powerful and universal God who is addressing humanity. The contrast between this God, on the one side, and man, on the other, is very explicit as well. If man is converted and helped to understand this contrast then the whole of humanity will be governed by God. "The reason for prophecy," Khomeyni says, "is to establish the rule of God in men's hearts. [If that is achieved] it will be extended to the governance of human society as well."[75]

This theme repeats itself in most of Khomeyni's writings speeches and sermons. "The prophets, without a single exception, all had as their mission the reformation [conversion] of man, " Khomeyni says.[76] The prophet of Islam brought the last and the most comprehensive message to humanity. Islam is sent to help man develop himself to his fullest capacity. As Khomeyni puts it:

> Islam has a thesis. It is to make a complete human being out of man. It has come to upgrade man from his current status. Man has natural aspects—Islam helps him develop them. Man has psychological needs—Islam provides for those. Man has spiritual wants—Islam has a cure for that. Man has a rational aspect—Islam helps him develop that. And man has a divine aspect—Islam provides for that. Islam and other religions have come to help this undeveloped man, with all his aspects, to grow and develop.[77]

Conclusion

This passage clearly portrays the main thrust of the present chapter. It shows the dichotomy of undeveloped man who will destroy everything if he is left on his own and the presence of an all-powerful God who acts as a lawgiver and saves man from that state by providing him with an all-comprehensive scheme. Khomeyni is theocentric insofar as God is the measure of all things and the source of all benevolence. He is anthropocentric insofar as man is the center of all attention. The irony of this paradox, however, is that Khomeyni's anthropocentrism derives not from man's inherent importance, but rather from man's status as the source of all obstacles between himself and salvation. If man is not converted, nothing else can be done. "One cannot reform a country," Khomeyni says, "if the people of that country are not reformed first.

. . . If man wants to overcome other battles [social, economic and political], he should first overcome the battle with himself (*nafs*).''[78] As with Plato, Khomeyni's political theory is fundamentally related to, and in many respects based on, the concept of the ''good man,'' a man whose true destiny is to follow the right path. Like Plato, Khomeyni sees the condition of humanity as that of citizens in the cave in a state of in-between (*bar sar do rāhī*), and like Plato's man, Khomeyni's must experience the good if he is to become perfect (*kāmel*). Unlike Plato, however, the redeeming experience of Khomeyni's man is not a philosophical conversion *per se*. It is something more than that. Khomeyni's man must dismiss the false deity (*ṭāghūt*) and conform his life to the Divine plan. Moreover, unlike Plato, who does not say why and how one of the dwellers of the cave is ''compelled suddenly to stand up and turn his neck round,''[79] Khomeyni states clearly that he is led out of ''his idol-temple'' by God through the prophets.[80]

Khomeyni's man has the potential of being led by the forces of false deity (*ṭāghūt*) or by the force of God. Without the prophet's aid man is doomed to follow the wrong path which darkens his heart. Led by the forces of the divine aspect of his essence and the guidance of the prophets, however, he can find and follow the right path. There are, therefore, only two types of order from which he chooses—either the right order of God's path or the wrong order of the worldly path. It seems appropriate to provide the verse of the Qur'ān which Khomeyni frequently quotes on this matter.

> Allah is the Protecting Friend of those who believe. He bringeth them out of darkness into light. As for those who disbelieve, their patrons are false deity (*ṭāghūt*). They bring them out of light into darkness. (II:257)

Khomeyni's philosophy of man can be shown graphically in a chart (Man's Two Paths, p. 49). As the chart shows, man is in the state of in-between. Because of his essence, man would tend to go toward the good, but is not able to do it on his own. If he is helped by the divine leaders he will follow the path to salvation and if he is helped by the false deity (*ṭāghūt*) he will walk the path to damnation. The following passage from one of the most important philosophers in Islamic political thought, Abu Nasr Muhammad al-farabi (Alfarabi) (ca. 870–950), best summarizes the discussion.

> Since what is intended by man's existence is that he attain supreme happiness, he—in order to achieve it—needs to know what happiness is, make it his end, and hold it before his eyes. Then, after that, he needs to know the things he ought to do in order to attain happiness, and then do these actions. . . . [Man] needs a teacher and a guide for this purpose.

> . . . This is found only in the one who possesses great and superior natural disposition, who his soul is in union with the Active Intellect [e.g., the Prophet].[81]

Considering that Khomeyni thinks it possible to attain happiness and justice in this world here and now, and considering that there is no prophet or Imām at the present time to guide man along the right path, how does he propose to achieve this? His answer is found in his views of politics, government and the state which will be the topics of the following chapter.

The highest of the high
people of heaven

The right path (*rāh Khodā*)

Guided by the prophets "Allah is the protecting friend of those who believe," (II:257)

and

Constant struggle against the self (*Jihād al-akhbar*)

Man in the state of
in-between
(*bar sar do rāhī*)

The wrong path (*rāh Sheyṭān yā Ṭāghūt*)

Guided by false deity (*ṭāghūt*) "For those who disbelieve, their patrons are false deities," (II:257)

and

Satisfaction of desires: love of self, love of the world and lust for power

The lowest of low
people of hell

MAN'S TWO PATHS

CHAPTER V
KHOMEYNI'S VIEWS OF POLITICS, GOVERNMENT AND THE STATE

Politics, in a general way, [is] the ordering of actions to an end that is being pursued.

Ibn Bajjah (Avempace)

Those who preside over the practice of religion should be looked up to and venerated as the soul of the body. . . . Furthermore since the soul is, as it were, the prince of the body and has a rule over the whole thereof, so those whom our author calls the prefects of religion preside over the entire body.

John of Salisbury

The end of the State is not mere life: it is rather, a good quality of life.

Aristotle

Ayat-Allah Khomeyni wants to reform man by establishing a just political order. This chapter will examine Khomeyni's view of politics, government and the state. A set of fundamental questions will be considered: How does Khomeyni define politics? Does his definition differ from the general understanding of this concept in Western political thought today? If so, how and why? In his approach to politics, what does he consider to be the ends and means? How does he view government? What are the functions of government? Who is responsible for controlling the machinery of government? How does Khomeyni perceive the state? Is his view any different from the post-Westphalian concept of territorial states? If it is, what is the basis of his understanding of the state? And finally, what are Khomeyni's views on the objectives and tools of the state?

Politics

"Politics for us," Max Weber wrote, "means striving to have power or striving to influence the distribution of power, either among states or among groups within a state."[1] This definition is not only that of Weber, but it represents an important trend in the study of politics today. For instance, Morgenthau, who is considered the father of modern political realism, writes, "All politics . . . seeks either to keep power, to increase power, or to demonstrate power."[2] Accordingly, the central issue of politics revolves around power and influence. Political science, therefore, concerns itself with the study of power.

There are others who define politics in terms of distributive justice. Politics, for David Easton, concerns the "authoritative allocation of values."[3] By this he appears to suggest that there exists a rational mechanism, which he calls a "political system," that will allocate all societal goods and services. Still others see politics as serving and pertaining to the elites in society. Harold Lasswell, for example, calls politics, "who gets what, when, how."[4] He goes on to investigate the nature of these elites and their functions in the society. The definitions offered by these thinkers, and the trends that they observe, relate in the final analysis to the way in which power becomes operational within the political society. This is not to suggest that, these thinkers have altogether similar views on politics but rather they acknowledge that power plays a major role.

On the other side, there are many who do not associate power with politics in any form. Indeed, politics for them comes to life only when power and the struggle for power have disappeared. The last stage of Communism is reached when the state and politics have undergone change and reached a condition of complete atrophy. Politics, in this sense, becomes the harmonious administration of the affairs of the community. The administration of things is substituted for the domination of man by man. This projection is not novel. In fact, to the great masters of political philosophy—Socrates, Plato and Aristotle—politics meant ministering to the affairs of the *polis*. Politics in this sense has a legal connotation. To put it differently, politics seems to require the recognition of certain higher laws irrespective of their source. Communism propagates the higher laws of dialectic and historical materialism. In classical Greek philosophy, the philosopher king emphasizes the higher law, attained by the rational faculty (*nomos*). Aristotle clarifies this idea when he says:

> The rule of law is therefore preferable . . . to that of a single citizen. . . . [E]ven if it be the better course to have individuals ruling, they should be made "law guardians" or ministers of the law.[5]

Similar to this latter tradition, Khomeyni's definition of politics is directly related to a higher law. This assertion is substantiated by his dichotomous theory of politics. According to him, there are two types of politics: "Divine" (*Khodā'ī*) and "non-Divine" (*ghyr khodā'ī*). Any politics wich is inspired by the Divine is accepted, and any other is rejected. The non-Divine politcs for Khomeyni has two sub-categories: Either it involves the mere struggle for power for the sake of self-glorification, in which case it is "Satanic;" or it provides valuable service for society, but fails to care for the other needs of man, and hence it is deficient. In the words of Khomeyni:

> Politics is said by some to mean deception, robbery, lying, and dominating the wealth and the life of the people.[6] This notion of politics has nothing to do with Islamic politics; it is Satanic politics. . . . Hypothetically, let us suppose there are people who . . . engage in a politics which benefits the people and secures the interest of the nation. The problem with this politics is that it has only a political dimension. . . . This politics is deficient.[7]

According to Khomeyni, ideal politics guides society to "that stage which is in the interest of the society as well as the individual."[8] The "ultimate aim," for Khomeyni, as shown in the previous chapter, is "the straight path" (the Qur'ān, I:6), (i.e., the realization of the revealed plan). "This politics," Khomeyni writes, "belongs exclusively to the prophets."[9] And because the prophets were sent to implement a "revealed" program, politics essentially becomes the implementation of that program. In short, politics for the individual means conformity to the laws and for the state it means the carrying out of that law.

"Politics" Khomeyni says "means administering the affairs of the country." He then adds, "In this sense, all people have the right (*ḥaq*) and even the duty (*taklif*) to participate in politics."[10] A degree of clarification is required here. "Participation" in Khomeyni's view does not have the same connotation as that recognized in the Western sense, i.e., the "natural right" of citizens to compete for the societal pie. It means, rather, that the law allows and grants the "right" (*ḥaq*) of participation to the people while it simultaneously sets limits (*ḥad*) to the extent of participation. What makes Khomeyni's policies so different from that of the West is this: Whereas the contemporary understanding of Western law considers it to be the product and the outcome of efforts by competing citizens, the law for any Muslim is "preexisting and eternal; it represents the absolute good."[11] For example, in the many referendums and elections which have occurred in Iran since the establishment of the Islamic Republic, Khomeyni has urged the people to participate in voting as a religious obligation. On being asked whether obedience to such minor laws as those relating to traffic constituted a religion obligation, and their breach a sin, he answered:

> Obeying the rules and regulations of the Islamic government [i.e., the Iranian government] is a religious obligation (*vājeb-e shar'ī*) and their violation is sin.[12]

This moralistic and legalistic understanding of politics is by no means exclusively Khomeyni's. All Islamic thought, including political philosophy, has one overriding goal: To insure that life is lived in accordance with the revealed program of the Divine, at all times. The primary function of that scheme is to distinguish between those aspects of human behavior which are included in that scheme (i.e., the good), and those which are excluded (i.e., the evil).[13] This notion of the revealed plan provides the basis for the unity of politics and religion in Islam. Under the revealed program, politics is intimately woven into the fabric of the religious order.

It is for this reason that Khomeyni attacks the notion of the separation of the "church" and "state." In fact, he considers the Western propagation of this idea to be a plot by the super-powers designed to undermine Islam. Note, for example, the following passage from his tract on Islamic government, the significance of which he has stressed repeatedly:

> This slogan of the separation of religion and politics, and the demand that Islamic scholars should not intervene in social and political affairs, have been formulated and propagated by the imperialists; it is only the irreligious who repeat them.[14]

Politics, therefore, is a branch of the revealed plan and a tool with which to implement that scheme. A look at Khomeyni's view of law will provide more insight into his view of politics.

Law

Any discussion of Khomeyni's view of law must rely on a chapter entitled "The Law," in his work *Kashf Asrār*.[15] The chapter was written partly in response to an oft-posed question: Does man have the right to formulate laws?[16] Khomeyni's answer to this question is an emphatic "No:"

> Man is only endowed with the right to possess his own wealth; if it is acquired lawfully (*mashrū'*). . . . In short, man has no right to legislation. Whatever law he formulates will be nothing but an academic exercise. Reason dictates that man is subject to no one's command except that of God who possessed the universe and the creatures within it.[17]

Another dichotomy in Khomeyni's thought is explicitly stated in this passage. According to Khomeyni, there are two types of law: man-made law (*qānūn basharī*) and divine law (*qānūn khodā'ī*). The man-made laws are not acceptable for two reasons. First,

> the lawgiver should be someone who is free from self-interest, sensuality and love of self, someone who does not practice oppression. There is no one but God who is free from these vices. Therefore, only God should legislate law.[18]

Second, man-made law

> invites man to material and worldly life only, and distract him from the immortal life. Such laws for man who possesses two lives [on earth and in heaven] and who requires provisions for both lives, are harmful.[19]

The divine laws, however, do not suffer from these deficiencies. "The Islamic law," Khomeyni writes, "takes into account the two aspects of man. It has rules and regulations which help man acquire both material provisions, and those required for heavenly life."[20]

When Khomeyni talks about the divine law he is specifically referring to Islamic law, the *sharī'a*. A few words of explanation are needed. The word *sharī'a* literally means, "the road to the watering-place", or "the clear path to be followed": but it has acquired a technical connotation which refers to the totality of Islamic moral, social, economic, legal and political law.[21] Generally, the *sharī'a* is divided into two sets of obligations and rules. One pertains to worship and devotional acts (*'ebādat*; i.e., man's relation with the divine), and the other governs social relations or mundane transactions (*mo'āmelāt*; i.e., man's relations with his fellow men). It is this feature of the *sharī'a* which led Professor Gibb to write, "As soul and body complement one another in the human organism, so do the two aspects of law complement one another in the social organism."[22] This complementary character of the *sharī'a* inspired Khomeyni's belief that Islamic law is the only correct and acceptable path for humanity. Speaking to the Council of Guardians of this subject he stated:[23]

> If one hundred million people, even if the whole world, were on one side and were saying something contrary to the ordinances of the Qur'ān, you should resist. It is your duty to propagate the laws of God even if the people rebel against you; this was the way the prophets lived.[24]

In summary, "politics" for Khomeyni demands individual conformity to the law, and implementation of it by the community. By "law," Khomeyni has in mind the *sharī'a*, the implementation of which will eliminate "injustice" (*bīdādgarīhā*), "thievery" (*dozdīhā*), and "calamitous unchastity" (*bī-'efatīhāye khānemānsūz*) from society.[25] "The implementation of the Islamic law," Khomeyni writes, "will create the virtuous city [*Madīne-ye Fāẕela*]."[26] How can such a desirable state be realized? The answer to this question is found in Khomeyni's theory of government.

Government

At the onset, a few words of explanation are needed regarding the terms Khomeyni employs to discuss government. He uses the words *ḥukūmat* and *velāyat* interchangeably in his arguments concerning the nature of government. However, an examination of his speeches and writings shows that he assigns a special meaning to each of these terms.

The term *ḥukūmat* is a derivative of the Arabic three letter verb *HKM*, which has a variety of meanings: to pass judgment, to adjudicate, to have authority, to govern, to rule, to dominate, and to command. In its political connotation it is used to mean "government," while in its legal connotation it is used to mean "judicial administration."[27] In both Shī'ī and Sunni history, the *fuquhā* have primarily invoked its legal connotation. For Khomeyni, the word *ḥukūmat* has a dual meaning. It refers to the machinery and institutions which govern the country (i.e., the political regime) and also connotes sovereignty (i.e., the ultimate source of power and law). For example, when he gave the following advice to one of the prime ministers, "Now that you have become the government (*ḥukūmat*) you should know that you are a public servant,"[28] he had the first meaning in mind. But when he stated that "There is only one government (*ḥukūmat*) in Islam and it is that of God,"[29] he uses the term in its second meaning.

The other term, *velāyat,* is a derivative of the Arabic root *valā,* which literally means "to be near." But it has also acquired the following meanings: to govern, to rule, and to protect.[30] For Khomeyni, however, *velāyat* does not mean "government" proper, although many people translate it for him as such. The title of his famous tract on the nature and function of Islamic government, *Velāyat-e Faqīh*, has been most frequently rendered as *Islamic Government.* By *velāyat* he has in mind the function of overseeing and supervising the implementation of the *sharī'ā. Velāyat* therefore means "guardianship." This is in fact the core of Khomeyni's thought on government.

According to Khomeyni, *hukūmat* in its connotation as the political regime of a country deemed necessary (*vājeb ḥasbīya*),[31] only because, security, order and implementation of the laws are pre-requisites of civil life. What type of political regime (i.e., monarchy, democracy, republicanism or constitutionalism) does Khomeyni then prefer? His view reaffirms Islamic thinking on this issue. Islam has not favored any particular regime—monarchy, tyranny, oligarchy, constitutionalism or democracy. As long as those in authority operate within the framework of the *Sharī'a*, the specific type of regime is unimportant. The Qur'ān only goes so far as to say, "O ye who believe! Obey Allah, and obey the messenger and those of you who are in authority" (IV:59), but it never specifies what it means by "those of you who are in authority." This ambiguity led the Sunni majority to argue that the phrase refers to the Caliphs, and led the Shī'īs to argue that it refers to the Imāms. Khomeyni seems to be very much aware of this ambiguity. If the Imāms were present, Khomeyni maintains, they would decide what form of regime it should be under. But now that the Imām is in occultation, Khomeyni has gone so far as to declare that the acceptable regime is to be that of "constitutionalism." The following passage summarizes his argument,

> Islamic government is neither tyrannical nor absolute, but constitutional. It is not constitutional in the current sense of the word, i.e., based on the approval of laws in accordance with the opinion of the majority. It is constitutional in the sense that the rulers are subject to a certain set of conditions in governing and administering the country, conditions that are set forth in the Noble Qur'ān and the Sunna of the Most Noble Messenger. . . . *Islamic government may therefore be defined as the rule of divine law over men.*[32] (emphasis added).

This passage does not provide any specific insight into Khomeyni's ideal regime. However, it allows room for concluding that Khomeyni does not object to the specifics of a government as long as it operates within the framework of the Law. He allows the contemporary political climate to dictate his choice of regime. Let us clarify this point by comparing his view on this issue during the 1940s with that of the 1970s. In 1943 he did not object to the institution of monarchy, as the following passage clearly indicates:

> The *'ulamā* never wanted to destroy the foundation of the government. If, at times, they opposed a ruler, *they opposed him personally,* because they considered him an obstacle in the realization of the country's interest. They have never to this day opposed the principal foundation of monarchy. In fact, most of the great *'ulamā,* such as Khaja Nasir al-Din [d. 1273], Allama Helli [d. 1327] Muhaquq Sani [d. 1532] and Majlesi [d. 1699], accompanied and assisted the monarch.[33] (emphasis added).

His lack of ambivalence and indeed his acceptance of monarchy, became clearer when he wrote "we have not said that the king should be a *faqīh*; the king should be a military officer, but should not violate the principles of Islamic jurisprudence (*fiqh*) which are the official laws of the country."[34]

Khomeyni's opposition to the institution of monarchy came in 1971. As the Pahlavi regime continued their policies of economic and social reforms in Iran, and as the people became more and more alienated from the regime, Khomeyni's animosity toward the government intensified. The celebration of the 2500th year of the reign of monarchy in Iran by the Pahlavis caused the final rift. On October 31, 1971, Khomeyni declared that a monarchical type of regime is incompatible with Islam.[35] Khomeyni referred to an "Islamic government," as an acceptable alternative.[36]

In the early stages of the 1978 revolution, the prevalent view of many Iranians was that the future regime would be a republican one. Khomeyni accepted the notion and declared that the future regime in Iran would be "the Islamic Republic, not one word less, not one word more."[27] He added that there would be nothing unique about the regime itself. Note for example his answer to the reporter of *Le Monde*, who asked what Islamic Republic meant:

> By "republic" it is meant the same types of republicanism as they are at work in other countries. However, this Republic is based on a constitution which is Islamic. The reason we call it the Islamic Republic is that all conditions for the candidates as well as all rules, are based on Islam. . . . The regime will be a Republic just like one anywhere else.[38]

In other words, the form of the regime is not in question as long as it operates within the framework of the *Sharī'a* and is supervised by the *faqīh*. The exact type of Republic to which Khomeyni was referring was never clarified. Moreover, the usual idea that in a republican regime the sovereignty lies with the people was not countenanced by Khomeyni. A look at his view of sovereignty will show this to be the case.

Let us return to the discussion of his definitions and explore the second meaning of *ḥukūmat,* (i.e., the notion of sovereignty). For Khomeyni, there are two types of sovereignty, human (*basharī*) and divine (*elāhī*).[39] A look at the world today and a review of history will show that most countries are ruled by human governments, Khomeyni says. Although they are labeled as Constitutional, Democratic, Socialist or Communist states, they are all actually dictatorships. There is no difference among them, Khomeyni maintains.[40] They are dictatorships because they are the result of man's rule over man. His disapproval of human government can be best summarized in this passage, which was written in 1943:

> Reason and experience alike tell us that the governments now existing in the world were establihsed at bayonet-point, by force. None of the monarchies or governments that we see in the world are based on justice or a correct foundation that is acceptable to reason. Their foundations are all rotten, being nothing but coercion and force. *Reason can never accept that a man who is no different from others in physical or spiritual accomplishments, and even perhaps inferior to them. . . , should have his dictates considered proper and just and his government legitimate. . . .*
> The only government that reason accepts as legitimate and welcomes freely and happily is the government of God.[41] (emphasis added).

Sometimes human governments do not engage in domination and oppression of the people and might even provide services for the people. Khomeyni still would not approve of such governments because they will be deficient in taking care of the spiritual needs of man. As he puts it:

> The worldly governments, regardless of their regime, only concern themselves with the establishment of order in their own country. . . . They do not concern themselves with what the people do in their own homes so long as it is not harmful to the government or to the country.[42]

In other words, human governments, even if they are not tyrannical, only concern themselves with political issues and, for the most part, the establishment of order. "Justice" for human governments, means the prosperity of the community, and order and security for the people. "No regime can be found," Khomeyni says, "which has the rectification (*tahz̄ib*) of people's souls as its aim.[43]

"Human" political regimes provide only political, economic, and social rules and programs but do not concern themselves with the private lives of their subjects. This is the sign of their deficiency. Only divine governments and Islam in particular provide ordinances for all aspects of life, be they related to spiritual life or to mundane affairs.[44] In a sermon delivered in Paris on November 11, 1978, Khomeyni elaborated on the differences between Islamic government and other types of regimes. "The other governments," he says, "only aim at social and political issues; they do not care about what one does when one is alone by himself, in his own home."[45] According to Khomeyni, an Islamic political society "is concerned with an individual's personal affairs as well as those of his family. It has ordinances for one's relations with neighbors, fellow citizens, fellow religionists, and non-believers."[46] This total concern of Islamic political society is indeed necessary because the *raison d'être* of man's existence is ultimate conformity to the divine scheme.

Khomeyni's political society, while appearing at first to resemble the usual description of totalitarianism in the twentieth century, is distinguished by its claim to a higher moral source.[47] His "totalitarianism" is based on the notion that the *Sharī'a* will dictate man's complete existence. And it is for this reason that Khomeyni does not concern himself as much with political regimes as with the nature and function of the divine laws' guardian and the theory of guardianship (*velāyat*).

It is also for this reason that government, in its meaning of "sovereignty," belongs only to God. Any other type of regime which claims sovereignty is unequivocally against Islam because it will hinder the implementation of the Islamic political order. This belief led him to say that "All non-Islamic systems of government are systems which reject the divine guidance, because the ruler in each case is a manifestation of false deity (*ṭāghūt*)."[48]

The Guardianship of the Faqīh

To secure the sovereignty of God on earch, His commands, namely the *Sharī'a*, should be implemented. To secure that implementation, God has appointed special representatives whose duty it is to safeguard the implementation of the law on the one hand and to guard thc people against wrong-doing on the other; hence the notion of guardianship (*velāyat*). As Khomeyni puts it, "government in its notion as sovereignty [of man] does not make sense in Islam."[49] Islam understands guardianship. "Even the prophets," Khomeyni says, "did not have sovereignty over people. . . . The exalted prophets understood that they had been sent to guide the people."[50] The guardianship, Khomeyni writes, "exists only as a type of appointment, like the appointment of a guardian for a minor. With respect to duty and position there is indeed no difference between the guardian of a nation and the guardian of a minor."[51] In addition to shepherding the people, another important responsibility is bestowed upon the office of guardianship, namely, the preservation of Islam itself. In this capacity, the primary function of the person who occupies this office is the preservation of the message. Note for example this passage by Khomeyni:

> Our goal is to fulfill our responsibility, which is the preservation of Islam. Even if we get killed, or kill someone in the process, we do so in order to fulfill that responsibility. . . . Indeed, it is of no importance if we get killed, because if we

> kill [on the path of God] and succeed we have God's blessings as well as worldly success, and if we get killed we will be taken to heaven.[52]

Guardianship in these two capacities is an integral part of political life for Khomeyni. Out of this conviction, he called for an Islamic revolution which would establish the institution of guardianship in Iran.[53] "By guardianship," Khomeyni writes, "we mean the administration and management of the affairs of the country, and the implementation of the sacred laws of the Sharī'a, which are serious and difficult duties but do not earn anyone extraordinary status."[54] One important feature of guardianship (*velāyat*) for Khomeyni is its validity in all times and places. Since God and his laws are eternal, guardianship will be eternal as well:

> Today and always . . . the existence of a holder of authority, a ruler who acts as a trustee and maintains the institutions and laws of Islam, is a necessity—a ruler who prevents cruelty, oppression, and violation of the rights of others; who is a trustworthy and viligant guardian of God's creatures; who guides men to the teachings, doctrines, laws, and institutions of Islam; and who prevents the undesirable changes that atheists and the enemies of religion wish to introduce in the laws and institutions of Islam.[55]

The Identity of the Guardians

One might ask who can be entrusted with such a stupendous task? Or, to put the question more simply, who can be the *vali*—the person who puts into practice the institution of the *velayat*? The ideal person or persons, Khomeyni believes, are the "ruler-prophets." Because of their special qualities, they have direct contact with the divine, relating His plan to men, and guiding the rest of humanity to a virtuous life. Since Muhammad is considered to be the last of the prophets, and the *sharī'a* is the most perfect plan, there will be no need for a new prophet. After the prophet's death, humanity needed infallible leaders (the Imāms) who were able to implement the divine plan. Only the Prophet, as Khomeyni and Shī'ī Muslims believe, was invested with the authority and the duty to appoint future leaders, which he has indeed done:

> We believe in government [*velāyat*] and believe that the Prophet (upon whom be peace) was bound to appoint a successor, as he indeed did. Was a successor designed purely for the sake of expounding law? The expounding of law did not require a successor to the Prophet. He himself, after all, had

> expounded the laws; it would have been enough for the laws to be written down in a book and put into the people's hands to guide them in their actions. It was logically necessary for a successor to be appointed for the sake of exercising government.[56]

Those heirs, as shown in chapter two, were the Imāms, the last of whom went into occulation in 940 A.D. and is expected to reappear, whenever God so commands him. According to Khomeyni, in the absence of the Imāms it would be illogical to suspend the institution of *velāyat*. It is the duty of certain categories of Muslim scholars to assume political responsibility and revitalize the institution of *velāyat*. He considers the revitalization of the Imām's political responsibility by the *'ulamā* to be the pre-requisite for implementation of other Islamic tenets. The *'ulamā*, therefore, should assume the role of guardians as part of their duty. (*'Ulamā* is the general name for the Islamic scholars, whereas the *fuqahā* are those Islamic scholars who have finished their studies and are authorized to pass legal judgment. In this discussion the two are used to refer to the same people.)

Khomeyni suggests that when God appointed the prophet as guardian, his authority extended to prophecy (*nabovvat*), cosmic guardianship (*velāyat-e takvīnī*) and the responsibility for overseeing the implementation of the law. Khomeyni calls the latter "rational and extrinsic matters (*umūr e'tebārī [va] 'oqalā'ī*).[57] Because of their special quality of infallibility, the Imāms inherited all the Prophet's authority, save the gift of prophecy. The *'ulamā*, however, inherited only the last aspect of the Prophet's authority (i.e, the function of overseeing and implementing the Law). As he puts it, "The guardianship of the *faqīh* is a rational extrinsic matter. . . . [I]t is not a privilege but a grave responsibility."[58] The following graph may help to explain Khomeyni's view:

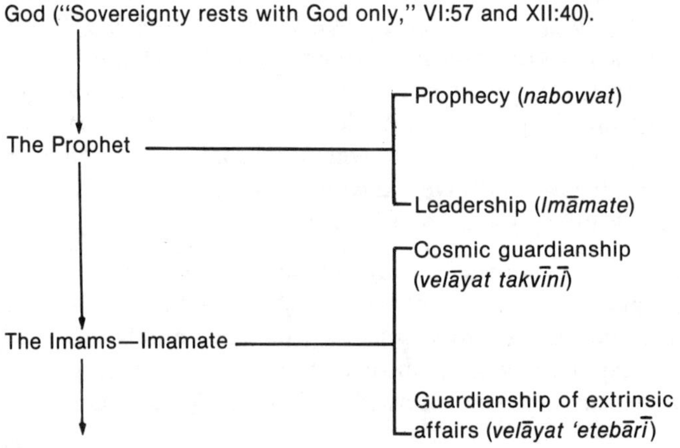

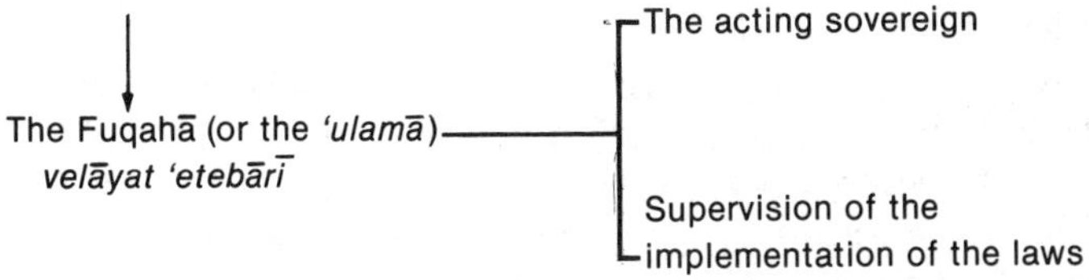

Before looking at the way Khomeyni justifies this position for the *fuqahā* and his perception of their characteristics, the following question should be considered. Should the *fuqahā* assume political and administrative positions in order to guarantee the implementation of the Law? Khomeyni's original answer to this question was "No." The *'ulamā*, according to Khomeyni, should not assume governmental positions. In an answer to a reporter, who asked whether the *'ulamā* can manage a country in this complex world, Khomeyni stated: " *'Ulamā* supervise the situation. The positions will be assumed by lay politicians. The *'ulamā* supervise so that nothing will go wrong."[59] The reason he does not, in principle, approve of the *'ulamā*'s direct access to political positions is that he thinks that their status, efforts and time are too valuable to be spent in trivial administrative and executive tasks.

> I have said from the beginning of the Revolution and from the time victory appeared in sight . . . , in Najaf and in Paris, that the religious leaders (*rohānīyūn*) have more important duties than getting involved in executive affairs.[60]

This view seems to contradict the fact that the president of the Islamic Republic of Iran is a religious leader. Khomeyni explains by saying:

> When we gained control of the country, we realized that we were mistaken. [We realized that] if the religious leaders do not assume executive posts, the country will be either swallowed by the Russians or by the Americans. . . . We are pursuing our interests and not the implementation of our words. . . . Therefore until the time that a group of capable non-religious leaders have been trained to assume these positions [we accept governmental jobs for the religious leaders]. . . . Regardless of what we are called, the country of *mollās*,[61] the regime of *ākhondīsm*[62] or any other name, . . . we will not abandon the battlefield.[63]

The supervisory function of the guardian, however, has more acceptability in the Islamic Republic; all political decisions, regardless of their significance, be they taken in a bank, in a factory, at a university or in a ministry, are being placed under the supervision of a religious leader.

The question to be considered at this stage is why and how the guardianship (*velāyat*) is considered to belong exclusively to the *'ulamā* and not to any other group. In Khomeyni's view, *velāyat* is an institution, an office or a function, which, excepting the Prophet himself and the twelve Imāms of the Shī'ī Islam, is not specified for any particular individual. The position can be occupied by any member of *'ulamā* who has reached the position of a *faqīh* because they have inherited that position from the Imām. To drive his point home Khomeyni cites many traditions from the Prophet as well as the Imāms. Here, two of his syllogisms and two of the traditions to which he refers will be discussed. The first syllogism proves that the *fuqahā* are the rightful leaders, and the second shows the extent of their authority. The first syllogism reads as follows:

> Were God not to appoint over men a solicitous, trustworthy, protecting reliable leader, the community would degenerate.[64]
> The *fuqahā* are the trustees of the Prophet.[65]
> [Therefore], "the *faqīh* must be the leader of the people."[66]

Khomeyni then adds that such a leadership is necessary "in order to prevent Islam from falling into decline."[67] The second syllogism asserts as follows:

> The Prophet has higher authority over the believers than their own selves. (XXXIII:6).
> The *'ulamā* are the heirs of the Prophet.[68]
> Therefore the *'ulamā* have higher authority over the believers.

In Khomeyni's words, "the same rule and governance that has been established for the Most Noble Messenger is also established for the *'ulamā*.[69]

Of the many traditions Khomeyni cites in support of his doctrine of guardianship, two are considered the most important. One is ascribed to the twelfth Imām and the other to the sixth Imām. The first tradition concerns a certain Muslim who called on the twelfth Imām for guidance on problems that he faced.[70] The Imām's response was as follows:

> In case of newly occurring social circumstances, you should turn for guidance to those who relate our traditions, for they are my proof to you, as I am God's proof.[71]

Many scholars before Khomeyni have interpreted the "newly occurring social circumstances" (*havādes̄-e vaqe'a*) as issues related to the legal problems of Muslims. Khomeyni, however, does not agree. "The phrase 'newly occurring social circumstances'," Khomeyni maintains, "does not refer to legal issues, rather, it pertains to new problems facing the Muslims."[72]

The second tradition is known because of its frequent invocation by many scholars. It is associated with the name of its original reporter,

'Umar ibn-Hanzala. Because of its fame and importance the tradition will be related in full.[73]

> 'Umar ibn-Hanzala says: "I asked Imām Sadiq (upon whom be peace) whether it was permissible for two of the Shī'īs who had a disagreement concerning a debt or a legacy to seek the verdict of the ruler or judge." He replied: 'Anyone who has recourse to the ruler or judge, whether his case be just or unjust, has in reality had recourse to *ṭāghūt* [i.e. the illegitimate ruling power]. Whatever he obtains as a result of their verdict, he will have obtained by forbidden means, even if he has a proved right to it, for he will have obtained it through the verdict and judgment of the *ṭāghūt*, that power which God Almighty has commanded him to disbelieve in.' " (They wish to seek justice from illegitimate powers, even though they have been commanded to disbelieve therein" [IV:60].)
>
> 'Umar ibn-Hanzala then asked: "What should two Shī'īs do then, under such circumstances?" Imām Sadiq answered: "They must seek out one of you who narrates our traditions, who is versed in what is permissible and what is forbidden, who is well acquainted with our laws and ordinances, and accept him as judge and arbiter, for I appoint him as judge over you."[74]

The significance of this tradition stems from its explicit recognition of the *'ulamā* as successors to the Imāms. However there is no consent among the Shī'ī thinkers on the functions of the *'ulamā*. Some used this tradition in support for their approval of the Constitutional Revolution (1905–11). Others used it to support the judicial authority of the *'ulamā*.[75] Khomeyni presents a more political interpretation of these traditions. He concludes from them that the *'ulamā* are the only group who are appointed indirectly by God to the position of guardianship.

The Qualifications of the Faqīh

The main qualification is the faithful concentration on one's lifelong program of religious studies. This program entails study of Islamic philosophy, jurisprudence, theology, history, Arabic and Persian languages and literature.[76] Khomeyni, of course, does not consider every student of religion to be qualified for this position, although being part of the Islamic religious institution is a pre-requisite. More specifically the guardian should be well-versed in Islamic sciences and should be a "righteous person" (*'ādil*). "In addition to general requirements such as intelligence and managerial ability (*tadbīr*)," Khomeyni writes, "there are two essential qualifications: knowledge of the law (*'elm be qānūn*) and "righteousness" (*edālat*)."[77]

These two qualifications are very subjective and there is no institutional mechanism for checking and insuring their realization. Note this passage by Khomeyni:

> If a worthy individual possessing these two qualities arises and establishes a government, he will possess the same authority as the Most Noble Messenger (upon whom be peace and blessings) in the administration of society, and it will be the duty of all people to obey him.[78]

How does one guarantee that such a person will not violate the *sharī'a* and will not monopolize the office for personal gain? There is no answer to this question. Khomeyni's optimism about man manifests itself here. One has to share his belief that a person who has become righteous and is well-versed in the *Sharī'a* will not do anything unlawful. But this optimism is not enough. It is true that the guardian is subject to the provisions of the law just as is any other member of the society. But the issue of "who stands guard over the guardians" is not resolved by any clear policy. In fact, the following comment on law and politics in early Sunnism seems to apply as easily to Shī'ī political thought and to Khomeyni's theory of guardianship:

> . . . The ruler was in no way above the law, nor did he embody the law, in the Hobbesian sense. He was clearly under the law, the instrument for its implementation . . . Theoretically, at least, a commandment entailing disobedience to God was not to be obeyed. . . .
>
> However, in the absence of specific procedures and institutions for the removal of an "illegal" ruler, the restraints conceived by the jurists proved worthless.[79]

It is true that Khomeyni says, "If a *faqīh* acts on his own he loses his guardianship (*velāyat*),"[80] but he does not provide an institutional guideline for such a case or a constitutional mechanism for controlling the *faqīh*.

There is, however, one practical restraint which could have great influence over the actual power of the guardian, namely, the leader's popularity. This is better known in Shī'ism as the qualification of *nāfez̄ al-kalema*, which literally means "the one whose opinion is respected."[81] Ayat-Allah Khomenyi is aware of it, despite the fact that he does not give it sufficient treatment.[82] It is also reflected in principle 5 of the Islamic Republic's Constitution, according to which a *faqīh* should "enjoy the confidence of the majority of the people as a leader."[83]

To put this issue in perspective, it seems that the guardian, in addition to having knowledge of law and righteousness should be very "influential" if he wants to assume the position of the supreme guardian of the nation. This latter element, however, makes the whole theory vulnerable to demagoguery and mob politics. It seems that the recognition of this vulnerability is responsible for the formulation of Article 107 of the Constitution, which calls for an Assembly of Experts to select Khomeyni's successor as the supreme guardian if a very influential *faqīh* does not "emerge."

To sum up Khomeyni's view of government, it is seen basically to be the mechanism for administration of the *Sharī'a*. It has two distinct features. One feature deals with the political regime, to which Khomeyni does not pay much attention. The republican form of regime, for example, was a product of the political situation of the pre-revolutionary climate. The other feature of government deals with the question of sovereignty. This is the area with which Khomeyni concerns himself most. Sovereignty belongs to God only. He has delegated some of His sovereignty to the Prophet, then to the Imāms and through them to the *fuqahā*. In Khomeyni view the *faqīh*'s duty is to guard the people so that they can live their life in accordance with the revealed law. But the law and its guardians have no utility without subjects, which brings us to the final major question of this chapter. What is Khomeyni's notion of political society?

The State

Most contemporary Muslim thinkers use the term *dawla* when they discuss the state. However, this term does not mean "state." It literally means "to alternate or to change periodically," and historically it has been used to mean "dynasty."[84] Even those Muslim contemporaries who employ the term to connote "state," interchangeably use it to mean "government." To avoid any confusion here let us say a few words about the way in which the word state is defined and used.

To the question "what is state" one can respond with a variety of definitions. Max Weber writes,

> [S]tate is a human community that (successfully) claims the *monopoly of legitimate use of physical force* within a given territory. Note that "territory" is one of the characteristics of the state.[85] (emphasis in the original).

Hans Morgenthau's definition proceeds along the same lines. For him, "State is but another name for the compulsory organization of society . . . ."[86] However, the state is more than just a monopoly of force, although this is one of its overriding characteristics. Among the various definitions of state in use today, the most generally accepted one is that offered by Professor Robert M. MacIver, according to whom

> *The state is an association which, acting through law as promulgated by a government endowed to this end with coercive power, maintains within a community territorially demarcated the universal external condition of social orders.*[87] (emphasis in the original).

It is easily inferred that "state," as used by political scientists today, refers to a political society which possesses a government, comprises a particular segment of the world's population, and exercises sovereignty domestically over a demarcated territory and internationally in its relations with other states. The two significant characteristics seem to be the concepts of sovereignty and of territoriality. And these two characteristics have dictated the path that states should take, namely, the preservation of their integrity and independence, or what is known in the history of the evolution of state as *raison d'état*. Friedrich Meinecke begins his classic *Machiavelism* on the history of *raison d'état* by calling this theory "The State's First Law of Motion."[88] Meinecke shows how *raison d'état* dictates both the path, goal and growth of the state:

> The well-being of the State and of its population is held to be the ultimate value and the goal; and power, maintenance of power, extension of power, is the indispensable means which must—without any qualification—be procured.[89]

Does Khomeyni's view of state resemble this? Does the state for Khomeyni mean a political society whose ultimate aim is to preserve itself as a whole through the means of power? Having seen his view of politics and government, the answer seems to be an unequivocal "No." Like all Muslim thinkers, Khomeyni's unit of political society is the *Umma*. The simplest definition of this concept identified *Umma* as "a certain segment of the population which has been sent a Prophet."[90] But this does not tell us much. Perhaps the following will shed some light on this important concept.

> The passages in the Kur'an [Qur'ān], in which the word *Umma* (plur. *Umam*) occurs are so varied that its meaning cannot be rigidly defined. This much however seems to be certain, that it always *refers to ethical, linguistic or religious bodies of people who are the objects of the divine plan of salvation*.[91] (emphasis added).

As the passage clearly and rightly shows, the basis of Islamic political society is the divine plan and not politics or territory.

It has been shown earlier that the central issue of politics is the *sharī'a* and its implementation. And it has been shown in the discussion of government that the central issue there is that of authority and the way in which it is realized in the form of guardianship. Therefore, the most significant characteristics of Islamic political society are leadership (*Imāmate*) and ideology (the *Sharī'a*). In contrast to the Western notion of state, territory plays a very small role in the Islamic *Umma*. It is true that patriotism and the defense of one's homeland are accepted and indeed encouraged in Islam. But one can argue that patriotism was and is encouraged for the protection of the Islamic stronghold. Note, for example, Khomeyni's words here:

> All these martyrs, invalids and homeless ones were for the cause of Islam. We suffered all these calamities for Iran only because it is an Islamic country.[92]

or

> This Iranian, Bakhtiyar,[93] who has resided in England . . . and claims to be an Iranian first and a Muslim second is practicing polytheism (*kofr*).[94]

As Professor Lambton asserts in discussing the nature of state in early Islam, "The basis of the Islamic state was ideological—not political, territorial or ethical and the primary purpose of government was to defend and protect the faith, not the state."[95] This passage, without any modification, applies to Khomeyni's view of the issue. In 1964, for example he said:

> Islam has dismissed racism. There is no difference between blacks, whites, Turks or non-Turks. The only point of reference and source of loyalty is Islam, in which righteousness is the only standard. "The noblest of you, in the sight of Allah, is the best in conduct.' [XLIX:13].[96]

In September 1979, he said:

> I have repeatedly emphasized that Islam does not recognize race, group, and so on. Islam is for all people.[97]

Similar to the Prophet's pragmatism at the time of the establishment of the first political society in Islam (622 A.D. in Madina), Khomeyni's political society includes all those non-Muslims who are recognized in the *Sharī'a* (the Jews, the Christians and the Zoroastrians) as well as those who do not present any threat to his Islamic Republic.[98] Like early Islamic practices which identified every institution in the state with God and used such expressions as *māl-Allāh* for public treasury, and *jund-Allāh* for the army, in Khomeyni's Islamic Republic such expressions as *ḥezb-Allāh* (the party of God), *yom-Allāh* (the special occasion for God), *jund-Allāh* (the army of God) and *ummat-Allāh* (the country of God) are frequently used. The political society, or the *Umma*, for Khomeyni is therefore by no means similar to the territorial state. It is, rather, a community of people who believe in an all-powerful God, who abide by an all-comprehensive program under the guardianship of the *faqīh* as God's agent.

The dichotomy of *Umma* vs. the state is very clear. The concept of *raison d'êtat*, therefore, at least in theory, plays no part in Khomeyni's thought. Instead the doctrine of the *raison d'ideologie* might be used to explain Khomeyni's view of state. It is the ideology, i.e., Islam, which must dictate both the path and the goal of the political society. To be sure, *raison d'êtat* in practice plays as much of a role in the behavior of Khomeyni's political society as it does in other political societies. It will be shown in the next chapter how the war between Iran and Iraq is justified by the doctrine of *raison d'ideologie*, while it is perfectly clear that the war is also a good case of *raison d'êtat* at work. This discrepancy may very well be an instance of the inevitable schism between theory and practice.

All in all, however, *raison d'ideologie* plays a significant role in Khomeyni's thought. Note for example the following passage:

> When the aim is Islam and the implementation of the Qur'ānic ordinances . . . everyone of these martyrs, despite their sorrowful death, are fruitful to the cause.[99]

The aim for Khomeyni is clearly not the preservation of individual's life but advancement of the ideology even if people must be "martyred." The following passage is even more striking:

> The preservation of the Islamic Republic is a divine duty which is above all other duties. It is even more important than preserving the Imām of Age (*Imām-e 'aṣr*),[100] because even the Imām of Age will sacrifice himself for Islam. All the prophets from the birth of the universe to the present were sent to strive for preservation of God's words. . . . Islam is a divine endowment. . . . Its preservation is an inexcusable individual obligation (*vājeb-e 'eynī*).[101]

Ideology, therefore, seems to be the central foundation of Khomeyni's political society. Other elements—namely territory, population and government—are important as well. But their role is instrumental. The territorial aspect of his political society is important insofar as it constitutes the basis of operation for society. For example, on the occasion of any political victory for the Iranian army in its war against Iraq, he congratulated the soldiers for their bravery in defending the land of Islam. On one of these occasions, in early July 1981, he said:

> Iran . . . is determined to propagate Islam to the whole world. *She takes pride in being the springboard for the advancement of Islam*. From Iran the divine revelation and the message of the Exalted Prophet will travel everywhere.[102] (emphasis added).

Khomeyni places greater importance on the human rather than the territorial element of state. He is quite aware of the danger of the lack of the people's support. He repeatedly warns the officials against aggravating the people. The following passage is typical of his message in that regard.

> Government can hardly function without the support of the people. . . . If one looks at the fifty years of the Pahlavi's monarchy and remembers their fate, one will realize what it means to rule without their support.[103]

The irony is that on the same occasion he urges the official to provide services for the people "for the sake of God."[104] It seems, then, that Khomeyni's concern for the people, as well as the display of his patriotism, is the result of the pressures of political reality. The unfortunate fate of the Pahlavi regime contributes to his concern for the people. Theoretically, however, the people should be thankful to the Islamic Republic for its policy of cleansing the society of its undesirable and corrupt elements, influences and practices.

Nationalism

To end the discussion of Khomeyni's view of the state, a few words should be added about his understanding of nationalism. "Every nation has a right to self-determination," Khomeyni said in October 1978.[105] This sentence suggests that he understands nationalism. But one should ask what he means by 'nation?' When he made that comment he was referring to Iranian people, and by "self-determination" he meant the right to establish an Islamic government. A careful study of his speeches and writings suggests that by "nation" he means the Islamic people who are bound together by the *Sharī'a*; he has *Umma* in mind and not simply Iran. "I remind you," Khomeyni says, "that for us language and territory do not make sense. Those who talk of languages are non-Muslims and are inspired by a false deity (*ṭāghūt*)."[106] On another occasion he summarized his argument by saying:

> Nationalism, in the sense that each country with its own special language should stand against another country with its special language, this runs contrary to the basis of the Prophet's call.
>
> The Prophets from the first to the last came to invite people to unity, friendship and brotherhood. . . . Islam came to establish community of brothers. "The believers are naught else than brothers" [XLIX:10].[107]

He becomes more specific about what he means by nationalism when he says "nationalism is this: pan-Iranism, pan-Arabism and pan-Turkism. This is contrary to God's will and words in the Qur'ān."[108] Khomeyni has been very consistent in this view all along.[109] He has also been consistent about the source of nationalism. Nationalism is a great trick of the West to undermine Islam. "After the introduction of nationalism by the Imperialists [the West]," Khomeyni says, "their lackeys propagated it in the Islamic world."[110] In fact any movement which in one way or another might prove to be a source of threat to Khomeyni's ideology, is without a trace of doubt inspired by forces outside the Khomeyni ideological milieu.

If nationalism, however, is seen more in the sense of solidarity, Khomeyni welcomes that eagerly. It is clear by now that indeed the source of vitality in Khomeyni's political society is the ideological solidarity of its members. The aim of Khomeyni's political society is to establish a conformity of viewpoints among its members, what Khomeyni calls *vaḥdat-e Kalamah*. It may be translated as the "unity of outlook." According to Khomeyni, the unity of outlook is the most important factor in the victory of the Revolution.[111]

Conclusion

It was in order to form a political society with one ideology—namely Islam—that Khomeyni defined politics as an individual's conformity to the *sharī'a* and its implementation by the society. For this reason, he defined government as the instrument by which the *Sharī'a* is to be implemented; and from his concept of government he developed the theory of guardianship to serve as the guarantor in that process. Finally, it was the formation of such a society which led Khomeyni to discard the Western understanding of "state" and to propagate *Umma*. But how does his political society interact with others? He answers this question in his theory of international relations to which our discussion turns next.

CHAPTER VI
KHOMEYNI'S VIEW OF INTERNATIONAL RELATIONS

And Allah will not give the disbelievers any way (to succeed) against the believers. (The Qur'ān, IV:141)

We do not live under anyone's protection. We live only under the banners of Islam, and no one has any influence over us.

Khomeyni

How does Khomeyni's Islamic community interact with other states and what type of relationship does the *faqīh* conceive for his state? Khomeyni's view of international relations will provide answers to this question. For its understanding, both theoretical and practical issues will be examined.[1] The chapter, therefore, centers around the following questions: what is Ayat-Allah Khomeyni's understanding of the existing territorial state system? How does his view of international relations compare with those based on a western perspective? Does he have his own theory of international relations? How should one evaluate his theory in terms of the actual behavior of the states? For example, what is the role of such concepts as the "exporting of the Islamic Revolution," the idea of "unity among Muslims" and the issue of war and peace in his thought?

The Territorial State System and Khomeyni's Understanding of It

The international system today is a system comprised of independent territorial states. Following the birth and growth of the modern notion of the state in the aftermath of the Treaty of Westphalia (1648), states have had a complex set of relationships which is now referred to by most scholars as the international system. The oldest definition is that of Samuel von Pufendorf, who thought that a system of states is "several states that are so connected as to seem to constitute one body but whose members retain sovereignty."[2] A more incisive definition, with regard to states' behavior, is provided by Hans J. Morgenthau, who defines it as the dynamic interaction among a group of independent states which engage in efforts "to maintain and to increase the power" of their own nations or "to keep in check or reduce the power of other nations."[3] However, the most comprehensive definition of the present international system may be that of Hedley Bull. According to him:

> A *system of states* (or international system) is formed when two or more states have sufficient contact between them, and have sufficient impact on one another's decisions, to cause them to behave—at least in some measure—as parts of a whole.[4] (emphasis in the original).

The defination refers to a system comprised of parties who have certain rights and engage in power relations with one another. Their contacts might be diplomatic, economic, cultural or military. They are engaged in political relationship in the broadest sense. In short, when we are talking about an international system we are referring to a system comprised of independent territorial states who recognize no political sovereign above themselves.

Does Khomeyni understand the system in the above sense? It does not suffice merely to propose a "yes" or a "no" answer, because he operates within a totally different philosophical framework. A study of his writings and speeches reveals that he thinks of the system in terms of what the British historian, Martin Wight called the "secondary states system." Martin Wight distinguished between two types of international systems. An international system is composed either of sovereign states or of suzerain-state systems.[5] The former system he called a "primary states system" and the latter a "secondary states system." Wight's understanding of a primary states system is equivalent to the earlier defination of the international system. However, the suzzerain-state system which comprises the secondary states system needs further explanation. By suzerain-state system, Wight meant a system in which one state asserts and maintains domination and supremacy over the rest. It is not imperial because the member states have a certain independence, nor is it a hegemonial relation because the preponderant state has more than power over the suzerain-states; it exercises authority as well. For Wight, the Roman Empire, the Abbasid Caliphate or Imperial China are good examples of suzerain-state systems. As he put it:

> Here [in these empires] there is indeed a group of states having relations more or less permanent with one another, but one among them asserts unique claims which the others formally or tacitly accept. This is the suzerain, the sole source of

> legitimate authority, conferring status on the rest and exacting tribute or other marks of difference. . . . we might distinguish these from international states-systems by calling them *suzerain* state systems.[6]

According to Khomeyni the international system today is a secondary states system comprised of two suzerain-state systems, one is the West (*gharb*) under the domination of the United States and the other is the East (*sharq*) under the domination of the Soviet Union. There is a basic difference between Khomeyni's understanding of the system and that of Martin Wight. Whereas the latter bases his argument on power and territorial states, the former bases his system on ideology. According to Khomeyni:

> There are only three paths: one is the 'straight path;'' [I:6] the others are the path of the East, "those who earn thine anger" [I:7] and the path of the West, "those who go astray" [I:7] . . . . The straight path is the path of Islam, which is the true path of humanity; it leads man to perfection, and belongs to God.[7]

Translated into political language, the world is comprised of powers who dominate it for their own interest. "The political situation of the world is such," Khomeyni says, "that all countries of the world are under the political supervision of super-powers, who supervise everywhere. The superpowers have plans to defeat all nations and groups to further their own advantages."[8] Although he uses the word "supervise" to express the relation of super-powers and other states, what he has in mind is a master-slave relationship. For example, he truly believes that the Shah was the "lackey of the Americans" or "the stooge of the Americans." He extends this analogy to the international scene and believes that the super-powers are the masters of the world, each in its own suzerain-state. By superpowers he has in mind the United States and Soviet Union, which according to him are the two sources of all the world's contemporary problems. Note, for example, Khomeyni's words:

> The threat to the world today stems from the two superpowers. They have manipulated the whole world under their own control and use it for their own interests. They formulate plans, some of which, such as the building of arsenals, are dangerous for humanity.[9]

The "interests" of the superpowers are nothing but self-aggrandizement and power, according to Khomeyni. "It is lust for power," Khomeyni writes, "which motivates America to commit crimes which have no equal in history.[10] It is the lust for domination and superiority which instigates the Soviet Union[11] to treat the oppressed people of the world unjustly."[12] The reason they define their interests in terms of power and superiority, Khomeyni says, is that their *raison d'être* is based on human ideologies. They pursue interests that are formulated according to man's capabilities alone. Moreover, they pursue only power because like all other states, their governments are based on force and on the idea of domination. As he puts it:

> Reason and experience alike tell us that the governments now existing in the world were established by bayonet-point, by force. None of the monarchies or governments that we see in the world are based on justice or [on] a correct foundation that is acceptable to reason. Their foundations are all rotten, being nothing but coercion and force.[13]

Because the United States and the Soviet Union are the most powerful countries in the world today, in Khomeyni's view, they have established suzerain-state systems around themselves and are in this way ruling the world. It is this belief which leads him to say that the future lies with "neither West nor East, only Islam;" or, more explicitly, "neither Soviet Union, nor America, but Islam and Muslims."[14] He continues:

> One cannot find a country today whose motto is "neither the East nor the West;" [all countries] rely officially or unofficially either on the Eastern Bloc or on the Western Bloc. Do not even believe the non-Aligned nations; it is rare that a country among them is really non-Aligned. Today we are confronted by the East and the West, by the Eastern Bloc and the Western Bloc. All the countries in all the regions of the world are under their domination.[15]

Only the Islamic Revolution and its Republic pursue a policy of "neither West, nor East." "We oppose international communism just as much," Khomeyni says, "as we struggle against the world dominators (*jahān-khārān*)[16] of the West under the leadership of the United States."[17]

In principle he has dismissed both superpowers as being the sources of evil and all the ills of world politics. In practice, however he has expressed harsher opinions about the United States than about the Soviet Union. The United States has been called time and again "the great Satan." "In this Revolution," Khomeyni declared, "America is the great Satan."[18] He has also declared that "our nation considers America its number one enemy."[19] The roots of Khomeyni's animosity go back to his perception of United States/Iran relations.[20] In other words, Khomeyni's attitude is colored more by existing political reality than by ideological convictions.

Based on Islamic tenets, Khomeyni should be more at odds with the atheistic Soviet Union than with the God-fearing America.

His direct attack against the United States came in the early 1960s after the Iranian government granted special status to the American military personnel stationed in Iran.[21] In a sermon he delivered immediately after the government made that decision, Khomeyni insisted that by this act Iran had made itself the servant of the U.S. He then added:

> America is worse than Britain; Britain is worse than America. The Soviet Union is worse than both of them. . . . But today it is America that we are concerned with. . . . All of our troubles today are caused by America and Israel. Israel itself derives from America; these deputies and ministers that have been imposed upon us derive from America--they are all agents of America, for it they were not, they would rise up in protest.[22]

This animosity intensified after the Revolution, because the United States opposed it. The Russians soon recognized the new regime and the Soviet-backed Tudeh Communist party approved of Khomeyni's every step. Perhaps this was why he concluded that anyone else who opposes that Islamic Republic must inevitably be the lackey of the Americans:

> These groups who cause trouble in universities, in mass media institutions, in agricultural areas and so on . . . and who claim to be communists; I think are American stooges. In every corner of the world the Americans have certain plans. In Muslim countries they train Marxists and pseudo-Marxists [to further their aim].[23]

The animosity toward the superpowers is quite understandable, particularly if one recalls his view of the "state." If political society, according to Khomeyni, is based on ideology and not on territory or politics, Khomeyni's understanding of the international system must be cast in terms of ideology as well. The boundaries between the states are ideological and not territorial. The following passage is indicative of Khomeyni's thought:

> These boundaries drawn around [territories of] the world to designate a country or a homeland are the product of the deficient human mind. . . . The world is the homeland of humanity. All people should reach the salvation of both worlds here. This will happen only by implementation of God's divine laws.[24]

Khomeyni's Theory of International Relations

When one looks at Khomeyni's view of international relations, his ideological conviction translates into a new dichotomy. It is true that the existing international system is for him a secondary states system composed of two suzerain-states, but when this view of the world is seen in relation to Islam, both super-powers join together to form an antagonistic front against Islam. Both the liberal humanism of the West and the Marxist Communism of the East are human ideologies (*makāteb-e ensānī*). In Khomeyni's mind, they both contradict the divine revelation of Islam. "No revolution [in history] has been attacked as much as the Iranian Revolution has been, . . . because, " Khomeyni says, "other revolutions have either tended toward the left or the right. If they tended toward the left, the leftists supported them, and *vice versa*. The Islamic Revolution has been Islamic from its birth."[25] By "left," Khomeyni has in mind the Eastern bloc, and by "right" he refers to the West. Islam is represented by the Iranian Revolution on one side and the forces of East and West on the other.

The correspondence between this dichotomy and that of *Dār al-Islām* (the abode of Islam) vs. the *Dār al-Ḥarb* (the abode of war, or the place of non-believers) is striking. The early Muslim jurists divided the world, in terms of its relation to the *Sharī'a*, into *Dār al-Islām* and *Dār al-Ḥarb*. The former meant those communities over which the *Sharī'a* had jurisdiction. Although they were not required to be Muslims, monotheism was a pre-requisite for becoming part of the Islamic society. It was a *pax Islamica* comprised of Muslims and non-Muslims, also, the latter having submitted to Muslim sovereignty.[26] *Dār al-Ḥarb* was the opposite of *Dār al-Islām* and it was used to refer to those communities who were hostile to the Muslim's security and interests.[27]

The dichotomy, in practice, was not as black and white as it appears in theory. Two other divisions were added to this original scheme. They were *Dār al-Ṣulḥ* (also known as *dār al-'ahd*), the area which has maintained a tributary relationship to Islam, and *Dār al-Movāde'a,* the area which has formed a truce with the Islamic State.[28] These additional categories were based on examples which had occurred during the reign of the Prophet (622–632). The first was modeled after the relationship of the Prophet with the tribes of Najran and Nubia, who were not totally under the *Sharī'a* but were protected by the Islamic community and agreed to pay certain taxes.[29] *Dār al-Movāde'a* seems to apply to those who concluded a truce of some sort with the Muslims. It refers to those areas which are neither at war with the Muslims nor are under the protection of Muslims. They might be those who have concluded a non-aggression pact with the Muslims. The cases in point are the truce with Quraysh in Hudaybiyah[30] (618 A.D.) and the truce with the Jews and other tribes in Medina in the form of a treaty better known as the "Constitution of Medina."[31]

Ayat-Allah Khomeyni also divides the world in terms of Islam into two realms. He uses different terminologies from the classical jurists: *Mostaẕ'afān* (the oppressed) vs. *Mostakbarān* (the oppressors). The word *Mostaẕ'afān* is the plural of the word *mostaẕ'af,* which literally means "deemed weak." But in its political sense refers to the Qur'anic verses "we were oppressed in the land" (II:97), and "who were oppressed in the earth" (XXVII:5). It has been shown that according to Ayat-Allah Khomeyni the world today is in the hands of the superpowers. Therefore, when he uses this term he seems to refer to subjugated peoples anywhere and not just to the Muslim countries who, according to him, are under domination. Khomeyni asserts:

> Beware that the world today will be that of the oppressed (*mostaẕ'afān*); sooner or later they will be victorious. God has promised that they will inherit and rule the earth.[32] Once again I declare my full support for all movements, groups and parties who struggle against the superpowers of left or right.[33]

The term *mostakbarān* is a derivative of the Arabic verb KBR meaning enhance, aggrandize, expand, and many other synonyms which relate to the notion of amplification. In the *Qur'ān,* however, it has been used to mean "disdain" (as in XXXIII:69 and LXIII:5). But in other places it is also applied to those who do not submit to God and are prideful and therefore rebellious [as in "But as for those who believe not in the Hereafter, their hearts refuse to know, for they are rebellious (oppressors)" (XVI:22); or "Lo! He loveth not the rebellious (oppressor)" (XVI:23)]. Note that there is no limit attached to any of the term's meanings. In Khomeyni's use, it refers to all forces who do not submit to God's plan and subjugate others, be they rich people in a single country or the powerful states themselves. In a more specific sense, he uses the term "oppressors" to refer to the enemies of the Islamic Revolution, whether inside or outside Iran. Thus, when he says, "The twelfth of Farvardin (April 1, 1979)[34] is the anniversary of the formal establishment of the government of the oppressed (*mostaẕ'afān*) over the oppressors (*mostakbarān*) in Iran," he has the oligarchy of the Pahlavi's Iran in mind.[35] When he says "these oppressors (*mostakbarān*) do not create anything, but cause corruptions," he has the powerful states in mind.[36]

The world for Khomeyni has two poles: that of the oppressed who have been deprived of their resources, and that of the oppressors who have subjugated the disinherited. When they are translated into political jargon they become the world of superpowers and those who associate with them, and the world of those who are powerless. If one is reminded of Khomeyni's view of the world today, according to which there is no power that is not dependent on the superpowers, the dichotomous scheme is reduced to the Islamic Republic of Iran as the only righteous force against the whole "corrupt" world.

In practice the Islamic Republic has not followed this dichotomy closely. Although Ayat-Allah Khomeyni has not so acknowledged, his silence on the subject of Iran's relations with certain states seems to indicate that he tolerates adjustments to this dichotomy. Syria, which has been friendly toward the Islamic Republic since the latter's formation, has never been accused of being a puppet to the Soviet Union, despite the former's close ties with that country. Japan, which is one of the world's most technologically advanced countries and also under the United State's defense umbrella, has seldom been condemned. Indeed, Japan has often been portrayed as a good model of a technologically advanced country which has been able to "preserve" its indigenous culture.

Are these states, and other countries which are in good standing with the Islamic Republic of Iran, in Khomeyni's mind in *Dār al-Movāde'a* (the abode of non-agrression truce) with Islam? He is not explicit on this question. While he has not stopped Iran from having friendly relations with non-Muslim countries (such as North Korea), in his rhetoric he appears to suggest that these relations are temporary in nature. The balance of power should be transformed to the advantage of the oppressed represented by the Islamic Republic of Iran. The following is typical of his thought on the issue:

> All the oppressed should join together and eradicate the roots of corruption from their countries. Security and peace in the world depends on the downfall of the oppressors. As long as these un-cultures (*bī-farhang*) dominators exist on earth, the disinherited will not acquire their God-promised[37] rightful heritage.[38]

God's promise that the disinherited will rule the world, and Ayat-Allah Khomeyni's optimism about man's ability to establish a just order, provide more substance to this dichotomy and the temporary nature of its existence:

> The relations between nations should be based on spiritual grounds in which distance plays no role; there are many neighbors who have no relations.[39]

As it stands today, Khomeyni maintains, there is only the logic of the oppressors which rules over the relations between the nations. In answer to a Japanese news reporter who, in reference to the taking of the hostages in the American embassy in Tehran (November 4, 1979) asked, "What do you think about those countries who worry that the hostage-taking in Iran may establish a dangerous precedent?" Khomeyni replied:

> It seems that the countries of the world are for you the same as they are for [President] Carter. . . . It is the logic of superpowers which sees the countries of the world as those whose leaders reside in castles and palaces. . . . Our difficulties are the problems of a plundered (*ghārat shodeh*) nation facing a plundering tyrant (*ẕālem-e ghāratgar*). Nothing makes sense beyond this dichotomy.[40]

By the "logic of the superpowers," Ayat-Allah Khomeyni means man-made laws (*qavānīn basharī*), human-inspired ideologies (*maktabhā-ye ensāni*), worldly governments (*ḥukūmathā-ye ensānī*), and the path to worldly life (*zendegī-ye donyā'ī*). Although the logic of "oppressed" people should mean subjugated people's grievances, for him, the logic of the disinherited comprises the divine laws (*qavānīn khodā'ī*), divine ideologies (*maktabhā-ye khodā'ī*) or religions, divine authorities (*velāyat*), and the path toward a higher life (*rāh-e khodā*). Khomeyni explains:

> Whatever is in accordance with Islam and its laws we will obey with humility. However, whatever contradicts Islam and the *Qur'ān,* be it constitutional law or international treaties, we will oppose it.[31]

* * *

> I hope that a party named the Party of the Oppressed (*ḥezb-e mostaẕ'afān*) will be established . . . and will rise against the oppressors (*mostakbarān*) and the plunderers (*chapāvolgarān*). . . . They then will establish the call of Islam, which is the government of the oppressed over the oppressors . . . on the earth.[42]

The second passage is of particular importance here, because it summarizes Ayat-Allah Khomeyni's international relations theory. There are two forces in the world; one is the oppressed, the other the oppresssor. The oppressed should rise and destroy the opresssors. But the struggle should not end there. If it does, the oppressed will act as the oppressors later. The remedy is for the disinherited to establish "the call of Islam" which will put an end to the logic of the oppressors.

The logic of the oppressors is the result of one culture, while the logic of the disinherited is the product of another. Khomeyni has not dealt with it on the international level, but in a sermon he has spoken of the working of the two cultures within Iran. One is the Islamic culture, which produces the logic of the oppressed, and the other is what he calls "the imported culture," i.e., the culture of the East or the West, which produces the logic of the oppressors.[43] He has argued that under the imported culture the Iranian universities, parliament, army, and all institutions in general were formed in order to serve the world plunderers.[44] On the contrary, the logic of Islamic culture has created such a country and has brought such a conversion in the people that everything works for God. "It is the Islamic culture," Khomeyni says, "that has caused young Iranians . . . to stand up to the world's powers, . . . has made them so courageous that they volunteer to fight for God . . . and has made a courageous nation out of us."[45]

Whereas the logic of Islam, when realized, means permanent security and peace, the logic of the oppressors means an endless struggle for domination. "The United States wants to destroy the Soviet Union," Khomeyni says, "and the Soviet Union wants to destroy the United States. The irony is that even if you give the whole world to one of them she will not be satisfied."[46]

Does Ayat-Allah Khomeyni want to destroy this logic? In some of the aforementioned passages he clearly sugggests that the "security and peace of the world depends on the downfall of the oppressors."[47] But is this a theoretical whim or a conviction which might become a concrete political goal and policy? In answering this question, let us look at some political issues which recurrently appear in his thought on international relations: the exporting of the revolution, Islamic unity, and war and peace.

Exporting the Revolution

Crane Brinton, in his classic work, *The Anatomy of Revolution,* shows that the revolutions under study "as gospels, as forms of religion, . . . are all universalist in aspiration."[48] Is Khomeyni's universalism the effect of revolutionary fervor? The answer is not clearcut. It cannot be explained as revolutionary fervor, because Khomeyni claims to be only the spokesman of a universal religion that has been revealed to humanity.

> The Iranian Revolution is not exclusively that of Iran, because Islam does not belong to any particular people. Islam is revealed for mankind and the Muslims, not for Iran. . . . An Islamic movement, therefore, cannot limit itself to any particular country, not even to the Islamic countries; it is the continuation of the revolution by the prophets.[49]

If the argument is carried to its logical conclusion, the export of the revolution will be one of its inevitable by-products. Ayat-Allah Khomeyni's statements such as "we do not see the revolution as an Iranian Revolution, rather it is an Islamic one," or "a movement by the oppressed against the oppressors," support this conclusion.[50] One does not necessarily have to resort to deductive reasoning. Time and again, Khomeyni has explicitly stated that one purpose of the Islamic Revolution is to spread Islam's message. The following few passages illustrate this point:

> The Islamic Republic intends to implement the ordinances of the Qur'ān and those of the messenger of God in all countries. Iran is the starting point. It intends to demonstrate to all countries that Islam is based on equality, brotherhood and unity.[51]
>
> * * *
>
> We will export our Revolution throughout the world because it is an Islamic revolution. The struggle will continue until the calls "there is no god but God" and "Muhammad is the messenger of God" are echoed all over the world. The struggle will continue as long as the oppressors subjugate people in every corner of the world.[52]
>
> * * *
>
> The aim is that Islam and Islamic laws shall govern us. . . . [The aim is] that, excepting God's laws, nothing and no one else shall rule. . . . We want the government of God (*ḥukūmat Allāh*) in our country and, God willing, to dominate in other countries.[53]

Khomeyni's ideals, therefore, are very clear. He would like to see Islam dominate the world. But let us consider two further questions. First, what does he mean by exporting the revolution? Second, how does he want to export it? With respect to the first question, Khomeyni answers as follows:

> When we say we want to export our Revolution we mean we would like to export this spirituality which dominates Iran. . . . We have no intention to attack anyone with swords or other arms.[54]

It is Iran's "enthusiasm" about Islam that Ayat-Allah Khomeyni wants to export. He believes that if the enthusiams were exported, the Muslim masses would rise up and rid themselves of the seemingly corrupt regimes which rule them now.

With respect to the second question, that is, "how" the Revolution will be exported, Khomeyni relies on propaganda and preaching. As he put it:

> The issue of propagation should have the highest priority; one can say that propaganda rules the world. The best device that can implement the revolution in Iran and export it into other places is sound advertising. Do not exaggerate anything. We have such a commodity that it requires no exaggeration.[55]

Khomeyni believes that if a small group from each country were enlightened, it would be sufficient to begin an Islamic Revolution. He told a group of delegates from religious communities of Islamic countries that they should try to "awaken their own nations."[56] And if they can do so, the same conversion that thas happened in Iran will happen in their countries. Moreover, he added on another occasion, "All the prophets began as lonely individuals, . . . but they persisted."[57] The Muslim countries should do the same.

On the subject of revolution, historians have argued that a religious call to spread a message becomes a "holy war." Why then does Khomeyni call for propaganda? There are two possible answers. First, according to the Shī'ī view, only the infallible Imāms are authorized to initiate offensive wars for the purpose of religious expansion. We will pursue this issue further when discussing war and peace. Second, he believes that the Islamic Revolution succeeded mainly because of the propaganda war against the Pahlavis. But he fails to recognize two facts. The first is that the revolution had other causes. The second is that he possesses great intuitive power for sensing the right political moment to further his end. Treatment of the first point is not within the scope of this work. The second point will be treated in the following chapter. So far as exporting the revolution is concerned, he says, "We are all waiting for the return of the Mahdi. . . . We should try our utmost to increase the power of Islam and to prepare the path for the Imām's return."[58]

Ayat-Allah Khomeyni's view of exporting the Revolution may be summarized in the following passage from his tract on *Islamic Government:*

> . . . [C]orruption must be swept away, and its instigators punished for their deeds. It is the same corruption that the Pharaoh generated in Egypt with his policies, so that the Qur'an says of him, "Truly he was among the corruptors" (28:4). A believing, pious, just individual cannot possibly exist in a socio-political environment of this nature and still maintain his faith and righteous conduct. . . . We have in reality, then, no choice but to destroy those systems of government that are corrupt in themselves and also entail the corruption of others, and to overthrow all treacherous, corrupt, opressive, and criminal regimes.
>
> This is a duty that all Muslims must fulfill, in every one of the Muslim countries, in order to achieve the triumphant political revolution of Islam.[59]

He then goes on to say that by "political revolution" he had in mind propaganda and training. "It is the duty of the *fugahā,*" he writes, "to promulgate religion and instruct the people in the creed, ordinances, and institutions of Islam, in order to pave the way in society for the implementation of Islamic law and the establishment of Islamic institutions."[60]

Unity of Muslims

Unity among Muslims is a recurrent theme in Khomeyni's messages, sermons, and writings. According to him, one of the guardian's main duties is the establishment of unity among Muslims. He cites the following tradition from Fatemah, the Prophet's daughter, to support his assertion.[61] "The *Imāmate* exists for the sake of preserving order among the Muslims and replacing their disunity with unity."[62] "In order to assure the unity of the Islamic *Umma,*" Khomeyni writes, ". . . we must overthrow the oppressive governments installed by the imperialists and bring into existence an Islamic government."[63] The grave difficulties that Muslims face today result from the fact that Muslims are not united. As he puts it:

> The problems of the Muslims vary, but the biggest problem is that they do not follow th Qur'ān. The Qur'ān says, "And hold fast, all of you together, to the cable of Allah, and do not separate" [III:103]. If the Muslims implement the advice given in this verse, all their political, social and economic problems will be solved, without any recourse to outsiders. . . . Why should Muslims not pay attention to the Prophetic tradition which declares, "Muslims are a united front?"[64]

According to Khomeyni, unity of Muslims is an intrinsic part of Islamic ideology and one of the natural products of its universalism. But what does he mean by it? Khomeyni answers this question as follows: "Our program, which is the program of Islam, is the realization of a unity of outlook (*vaḥdat-e kalama*) among Muslims, political unity among Muslim countries, and brotherhood with other Islamic sects (*feraq*)."[65] Ayat-Allah Khomeyni proposes three objectives in this passage: ideological unity, political unity, and the resolution of differences between Islamic sects.

The issue of ideological unity seems to be the same as exporting the Revolution. Let us look instead, then, at the other two objectives, beginning with the unity among the different sects. The most significant rift in Islam is the Shīʿī/Sunni schism. While Al-Afghani (1839–1897), who is considered the father of pan-Islamism simply overlooked the ideological differences, Khomeyni deals with it directly on many occasions.[66]

He has tried to resolve the differences between Sunni and Shīʿī Islam by dismissing them as representing only two different schools of jurisprudence. Note, for example, the following passage from one of his sermons to a group of Sunni Muslims:

> We are all brothers and we are united. Nonetherless, your *'ulamā* issued one legal ruling (*fatvā*), you followed him; then you became Hanafi. Another group followed Shafe'i's ruling and yet another followed the exalted Imām Sadeq.[67] The followers of the latter became Shī'ī. These are not reasons for disunity. . . . We are Muslim, monotheist and followers of the Qur'ān. We should work for God and the Qur'ān.[68]

Many Muslims would consider this a simplistic presentation of so complicated an issue. The historical rift between the Shī'ī and the Sunni Muslims has developed to such an extent that it is doubtful any simplistic approach could resolve it. Moreover, Ayat-Allah Khomeyni himself has treated this rift with more zeal in his earlier writings. He has attacked the early Sunni leaders for usurping the rulership of the newly established Islamic Community in the aftermath of the Prophet's death (632).[69] The fact that in his recent works and sermons he has treated the issue so lightly might be explained by the political problems that the Sunni minority created in the Islamic Republic of Iran. The treatment of the third objective, that is, the political unity among Muslim countries, might shed some light on this question as well.

Two questions should be considered here. If the countries Khomeyni has in mind are all Muslim why are they not already united? And now does Khomeyni plan to unite them? For Khomeyni the answer to the first question is self-evident. It is the outsiders who do not want to see Muslims united. "The central aim of the colonialist powers, " Khomeyni maintains, "is to destroy the Qur'ān, Islam, and the *'ulamā*. . ., [because] these are the only obstacles in the way of taking over the resources of the Islamic countries."[70] To that end, the powers partitioned the homeland of Islam into small countries in the aftermath of World War I, and they established a "germ of corruption" (*jarsūme-ye fasād*), Israel,[71] in the Middle East in the aftermath of World War II:

> Russia, Britain, Austria, and other imperialistic powers united, and, through wars against the Ottoman,, each came to occupy or absorb into its sphere of influence part of the Ottoman realm. . . . [T]he imperialists at the end of World War I divided the Ottoman State, creating in its territories about ten or fifteen petty states.[72]
>
> * * *
>
> The Ottoman Empire was an Islamic state whose domination spread far to the West and to the East. They [the colonial

> powers] realized that they could not gain control over the Muslim resources with this state in existence. Therefore, after the war, the victorious forces partitioned the Ottoman Empire among an Amir [ruler], a Sultan [king] and a president.[73]
>
> * * *
>
> Israel was born out of the collusion and agreement of the imperialist states of East and West. It was created in order to suppress and exploit the Muslim peoples, and it is being supported today by all the imperialists.[74]
>
> * * *
>
> The heads of the Islamic countries should note that they [i.e., the superpowers] have created this germ of corruption in the heart of the Islamic countries, not just to suppress the Arabs; its threat is against all of the Middle East. They have plans for Zionism to dominate the Islamic world and to take over the resources and fertile lands of the Islamic countries.[75]

These political strategies perceived by Khomeyni, added to the call for unity among Muslims, make the political unity of Muslim countries a necessity for him. This brings us to the question of tactics. Ayat-Allah Khomeyni never specifies the way in which he wants to bring political unity into practice. Does he suggest a federation of Muslim countries? In light of Khomeyni's belief that the Islamic Republic is the only true Islamic state, it is optimistic to think that such a federation could ever materialize. Maybe what Khomeyni has in mind is a suzerain-state system comprised of states who have brought about an Islamic Republic for their own country, modeled after Iran, and over which the Islamic Republic of Iran will act as the ultimate source of legitimacy. Such a scheme appears close to what he has in mind:

> Whereas the Muslim states should gather around this center (the Islamic Republic) and incline toward Islam . . . they either do not pay attention or the love of self (*nafs*) inhibits them from doing so. . . . The Islamic Republic wishes that all Islamic countries, and their governments . . . would wake up from this benumbing dream.[76]

In other words, the Islamic countries imagine that they are independent and free and therefore they have this "benumbing dream" that they are progressing. They should be undeceived and guided back to Islam.[77] The last point takes us back to Khomeyni's view on the exporting of the revolution; in both cases, no specific program of action is provided. This ambiguity is very well reflected in the Constitution of the Islamic Republic. Priciple 11 of the Constitution, for example, deals with this issue in the following manner.

> Based on the ordinances of the Qur'ān, that "Lo! that your community is a united one and I am your Lord, so worship me" (XX:92], the Islamic Republic of Iran is to base its overall policy on the coalition and unity of the Islamic nation. Furthermore, it should exert continuous effort until political, economic and cultural unity is realized in the Islamic world.[78]

War and Peace

A look at the issue of war and peace provides greater insight into Ayat-Allah Khomeyni's world order than the two previous issues, particularly in view of the war between Iran and Iraq. Whereas exporting the revolution and unity of Muslims were, for the most part, abstract issues, the war between Iran and Iraq gave greater substance to the issue of peace and war in Khomeyni's mind. Let us first look at Khomeyni's general view of war and then at his view of the war between Iran and Iraq.

While history has shown that war and peace are facts of life and that they have been one of the significant issues in political life, Khomeyni claims that war is a temporary issue in human relationships. War will be eliminated when God's divine plan rules the world. In the meantime, he maintains, there are two types of war: Satanic wars (*jang-e ṭāghūtī*) and monotheistic wars (*jang-e toḥīdī*). The Satanic wars are those which are initiated by man himself and are motivated by man's worldly desires. As is the case with all other issues and concepts in Khomeyni's thought, "wars" fall into the categories of divine and non-divine. Note Khomeyni's explanation:

> The wars are also either *ṭāghūtī* or *tohīdī*. The wars, launched by the prophets, the Imams, and the believers, were to convert the rebellious people and reform them; these were divine wars. Then there are wars which are caused by desire for status, for power, for domination of othe societies, and for the other interests of the superpowers; these wars are Satanic and *ṭāghūtī*.
>
> The world, thus, has only two paths. Every move man initiates, be it from his heart, from his soul or by his organs, is either toward the "straight path" [I:6] and God, or toward the wrong path and *ṭāghūt*.[79]

Ayat-Allah Khomeyni accepts the apparent paradox that the prophets may engage in wars, because such wars are fought on behalf of a "good" cause. War as an instrument of God's will is acceptable. Of course, like other instruments, war for Khomeyni is a temporary episode in human life. When the whole of humanity has learned to serve God, war will vanish. The prophets, for example, never fight. "If all the people in the world were prophets," Khomeyni maintains, "no dispute would ever arise."[80] But one does not have to be a prophet; "true believers" have no difficulty in living in harmony either. Khomeyni asserts:

> True believers will not go to war with each other; if war breaks out between two people, they must realize that they are not believers. Where there is no belief, but only attention to self, concern for the self and its desires, there trouble arises.[81]

According to this view, the believers never fight, because they have found peace and security in their hearts and have submitted to God. Even if they make peace, those people who have not submitted are planning in their hearts to struggle further. They make peace while they are waiting for a future opportunity, Khomeyni believes.[82] The best illustration of this belief occurred in the aftermath of World War II:

> When in the end of World War II the allies defeated the other side, the Soviet Union and England were allies. Churchill believed that now that England had defeated the enemy they should attack their own friend, the Soviet Union. The British parliament stopped him,[82]

The reason, he argues, is that man's love of self (*nafs*) is the source of all wars, and the world powers, then and now, have never submitted to a divine plan which would deter them from egotism. Therefore, as long as humanity has not been converted to make God the measure of all things, wars continue. That is why, Khomeyni maintains, Islam has two types of war. The first is *Jihād* (holy war) and the second is *Defā'* (defense); offensive war and defensive war. As he puts it:

> There are two types of wars in Islam: one is *Jihād*; that is, the war of expansion . . . and the other is *Defā'*, struggle to preserve one's independence.
>
> *Jihād* means expansion and the taking over of other countries, which will be carried on by the Imam himself or under his command. In that case it will become everyone's duty . . . to fight and to spread the Islamic laws throughout the world. . . .
>
> The second type, what we call *Defā'*, is a war to defend one's independence, which does not require the Imam nor his command.[84]

This view corresponds to the traditional Shī'ī view of war developed by Shaykh Tusi (d. 1067).[85] Following the occultation of the twelfth Imām in 940 A.D. it was accepted that initiatiting any type of war was the duty and prerogative of the Imāms. But during the rule of the Shī'ī dynasty, the Buwayhids (932–1055), had to deal with the practical problem of living under pressure from the Sunni dynasty. Shaykh Tusi therefore formulated a theory which made defensive war permissible in the absence of the Imām.[86] This theory became the basis for all subsequent Shī'ī views on the subject.

The distinction between an offensive war, for the expansion of the *Dār al-Islām,* and its defense acquired significance in Shī'ī Islam. The former cannot be launched without the Imām's presence or his direct command; Ayat-Allah Khomeyni has not claimed any direct connection with the Imām. This doctrine made the defense of Islam's stronghold a religious duty incumbent upon every capable Muslim. This appears to be the reason why Khomeyni casts Iran's offensive attack on Iraq on July 13, 1982, in the framework of a purely defensive measure:

> We have no intention of fighting against any country, Islamic or non-Islamic. We desire peace and amity among all nations. Up to date we are engaged only in self defense which is both a God-given and a human right. We never intend to commit aggression against other countries.[87]

The war between Iran and Iraq began following the latter's invasion of Iran on September 22, 1982, but has grown into a very complicated political problem. Regardless of its complexity and its historical and legal roots, Khomeyni does not perceive it as a dispute to be resolved; rather, it is a clear case of aggression in which the aggressor should be punished. It is a case of right against wrong. As he puts it:

> The issue is not a dispute between two governments. It is the aggression of the Ba'thist non-Muslim (*gheyr-Muslim*) Iraqi against an Islamic government; it is a case of the rebellion of polytheism (*kofr*) against Islam. It is incumbent upon all Muslims to fight this aggressor.[88]

The question is, could he see the war in an other way? The answer seems to be "no", because it has been shown that, according to him, true believers only fight on God's behalf and not with each other. In Khomeyni's mind, it is the Iraqi regime which is not fighting for God and not the Islamic Republic. However, Khomeyni has other reasons for his claims. Other religious leaders have accused the Ba'thist regime of being non-Islamic. "The Iraqi regime claims they are Muslims, . . . and asks me," Khomeyni says, "why I have accused them of non-belief. My answer is that before I said anything, Ayat-Allah Hakim (d. 1970) had accused them of non-belief. The people of Iraq are Muslim but the ideology of this Ba'thist regime is non-Islamic."[89] The dichotomy of the Ba'thist ideology vs. Islam is very clear. There have been times, though, when Khomeyni has accepted Iraqi Ba'thists as Muslims. Even then he did not see the dispute as a political or a military problem. It became a clash between two Muslims and needed to be resolved by the *Sharī'a*. When Khomeyni does not accuse the Iraqi regime of being a "bunch of non-believers,"[90] or "the stooges of the Americans,"[91] and treats the Iraqi regime as an Islamic government, the Qur'ān should be their arbitor. In response to the effort of certain Islamic countries to find a solution for the dispute, Khomeyni said:

> We declare to all Islamic as well as Arab and non-Arab countries that the Qur'an will be our arbitor. . . . Those countries who claim to adhere to the Qur'an should gather here or send their representatives. We shall then open the Qur'an, read a verse from *surah al-Ḥujurat* and act upon it. That verse says "And if two parties of believers fall to fighting, then make peace between them. And if one party of them doeth wrong to the other, fight ye that which doeth wrong till it returns unto the ordinance of Allah; then, if it returns, make peace between them justly, and act equitably: [XLIX:9].[92]

The dichotomies vanish the moment an issue is considered to be within the realm of Islam. In fact, duality of any sort is considered a heresy in Islam. It exists only when the Islamic legal, political, social, economic, moral and religious milieu is confronted with a non-Islamic one. This was very clear in the earlier discussion of Ayat-Allah Khomeyni's view of the existing international system. The forces of oppressors stood against the oppressed, which meant, in the final analysis, the Muslims vs. the non-Muslims. When the issue of exporting the revolution was examined, it was seen as a hope for the establishment of a party of the oppressed who could destroy the oppressors. When the issue of unity among Muslims was discussed, it was seen to mean the unification of Islam against the outsiders. This paradox in Khomeyni's thought manifested itself most clearly on occasions when the Iran-Iraq war was discussed. If the Iraqi regime is seen as the non-Muslim Ba'thist, then the Iran-Iraqi war is seen as an "unresolvable dispute between Islam and anti-Islam."[93] But if the Iraqi regime is seen as an Islamic government, the dichotomy vanishes and the war becomes a legal dispute within the jurisdiction of the *Sharī'a*.

Conclusion

To summarize, Ayat-Allah Khomeyni's theory of international relations can only be understood in terms of his ideological convictions, according to which, the world has two poles: those who follow the worldly path and therefore constantly struggle for domination and power, and those who follow the path of God and thus live under the absolute authority of God. This situation is representative of that stage in human history where people have not been converted to learn that their true *raison d'être* is to walk the right path. In other words, Khomeyni's world order calls for a complete transformation of the existing international system into a new one, in which the relationships of men or their unit of political organization is not based on power but is regulated by the divine scheme. In the process of achieving that transformation, Khomeyni seems to view Iran and the establishment of the Islamic Republic as the starting place and the means of determining right and wrong. How he brought into existence that regime is seen in Khomeyni's political practice, the theme of the following chapter.

CHAPTER VII
AYAT-ALLAH KHOMEYNI: THEORIST AND PRACTITIONER

Knowledge without practice is like a tree without fruit.

Persian Proverb

So far this study has examined and attempted to present a systematic picture of Ayat-Allah Khomeyni's world view and political theory. The study has shown that his world view is centered on the conviction that it is possible to create "good men," and the most important aspect of that vision concerns the notion that such a thing is possible only through the implementation of Islamic law by the *faqīh*. The present chapter has two further objectives. First, it presents, in summary a concise statement of Khomeyni's vision. Second, it shows how Ayat-Allah Khomeyni has behaved as a political leader and practitioner. It is therefore, a chapter which deals with Khomeyni the thinker and Khomeyni the leader and political actor.

As a thinker, Ayat-Allah Khomeyni assumes that it is possible to establish a just political order because man is essentially good. Owing to his nature, man is able to elevate himself to a higher spiritual status. On the other hand, man has many weaknesses which push him toward committing errors and toward leading a nondivine life. Out of these two versions of human nature emerge the dichotomies of the undeveloped vs. the developed man, the right path vs. the wrong path, and God vs. Satan. A corollary is the dichotomy of the right political order inspired and dictated by the divine and the wrong political order inspired and dictated by man himself. Man is endowed with the choice of taking either of two paths and Ayat-Allah Khomeyni saw the possibility of creating a society where each person happily chooses to follow the right path. Based on this optimism, Khomeyni has formulated his theory of politics.

The central issue is Khomeyni's vision of a political society in which everyone would like to live. The most important role in such a society is that of the guardian. Consequently, Ayat-Allah Khomeyni does not concern himself much with political regimes (i.e., the means of politics). It is the political situation of the time which dictates the accepted form of the regime. That is partly explained by the fact that there is no clearly specified type of regime in Islam appropriate for society. Islam has only provided the laws which are to govern such a society. According to Sunni political thought, even the issue of sovereignty has not been clarified. It is the Shīʿīs who believe that sovereignty has been delegated by God to the Prophet, then to the Imāms and, according to Khomeyni and some of his predecessors, to the *fuqahā*.

This belief provided the impetus for Ayat-Allah Khomeyni to formulate his doctrine of the guardianship of the theologian jurisconsult (*Velāyat-e Faqīh*). Politics and state are merely instruments in the hand of the guardian for the establishment of the cultural milieu under which people will be taught to walk the right path.

When Khomeyni's vision is confronted with the political realities beyond his own ideological world, a dichotomy of the oppressed vs. the oppressors emerges. The relevance of this dichotomy to certain important issues such as exporting the revolution, unity among Muslims and war and peace shows that Khomeyni's argument essentially means "Islam vs. the outsiders." The centrality of Islam as the source of Khomeyni's vision became all the more apparent when his view of the Iran-Iraq war is examined. So long as the Iraqi regime is perceived as a non-Muslim Baʿthist, the dichotomy of Islam vs. the outsiders is relevant and predominant. But when the Iraqi government is taken to be the God-fearing Islamic government of an Islamic country the dichotomy vanishes and the *Sharīʿa* becomes the ultimate arbiter.

The virtuous city in Khomeyni's mind is a political society where the guardian will fully implement the Islamic law. He thinks that the Islamic Republic of Iran is such a city. But how has he put his vision into practice? Since his emergence as the leader of the revolution and subsequently, as the most powerful protagonist on the Iranian political scene, Khomeyni has allowed himself to be guided by what Weber calls an "ethic of ultimate ends."[1] According to Weber:

> We must be clear about the fact that all ethically-oriented conduct may be guided by one of two fundamentally differing and irreconcilably opposed maxims: conduct can be oriented to an "ethic of ultimate ends" or to an "ethic of responsibility." This is not to say that an ethic of ultimate ends is identical with irresponsibility, or that an ethnic of responsibility is identical with unprincipled opportunism. Naturally nobody says that. However, there is an abysmal contrast between conduct that follows the maxim of an ethic of ultimate ends—that is, in religious terms, "The Christian does rightly and

> leaves the results with the Lord"—and conduct that follows the maxim of an ethic of responsibility, in which case one has to give an account of the foreseeable results of one's action.[2]

Ayat-Allah Khomeyni has demonstrated both in theory and practice tht he follows the "ethic of ultimate ends." He always has his mind on the ultimate goal he is seeking, and evaluates political events accordingly. This is not to suggest that for Khomeyni the end justifies the means; instead, he emphasizes the intention and the end (i.e., his perfect society symbolized by the theory of guardianship) far more than he emphasizes the means (i.e., the political regimes). Moreover, his end is defined and refined by Islam as interpreted by the Shī'ī *fuqahā*. According to Ayat-Allah Khomeyni, only a good end can explain and justify the means. Not every action is an acceptable one. Only the end distinguishes between a good and bad action. As he puts it:

> What distinguishes two acts is the intention; "lo! an act is not but its intention."[3] Imagine that two persons use their swords to kill someone. The nature of the act is the same. But for one of them this is a devotional act (*'ebādat*) and for the other it is the source of corruption and destruction. . . . The thing that distinguishes action is their ends which instigate us to commit those actions.[4]
>
> * * *
>
> From the beginning of the world there have existed two parties; the one, the party of God, the other the party of Satan. . . . The issue is not that one party is good and the other is bad. [There is no] *difference in the nature* of the two parties. The measure of goodness are the ideals of the party. If the ideals are not good the party is Satanic.[5] (emphasis added).

These passages are taken from sermons which were delivered two years apart. As both passages suggest, it is the "ethic of ultimate ends" which is for Ayat-Allah Khomeyni a dependable measure of judgment and a guide for political actions. Let us consider an actual example. After the revolution, the contacting of American officials was not considered a proper act. Without Khomeyni's prior knowledge, Mehdi Bazargan, the first Revolutionary Prime-Minister, met with Zbigniew Brzezinski, the national security advisor to President Carter, on November 2, 1979.[6] On September 17, 1980 another important meeting took place between an Iranian oficial and Warren Christopher, the American under secretary of state, this time in Bonn.[7] Although the nature of both acts is the same, the first was condemned and the second was approved. The first was perceived as a way of inviting the Americans into Iran, and the second was for the cause of Islam. Thus, only those ends which are prescribed by religions and in particular by Islam (in this case prescribed by the guardian) can justify the means.

The question is, how does one stop the damage done by those people who make Islam a pretext for pursuing their personal interest? Ayat-Allah Khomeyni's answer would be to trust the guardian. But to the question, "who guards the guardian?" Khomeyni provides no answer; he would have one share his optimistic belief that the theologian jurisconsult will not step beyond the boundaries of the *Sharī'a*. This is precisely why he has done his utmost to ensure the realization of his theory of guardianship—a theory which has proved to be his lifelong goal.[8]

It is revealing to point out that many people, including Bazargan, subscribe to the erroneous view that Khomeyni's actions were erratic and impulsive, lacking an overall design and goal. In an interview with Oriana Fallaci, Bazargan stated:

> Something unforeseen and unforeseeable happened after the revolution. What happened was that the clergy supplanted us and succeeded in taking over the country. . . . In fact, it cannot even be said that they had it in mind to monopolize the country. They simply seized the opportunity offered by history to fill the vacuum left by us.[9]

Contrary to this view, Khomeyni knew full well his ultimate end and seized every opportunity to realize that end. In fact, one of Khomeyni's greatest strengths has been his sense of political timing and abilty to seize the opportunity.

From the early days of the revolution, he vigilantly watched the political developments, zealously maintained his theory of guardianship, and patiently, in step-by-step tactics, implemented it, until December 9, 1982, when, with the election of the Assembly of Experts for selecting the future guardian, he achieved the final phase in the institutionalization of his vision. According to the constitution of the Islamic Republic a certain *faqīh* or a council of *fuqahā* should always exist as the acting sovereign in the country without whose approval nothing can be achieved. The election of the Assembly of Experts, whose *raison d'être* is also provided for in the Constitution, guarantees that the institution of guardian will continue after Khomeyni. This appears to be the main reason why Ayat-Allah Khomeyni declared (on December 22, 1982) that the revolution was over. He said:

> We feel secure within our borders and because of this we should now serve the people. *We should not say that we are in a state of revolution any longer. No. The state of tranquility has arrived.*[10] (emphasis added).

An examination of major events in the process of establishing the rule of the *faqīh* puts this point in political and historical perspective. Early in the revolution Ayat-Allah Khomeyni's messages were meant basically to encourage the revolutionaries to continue until the old regime was destroyed. In October 1978 he enumerated the details of his plan as follows:

> Note that our immediate and preliminary goals . . . are: (1) the elimination of monarchical types of regime. . . . (2) expulsion of all figures who were in high positions during the reign of the Pahlavis. . . . (3) elimination of all foreign influences. . . . Our main goals will be announced later and, God willing, we will put them into practice with the continuation of our national Islamic revolution.[11]

A month later he added the formation of an Islamic Republic as another objective and thereby he announced what he called the "three point program."

> Our Islamic goals [in the Revolution] are (1) elimination of the monarchical type of regime [in Iran], (2) the destruction of the reign of the Pahlavi dynasty, whose illegitimacy is obvious . . . and (3) that the political regime of Iran will be an Islamic Republic.[12]

These three points became Khomeyni's ultimate end during the early phase of the Revolution. He reiterated them often, showing no sign of compromise whatsoever.[13] The following two events provide evidence of his inflexibility. In mid-October 1978, the rumor spread that Bazargan was travelling to Paris to work out some sort of accommodation between the Shah's regime and Ayat-Allah Khomeyni. The latter blocked any path of compromise a few days before Bazargan reached Paris. On October 17, he dismissed any understanding with the old regime as constituting a betrayal of the Revolution.[14] The second event relates to the journey to Paris made by Karim Sanjabi, the leader of National Front. After Sanjabi had met with Khomeyni, the official organ of the National Front declared that a *modus vivendi* had been worked out between Khomeyni and Sanjabi according to which the revolution embodied both the "national and Islamic movements."[15] Subsequently, when Khomeyni emphasized only the Islamic aspects of the Revolution and called for Islamization of the Iranian society, many people argued that Khomeyni had betrayed their national revolution.[16] A look at Ayat-Allah Khomeyni's speeches and interviews suggests that such was not the case. For example, in an interview with German television on November 16, 1978, Khomeyni denied any understanding between himself and Sanjabi. The reporter asked, "you had a meeting with Sanjabi recently, did you conclude any coalition with him?" Khomeyni answered:

> I have certain goals which I will never compromise. I enumerated them for him. I have no coalition with any group. I am with the Iranian people. Whoever agrees with our points (independence from foreign influence, absolute freedom and the establishment of the Islamic Republic) is one of us and one of the Iranian people. If anyone disagrees [with these points] he has moved away from the interests of Islam and we will have nothing to do with him. Those who agree with us are in harmony with us. However, we have no special relation with anyone.[17]

The Iranian political leaders and intelligentsia chose not to notice.[18] Khomeyni's subsequent actions proved their naivete. On January 13, 1979, he announced the formation of the Revolutionary Council, whose duty it was to prepare the path for the establishment of the Islamic Republic.[19] The identity of the Council's members was not revealed at first, but when the members became known, it was discovered that none of the national political leaders were involved, save Bazargan. Nearly all of its members were either religious leaders or the very close associates of Khomeyni.

He carried over his uncompromising attitude to other issues. Following the triumph of the revolutionaries, the next important issue was the title of Iran's future regime. It has been demonstrated that the establishment of an Islamic Republic was part of Khomeyni's "three points program." Bazargan, on the other hand, advocated the title, "The Democratic Islamic Republic."[20] Moreover, Bazargan appointed people from the National Front, in his provisional government who had openly opposed the idea of an Islamic Republic and called simply for a Republican form of regime.[21] Soon after the downfall of the Shah, the nation's political structure dissolved into a multitude of groups, including those who supported the realization of an Islamic form of polity as outlined by Khomeyni. The latter group soon formed the Islamic Republican Party, which proved to have a decisive role in the political life of the nation.[22] Hindered by the formation of so many groups and the loss of unity, Khomeyni constantly asked for solidarity and the continuation of the revolution. He did not forget, the main objective, however—the establishment of the Islamic Republic. The following is typical of the tone of his sermons during this phase:

> I ask the nation to continue its revolution until the establishment of a just Islamic political order. . . . No Republic, no Democratic Republic, no Democratic Islamic Reppublic; only an Islamic Republic. I request that the nation be vigilant. Do not allow your sacrifices and efforts to be wasted. Do not be

> intimidated by the word "Democratic." These forms are western; do not accept them.[23]

Although Ayat-Allah Khomeyni's emphasis on an "Islamic Republic *only*" was an implied criticism of Bazargan, he was very careful not to attack anyone directly. He seems to have been quite aware of the power of the other groups. As the Revolution became consolidated, he changed his tone. About three weeks before the referendum for the future regime of Iran, he said:

> I will vote for the Islamic Republic and I ask you to vote for the Islamic Republic, not one word less, not one word more. Those who talk about "Republic" alone mean no Islam. Those who talk about "Democratic Republic" mean not the Islamic Republic. They want to reinstitute the same old practices in a different form.[24]

During a two-day referendum (March 29-30, 1979), the Iranians overwhelmingly approved the Islamic Republic as the future regime for Iran. The next step was to adopt the new constitution. Two problems arose when a future constitution was debated: the issue of a constitutional assembly and the interrelation between divine and popular sovereignty.

Most of the political parties which had been formed right after the revolution were calling for the establishment of a grand assembly to review the future constitution, and to formulate a constitution which would secure popular sovereignty. Ayat-Allah Khomeyni's optimism about Islam and his belief that Islam would satisfy everyone was shattered by the establishment of so many different parties and so many different demands.[25] In response he began to attack them. The birth and growth of so many groups were not seen as a legitimate expression of pluralism, but rather as a new conspiracy by outsiders. "When they [i.e., any outsiders] sensed the unity of the Iranian people," Khomeyni said," . . . they planned to disunite our nation. . . . More than a hundred factions have been formed."[26]

These groups were calling for a constitutional assembly whose four hundred or so members would be from all components of Iranian society, whereas Ayat-Allah Khomeyni wanted a relatively small Assembly of Experts, who would draft and approve a Constitution in a short time.[27] As he puts it:

> We are trying to formulate a constitution and present it to the nation. . . . These people want a constitutional Assembly of 600-700 members. . . . Their whole plan is to eliminate Islam and the constitution and to bring about the old situation.[28]

Despite the boycott of the election by many political parties, an Assembly of Experts dominated by religious scholars was elected on August 5, 1979, and immediately began deliberation of the constitution.

Faced by the opposition of so many groups and obstacles he had never anticipated, Ayat-Allah Khomeyni's good intentions were challenged. He declared on August 17, 1979:

> If we had been truly revolutionary we would not have allowed them [the opposition parties] to be established. We should have established one party, the party of the oppressed. . . . I will warn these corrupt groups all over the country that if they do not stop we will deal with them differently. . . . It is the duty of the revolutionary tribunal to ban all these newspapers and magazines which do not reflect the path of the nation and to arrest their writers and put them on trial.[29]

Before total institutionalization of the theory of guardianship, the remaining political goals were: ratification of the constitution; election of the president; election of the deputies of the parliament; and institutionalization of the position of leadership—that is, the grand guardian. These goals were published as the official program of the nation by the Revolutionary Council, which had become both the *de jure* and the *de facto* regime on November 7, 1979.[30]

Principle 5 of the new Constitution recognized sovereignty (*velāyat*) as belonging to the *faqīh* and principles 107–112 granted him unlimited power and the highest position in the country. Many groups, notably the Mojahedin, boycotted the referendum, and the Muslim Nation Party (*Ḥezb Khalq Musalmān*) (MNP) of the Azerbaijan province under the patronage of Ayat-Allah Shari'at-madari pointed out that the constitution contained "an important flaw."[32] Ayat-Allah Khomeyni was quick to label them "hypocrites" who pretend to be Muslim and yet attack Islam.[32] The opposition to the Constitution did not amount to much; it was approved in a referendum on December 2, 1979.

The next step in the process was the election of the future president. Shortly before the election, Khomeyni enumerated the essential qualifications for a future president:

> Those who register to be a candidate should note: they should be most devoted to Islam, have a clean record, have no inclination toward either the East or the West, care for the nation, and have had no position in the previous regime.[33]

Moreover, on another occasion he stated that those who had not approved of the theory of guardianship and had not participated in the constitutional referendum were not qualified to become candidates.[34] This obstacle, plus the other stipulations, automatically disqualified a good many of the national political leaders. On January 25th, Abolhassan Bani-Sadr, the first president of the Islamic Republic, was elected. Soon after he installed the president in his post, Ayat-Allah Khomeyni began campaigning for the parliamentary elections. Note this passage:

> I hope that you will continue the great Islamic Revolution to the end, that is, the establishment of the sovereignty of God over all aspects of life in the country. . . . [I hope] you send the disinherited into the Islamic Assembly.[35]

Khomeyni emphasized an "Islamic Consultative Assembly" rather than a National Consultative Assembly, the title given to the Iranian Parliament after the Constitutional Revolution (1905–11). Moreover, the Ministry of the Interior set the condition that deputies must get an absolute majority of votes to be qualified to enter the Parliament.

Despite protest against the concept of an absolute majority by various political groups, the election was held on March 14, 1980. The Islamic Republican Party won an overwhelming majority, thereby leaving the nationalist politicians out of the political process. At the opening of parliament on May 28, 1980, Ayat-Allah Khomeyni told the newly-elected members, "You have been elected to implement Islamic Justice, . . . and to follow the policy of 'neither East nor West' in all areas of domestic as well as foreign policies."[36]

Having secured the principle of guardianship in the constitution, practically eliminating all nationalist, and secular politicians, and finally having realized the formation of an *'ulamā*-dominated parliament, Khomeyni began talking about cultural revolution, by which he meant greater Islamization of Iranian society. He declared the beginning of his formal Islamization of Iran on July 13, 1980. He appointed a seven-member committee to establish the future direction of Iranian universities "based on Islamic culture."[37] Groups such as the Mojahedin called for an open demonstration in protest against the government's overall policies. Khomeyni reacted by calling the group "hypocrites."[38]

He warned that this group was more dangerous than were the nonbelievers, and wanted the government to purge all those elements which were not in support of Islam (by which he meant his theory of Islamic political society).[39] Later his displeasure was translated into governmental policy. On July 8, 1980, the government banned all political demonstrations "for reasons of security."[40] As the situation grew acute, Ayat-Allah Khomeyni reacted more strongly than before. On July 20th, he declared:

> We did not act like revolutionaries. . . . We had no experience. . . . We should have appointed a decisive group. . . . Now that the new administration is being formed, I warn the Consultative Assembly to approve of only those people who

> are one hundred percent Islamic and steadfast. . . . Only one hundred percent ideologues (*maktabi*) and steadfast ministers should be selected.[41]

An unanticipated issue arose. The president of the Republic, Bani-Sadr, emerged, to use the media's term, as "the leader of the opposition." He criticized the policies of the government and appealed to the nation for support in a political rally at Tehran University on March 6, 1981.[42] Then Ayat-Allah Khomeyni appointed a three-man reconciliation committee in order to resolve the political differences among leaders in the country and, at the same time, prohibited the politicians from public debate until the political problems were resolved.[43] Bani Sadar criticized the policies of the government further, and kept arguing that he was a popularly-elected president and the nation had supported him. Khomeyni perceived Bani Sadar's emphasis on "the nation" as a return to the tradition of popular sovereignty, and reacted quickly. In a long sermon delivered on May 27, 1981, he attacked all those who opposed the Parliament and the administration:

> The nation wants Islam. . . . The nation is with Islam. If you disagree with Islam go to Europe, America or wherever else you like. . . . Do not constantly say, "the nation supports me." The nation neither supports me nor you, it supports Islam.[44]

A few days later the three-man commission found Bani-Sadar guilty of violating the constitution. The Revolutionary Prosecutor banned his newspaper *Enqelāb Eslāmī* along with six other newspapers. When Ayat-Allah Khomeyni dismissed Bani Sadar as acting commander-in-chief of the armed forces on June 10,[45] the latter issued a statement saying that a "coup" against him was under way.[46] Bani Sadar was soon removed formally from office after a vote of impeachment by the parliament on June 21. With the removal of Bani Sadar, the opposition parties, particularly the Mojahedin which was the most significant and organized group, lost faith in the Islamic Republic. On June 21, Mojahedin openly declared an armed struggle against the regime.[47] Soon a bomb destroyed the headquarters of the Islamic Republican Party, killing over seventy people, including important party leaders.

While blaming the super-powers and their lackeys for the incident, Ayat-Allah Khomeyni consoled the people by stressing martyrdom as the practice of prophets. In other words, he again emphasized the end as the only legitimate guide for actions, even if one should perish in achieving it. "Why should we doubt our actions? Are we not self-sacrificing devotees to our aim?" Then, addressing the opposition, he continued, "The big problem with you and your supporters is that you do not recognize the power of Islam and the motivation for sacrifice it has created in the people."[48]

The bombing of the party's headquarters generated sympathy for the Islamic Republication Party. Its candidate, Mohammad Ali Raja'i, was elected the second president of the Islamic Republic on July 25, 1981. The new president did not remain in office long. A bomb killed both him and his Prime-Minister on August 30, 1981. Yet, despite constant bombing and strife, a new president was again elected on October 2, 1981. President Ali Khmene'i soon formed his new administration under the Premiership of Mir Hossein Musavi, and the Parliament approved it on November 3, 1981.

The new government followed an extreme and severe policy of eliminating the opposition. When international criticism of the executions and arrests reached Ayat-Allah Khomeyni, he said:

> It is reported that they [the Islamic Republic of Iran] kill people. People imagine that Iran executes human beings. To this day Iran has not killed even one human being. Iran only deals with those beasts who attack Islam, the nation, and humanity. It rectifies and edifies them by training or imprisonment. And if that is not possible it eliminates them. This is a method that prophets have followed from the beginning of existence to the present.[49]

Although Bani Sadar and Rajavi, the head of the Mojahedin, continued their campaign against the regime from France, with the death of the Mojahedins' leader in Iran on February 8, 1982, the opposition began to subside and the Islamic Republic, as Ayat-Allah Khomeyni desired, began a process of consolidation. Khomeyni, who earlier had been urging and encouraging everyone to become involved in politics, began urging the Army and the Revolutionary Guard corps to stay clear of politics:

> I say that the armed forces must not enter into any political party. If the Army, the Revolutionary Guard Corps or other forces engage in party activities, that day marks the end of an effective armed forces. Do not enter into political groups or parties. It is your religious duty either to be in the army or to get involved in politics.[50]

With successful and effective undermining of the opposition, Ayat-Allah Khomeyni began to talk about the last point in his theory of guardianship, namely the institutionalization of the process of succession:

> What is at stake today for our nation is the issue of the Assembly of Experts to select the leader [supreme guardian]

. . . . I have heard that some quarters argue that there should not be an Assembly of Experts because it weakens the leadership. The Assembly of Experts is in fact a source of strength for the institution of leadership. . . . This is a duty . . . to vote for the election of the members of the Assembly.[51]

The election for the Assembly of Experts was held on December 9, 1982, and with it, Ayat-Allah Khomeyni's theory of guardianship was fully institutionalized. Soon after, in an eight-point message, he called for the restoration of people's civil and economic rights, thereby declaring the "Thermidorian" phase of the Islamic Revolution.[52] His self-confidence and feeling of security are well reflected in the following passage from his sermon of December 25, 1982:

We should establish and continue our relations with those foreign countries which do not intend to subjugate us. We have no need to have relations with those countries who intend to swallow us through their relation with us. While we aim for self-sufficiency we should deal with these latter countries very cautiously.[53]

Ayat-Allah Khomeyni as a thinker relates everything he knows and everything he wants to his understanding of Islam and more specifically his theory of the guardianship of the *faqīh*. He has allowed this "single organizing principle" to tell him what the ultimate ends were. When he decided that this end was the realization of the guardianship of the *faqīh*, he did everything in his power to bring about that end. If in that process undesirable consequences resulted, it was not because of his wickedness but rather because of his self-righteousness, which led him to follow an ethic of ultimate ends in his political practices. Was he ever conscious of it? I believe that he became aware of it late in the game. On December 25, 1982, he said:

When these gentlemen say, "why did you confront America and in so doing bring about this war?" I say we have known that this might happen. These gentlemen should question the Prophet himself, who faced Abu-Sufyan,[54] a conflict which resulted in his losing an uncle and many great men. . . .[55]

Will Ayat-Allah Khomeyni's vision in the end bring about the virtuous nation which he promises? This is a momentous question to which only history will provide the answer.

NOTES TO THE CHAPTERS

Chapter I

1 A great number of books have been published on the subject of the causes of the revolution in Iran since 1979. A list of some of the more significant ones are as follows: For economic causes of the revolution, see Homa Katouzian, *The Political Economy of Modern Iran: Despotism and Pseudo-Modernism, 1926–1979.* (New York: The New York University Press, 1981); and Farhad Kazemi, *Poverty and Revolution in Iran: The Migrant Poor, Urban Marginality*. (New York: The New York University Press, 1981). For political causes, both internally and externally, see Fereydoun Hoveyda, *The Fall of the Shah*. Trans. from French by Roger Liddel, (London: Weidenfeld and Nicolson, 1980); R. K. Ramazani, *The United States and Iran* (New York: Praeger, 1982); Barry Rubin, *Paved with Good Intention: The American Experience and Iran*. (Oxford: The Oxford University Press, 1980); and Sepehr Zabih, *Iran's Revolutionary Upheaval: An Interpretive Essay*. (San Francisco: Alchemy Books, 1979). For historical causes, see Richard Cottom, *Nationalism in Iran, Updated Through 1978*. (Pittsburgh: The University of Pittsburgh Press, 1979); and Nikki Keddie, *Roots of Revolution: An Interpretive History of Modern Iran*. (New Haven: Yale University Press, 1981). For social as well as political causes, see Robert Graham, *Iran, the Illusion of Power*. Revised ed. (London: Croom Helen, 1979); and Fred Halliday, *Iran: Dictatorship and Development*. (New York: Penguin, 1979). And finally, for religious and also social causes, see Shahrough Akhavi, *Religion and Politics in Contemporary Iran: Clergy-State Relations in the Pahlavi Period*. (Albany: The State University of New York Press, 1980); Michael Fischer, *Iran, from Religious Dispute to Revolution*. (Cambridge: Harvard University Press, 1980); and S. A. A. Rizvi, *Iran, Royalty, Religion and Revolution*. (Canberra, Australia: Ma'rifat Publ, 1980).

2 The concept *Velāyat-e Faqīh* has been variously translated as "the government of the jurist," "the government of jurisprudent," and "the guardianship of jurisconsults." As the title of Khomeyni's book it has been translated as "Islamic government." It has been translated here as "the guardianship of the theologian jurisconsult." The reasons for translating *Velāyat* as "guardianship" are found in chapter V of the present work. The reasons for translating the word *faqīh* as "theologian jurisconsult," are as follows. A *faqīh* is a person who has mastered the sciences of theology (*kalām*) and

jurisprudence (*fiqh*). "Jurisconsult" is defined in the Oxford dictionary as "a person who is skilled in law and is authorized to give legal advice." These are precisely some of the qualifications and functions of a *faqīh*. Thus, the translation of *Velāyat-e Faqīh* into "the guardianship of the theologian jurisconsult" seems closest to the meaning of the concept.

3 Richard Falk. "Trusting Khomeini," *The New York Times* (February 10, 1979): A-27.

4 Richard Falk. "Khomeini's Promise," *Foreign Policy* No. 34 (spring 1979): 32.

5 Mansour Farhang. "The Outlook Interview," *The Washington Post* (November 28, 1982): C-3.

6 Rubin W. Carlsen. *The Imam and His Islamic Revolution*, (Victorio, Ca: The Snow Man Press, 1982), pp. 110–115.

7 See Bruce Mazlish. "The Hidden Khomeini," *The New York* (December 24, 1979): 49–54.

8 *Ibid*., p. 50.

9 *Ibid*., p. 54.

10 *Time*, (January 7, 1980): 22.

11 See Ruhollah Khomeyni. *Islam and Revolution: Writings and Declarations of Imam Khomeini*, Translated and annotated by Hamid Algar. (Berkeley: Mizan Press, 1982) (hereafter cited as *Islam and Revolution*), pp. 64–65. This is a valuable and reliable translation of Khomeyni's major tract on the nature of Islamic government and a selection of his sermons, lectures and speeches. I shall be using Algar's translation throughout, except in cases in which I disagree with his rendering of crucial terms.

12 The most significant issue for those who examine Khomeyni's works has been his opposition to the monarchical type of regime. See for example: Willem M. Floor, "The Revolutionary Character of the Iranian Ulamā: Wishful Thinking or Reality?" *International Journal of Middle East Studies* vol. 12 no. 4 (December 1980) (hereafter cited as Floor. "Ulamā,"): 501–524; Yann, Richard, "Contemporary Shī'ī Thought," in Nikki Keddie, *Roots of Revolution* (New Haven: Yale University Press, 1981) (hereafter cited as Richard. "Contemporary,"), pp. 205–209. The most important work according to those who study Khomeyni's works is his *Islamic Government*. See for example Mangol Bayat, "The Iranian Revolution of 1978–79: Fundamentalist or Modern?" *The Middle East Journal* Vol. 37 no. 1 (winter 1983) (hereafter cited as Bayat. "The Revolution,"): 30–42; Norman Calder, "Accommodation and Revolution in Imāmi Shī'ī Jurisprudence: Khumayni and the Classical Tradition," *Middle East Studies* Vol. 18 no. 1 (January 1982) (hereafter cited as Calder. "Accommodation,"): 1–20; George Carpozi, Jr. "Islamic Government by Ayatollah Khomeyni," in Khomeyni, *Islamic Government*, trans. by Joint Publication Research Service (New York: Manor Books, Inc., 1979), pp. 123–154; and Hamid Enayat, "Khumayni's Concept of the 'Guardianship of the Jurisconsult'," in *Islam in the Political Process* edited by James Piscatori (New York: Cambridge University Press, 1982) (hereafter cited as Enayat. "Khumayni,"), pp. 160–180.

13 See Khomeyni, "Lecture on *Surah al-Fathia*," in *Islam and Revolution*, p. 416. I have replaced the work *Fuqahā*, which appears as such in Algar's translation, with "theologian jurisconsults."

14 Sermon delivered on September 17, 1979. See *Rahnemūdhā-ye Imām dar Tābestān-e 1358* (Tehran: Nās Pub., n.d.) (hereafter cited as *Rahnemudhā; Tābestān*), p. 194. Except those passages quoted from *Islam and Revolution*, the translation of Khomeyni's words is that of the author.

15 Among other verses see "Lo! He loveth not the oppressor," (XVI:23) and "they will say: We are oppressed in the land" (IV:97).

Chapter II

1 "Juridical Trend" here refers to that trend in Islam which is represented by the works of the *fuqahā*. In reviewing Islamic political thought one may look at the philosophical trend, by studying the philosophers (*falāsefa*), or the literalist trend, by studying the literalists (*odabā*), or the juridical trend, by studying the theologian jurisconsults (*fuqahā*). Because Khomeyni is a *faqīh*, I have chosen to review the Shī'ī political thought in the thought of certain major *fuqahā*.

2 See Enayat. "Khumayni," p. 161. I have reservations about Professor Enayat equating modernization with Westernization. The spread of modernity, although it originated in the West, is now a world phenomenon which, as some scholars suggest, was an inevitable occurrence in human history. See for example, Marshal Hodgson, *The Venture of Islam,* (Chicago: The University of Chicago Press, 1974) Vol. 3, pp. 165-208.

3 Nomocracy is a derivative of the Greek word *nomos* meaning "law and custom." It is interesting that the same word, with a slight variation in pronunciation, *nāmūs,* is used both in Arabic and Persian. See *Loghat Nāmeh Dehkhodā,* Vol. XXVI, s.v. "*Nāmūs*," and *Hasting Encyclopedia of Religion and Ethics,* Vol. IX, s.v. "Nomism."

4 For this distinction in the Shī'ī thought see Muhammad Hossein Na'ini, *Tanbīh al-Umma va Tanzīh al-Mella,* annotated and edited by Mahmud Taleqani. (Tehran: Ferdousi, 1374Q/1955) (hereafter cited as Na'ini. *Tanbīh*), pp. 8-12. For this distinction in the Sunni thought see Ibn Khaldun, *The Muqaddimah,* Trans. Franz Rosenthal (Princeton: Princeton University Press, 1967) Vol. II, pp. 233-305.

5 The view that, first the Caliphs and later the Umayyads initiated innovations in Islam is a prevalent theme in the thought of all Shī'ī thinkers from the early history of Islam to the present. A prominent Ayat-Allah goes so far as to attribute the present confusion and alienation in the Muslim world to the reign of the third Caliph (644-656). See Mahmud Taleqani, *Islām va Mālekiyat* (Tehran: Nashr Ketab, 1354/1975 (hereafter cited as Taleqani. *Islam*), pp. 193-97. For an English translation of this work see Mahmud Taleqani, *Islam and Ownership* translated and annotated by Ahmad Jabbari and Farhang Rajaee (Lexington, KY: Mazda Pub., forthcoming).

6 S. Husain M. Jafri, *Origins and Early Development of Shī'ī Islam* (New York: Longman, 1976), p. 50.

7 *E.I.*, 2nd ed., s.v. "Hisham b. al-Hakam," by W. Madelung.

8 Hasan ibn Yusuf ibn 'Ali ibn al-Mutahar al-Helli, *al-Bab al-Hadi 'Ashar,* trans. William McElwee Miller (London, The Royal Asiatic Society, 1928), p. 62.

9 *Ibid.*, p. 68.
10 *Ibid.*, pp. 64-70
11 See Murtaza Mutahari, *Jahān Bīnī Islamī*, Vol. IV (n.p.: Muslim Student Association, 1359/1980-81) (hereafter cited as Mutahari. *Jahān*), pp. 188-94; 'Ali Shari'ati, *Ensān va Islām* (Tehran: Enteshar, n.d.), pp. 1-17; and Taleqani. *Islām*, pp. 143-46. In writing on the viceroyship of man, they refer to the following verses of the Qur'ān: VI:165; X: 14; and XXXV:39.
12 See Mutahari. *Jahān*, pp. 195-96. On the wickedness of man the reference is to the Qur'ān XVII:100; XVIII:54; XXXIII:72; and LXX:19.
13 According to Shī'ī creed, God has designated fourteen infallibles: the Prophet, his daughter Fatemah, and the Twelve Imāms.
14 According to Shī'ism the political situation of the time forced the Imām to conceal his son. Note the following passage from Shaykh Mufid, one of the Imām's special deputy:

> He [the eleventh Imām] had concealed his birth [the twelfth Imām's] and hidden his affairs because of the difficulties of the times and the intensity of the search by the authorities of the time for him.

Shaykh al-Mufid, *Kitab al-Irshad* trans. I.K.A. Howard (London: Balagha Books, 1981), (hereafter cited as Mufid. *al-Irshad*), p. 523.
15 The Buwayhid rulers were a short-lived Shī'ī dynasty who established themselves in Southern Iraq and Iran. They occupied Baghdad in 945 but did not abolish the Caliphate. In fact despite their Shī'ī background and leanings they accepted the nominal supremacy of the Sunni Abbasid Caliph.
16 For an account of the Occultation by a religious scholar see Mufid. *al-Irshad*, pp. 524-555. For a well researched and scholarly presentation of the Occultation see A.A. Sachedina, *Islamic Messianism,* (Albany; State University of N.Y., 1981) (hereafter cited as Sachedina. *Islamic*), pp. 78-180.
17 Hamid Algar, *Religion and State in Iran* (Berkeley: University of California Press, 1968) (hereafter cited as Algar. *Religion*), p. 3.
18 According to the Shī'ī creed there should always exist a proof (*ḥujja*) of God on earth. The Imāms, in part, are explained as the God's proof on earth.
19 For detail see, Abbas Iqbal, *Khāndān Nobakhtī* (Tehran: Nashr Ketab, 1345/1966), pp. 212-213; M. Javad Mashkur, *Tārīkh Shī'a* (Tehran: Eshraqi, 1355/1976), pp. 137-146; and Sachedina. *Islamic,* pp. 86-99.
20 Ali Davani, the translator of Vol XIII of Majlisi's *Beḥār al-Anvār,* loc. cit.; Sachedina. *Islamic*, p. 101.
21 Eskandar Beyg Monshi, *Tarīkh 'ālam Ārāye 'Abbāsi* (Tehran: Amir Kabir, 1334S/1951-52), Vol. 1, pp. 8-22.
22 Hamid Algar, *Islamic Revolution in Iran* (London: Open Press, 1980), p. 4.
23 Ann K.S. Lambton, "Quis Custodiet Custodes," II, *Studia Islamica* VI (1956) (hereafter cited as Lambton "Quis,"): 126.
24 There are seven works of the collections of traditions among Shī'is. Four of them, which are the most important ones, were compiled in the tenth and eleventh centuries. They are as follows: *Usūl al-Kāfī*, compiled by Abu Ja'far Muhammad ibn Ya'qūb Kulayni (d. 940); *Man la-Yaḥẓoro*, compiled by Abu Ja'far Muhammad ibn 'Ali ibn Hassan (ibn Babuya) (d. 911); *Tahẕib al-Aḥkām*, and *Estebṣār*, compiled by Shaykh Ṭusi (d. 1067).

In the seventeenth century the same traditions were recompiled and reproduced in three works: *Vāfī*, compiled by Mulla Fayẓ Kashani (d. 1680); *Behār al-Anvār*, compiled by Mulla Baqir Majlesi (d. 1699); and *Vasā'il al-Shī'a*, compiled by Muhammad ibn Ḥassan Ḥur 'Amoli (d. 1692-93).

25 Mirza Muhammad Tunekabuni, *Qeṣaṣ al-'Ulamā* (Tehran: 'Elmiya, n.d.) (hereafter cited as Tunekabuni, *Qeṣaṣ*.), p. 343.

26 Cf. Lambton "Quis," p. 126 and G. Scarcia, loc. cit.; Algar. *Religion*, p. 28.

27 Muhammad Muhit Tabataba'i, *Naqsh Jamāl al-Din Asadābādi dar Bīdārī-e Mashreq Zamīn* (Qum: Dār-al-Tablīgh-e Eslāmi, 1350/1970–71), p. 85.

28 *E. I.*, 2nd ed., s.v. "Akhbariyya," by W. Madelung (hereafter cited as "Akhbariyya.").

29 *Ibid.*

30 See note 24.

31 Algar. *Religion,* p. 7; and Ali Davani, *Vaḥīd Behbahānī,* (Qum: Dar-al-'Elm, 1337/1958–59) (hereafter cited as Davani. *Vaḥīd*), p. 144.

32 According to Shī'ī jurisprudence the source of the law are the Qur'ān, the traditions of the Prophet and the Imāms, *ijma'* (consensus) and *'agl* or *ijtihād* (independent reasoning).

33 Behbahani was born in Isfahan in 1705–06 in a religious family. He studied with his father until 1722 when the city was sacked by the Afghans. He then travelled to Najaf and continued his studies there. Later he migrated to Behbahan and stayed there for a long time, thus acquiring the name Behbahani. It is very likely that the migration of the *akhbārī 'ulamā* from Bahreyn to Behbahan inspired his travel to that city. It was for the same reason that he travelled to major Shī'ī centers (*'atabāt*) in 1746. He died there in 1793–94. (Biographical data extracted from Davani, *Vaḥīd,* pp. 124–156; and Tunekabuni, *Qeṣaṣ,* pp. 195–204).

34 Muhammad Baqir Vahid Behbahani, *al-Rēsālah fī al-Iitihād wa al-Akhbār,* in a collection of sixteen tracts by Behbahani under the title *al-Fawā'id,* (hand written manuscript, Mar'ashi Library, Qum, Iran).

35 *Ibid.,* section two.

36 *Ibid.*

37 The best account of *taqīyya* in Shī'ī political thought is presented by Hamid Enayat in his *Modern Islamic Political Thought,* (Austin: Texas University Press, 1982) (hereafter cited as Enayat. *Modern*), pp. 175–81. This is one of the best treatment of the subject by a scholar who masterfully has succeeded in presenting both an expressive and an impressive account of the diverse trend in the Muslim world in modern history.

38 Behbahani, loc. cit.; Davani. *Vaḥīd,* p. 91

39 "Akhbariyya."

40 Mirza Muhammad ibn 'Abd al-Nabi Akhbari, loc. cit.; Mahmud Shahabi, *Taqrīrāt Usūl* (Tehran: 'Elmi, 1344/1965–66) (hereafter cited as Shahabi. *Taqrīrāt*), p. 64

41 Davani. *Vaḥīd,* p. 338.

42 *Ibid.,* p. 153; and Tunekabuni. *Qeṣaṣ,* p. 204. This is highly significant because the Shī'īs believe that, at the beginning of each century, a renewer will rise up and strengthen their faith. In fact many people consider Ayat-Allah Khomeyni as the renewer for the 15th century Islamic calendar.

43 Shaykhism was founded by Shaykh Ahmad Ahsa'i. His opponents were known as *Bālāsarī.* See Denis MacEoin "From Shaykhism to Babism," Ph.D. dissertation, Cambridge University, 1979, (hereafter cited as MacEoin. *Shaykhism*), pp, 50–82; and Murtaza Modarresi Chardahi, *Shaykhīqarī-Babīgarī,* (Tehran: *Forughi,* 1345/1966–67) (hereafter cited as Modarresi. *Shaykhīgarī*), pp. 27–51.

44 Mulla Ahmad Naraqi was born in Naraq a village near Kashan in 1771–72. In his youth he travelled to Karbala with his father Mulla Mehdi Naraqi (d. 1794–95), a prominent *'ālim* (pl. *'ulamā*) himself. There, he attended the classes of Aqa Baqir Behbahani who was in the last years of his life. Upon his father's death, Naraqi returned to Kashan and assumed the religious leadership there. His works are mostly on principles of jurisprudence (*usūl al-fiqh*) and jurisprudence proper. One of his works, *Sayf al-Umma,* is a polemical work refuting Henry Martyn, a British missionary who arrived in Iran in June, 1811, pretending to be a Muslim. (The biographical data is extracted from Davani, *Vaḥīd,* pp. 297–299 and Tunekabuni, *Qeṣaṣ,* pp. 129–132).

45 Shaykh Murtaza Ansari was born in Dizful in 1799. His lineage goes back to Jabir ibn Abd-Allah Ansari (d. 697), a companion of the Prophet (hence his last name). He spent most of his youth travelling back and forth between Iran and Iraq to study with the religious leaders of his time in both countries. He studied with Naraqi, Seyyed Muhammad Mujahid (d. 1826), Mullah Muhammad Sharif al-'Ulamā (d. 1829), Shaykh Musa Kashif al-Qita' (d. 1826) and Seyyed Muhammad Baqir Shafti (d. 1853). Upon his death in 1849, Shaykh Muhammad ibn Baqir Najafi, the *marja'* of the time, chose Ansari as his successor. Very soon he was recognized by all the Shī'īs; for the first time the Shī'ī community was centralized.

This short account of Ansari's life is extracted from *E. I.*, 2nd ed., s.v., "Ansari," by Abdul-Hadi Hairi (hereafter cited as E. I., "Ansari"); Abdul-Hadi Hairi, *Shī'īsm and Constitutionalism in Iran* (Leiden: E. J. Brill, 1977) (hereafter cited as Hairi. *Shī'īsm*), pp. 63–65; and Tunekabuni, *Qeṣaṣ,* pp. 106–107.

46 I am greatly indebted to Professor Sachedina, who was so generous as to assist me in reading the Arabic works of these two scholars, and who shared with me his own notes on them.

47 Ahmad ibn Muhammad Mehdi Naraqi, *'Awā'id al-Ayyām,* (Tehran: n.p., 1321/1903–04) (hereafter cited as Naraqi. *'Awā'id*).

48 *Ibid.,* p. 185,

49 *Ibid.*

50 *Ibid.*

51 *Ibid.,* pp. 185–195.

52 *Ibid.,* p. 195.

53 *Ibid.,* pp. 195–96.

54 *Ibid.,* p. 205

55 Most scholars maintain that looking at the financial management of a special tax in Shī'īsm, known as the share of the Imām, which falls in Naraqi's last category, would better help to understand the extent of *'ulamā*'s power. Professor Sachedina, for example, argues that this issue is more significant than others. [See his "Al-Khums: The Fifth in the Imāmi Shī'ī Legal System,"

Journal of Near Eastern Studies Vol. 39 no. 4 (October 1980): 275–289]. think, however, that looking at the issue of the acting sovereign's role bette serves the purpose.

56 Naraqi. *'Awā'id,* pp. 186–87.

57 *Ibid.,* p. 186.

58 Cf. Ruhollah Khomeyni, *Nāme'ī az Imām* (Tehran: n.p., 1354/1975–76) (hereafter cited as *Nāme'ī az Imām*), pp. 53–100.

59 See note 44.

60 Tunekabuni. *Qeṣaṣ,* p. 130.

61 *Ibid.*

62 In Shī'ī jurisprudence a Muslim either is an authority in the matters of religion or a follower of one. The former is known as *mujtahid* or the *marja' al-taqlīd.* The latter phrase literally means the source of following and refers to a competent authority to whom a person refers in matters of religion firmly believing him to be right therein.

63 Shaykh Murtaza Ansari, *Al-Makāsib* (Tabriz: n.p., 1375Q/1955).

64 *Ibid.,* p. 153.

65 *Ibid.,* p. 155

66 See Hairi. *Shī'ism,* p. 60.

67 Algar. *Religion,* p. 164.

69 Loc. Cit,; *E. I.,* "Ansari."

69 On Babism consult, *inter alia,* Algar. *Religion,* pp. 137–52; *E. I.,* 2nd ed., s.v., "Bab," by G. H. Bousquet; MacEoin, *Shaykhism*; and Modarresi. *Shaykhīgarī.*

70 Abbas Effendi, *A Traveller's Narrative,* trans. E. G. Browne, reprint (Amsterdam: Philo Press, 1975), pp. 86–87.

71 Mirza Fath-'Ali Akhundzadeh, loc. cit.; *E. I.,* "Ansari."

72 The following English sources are good references for the events of the Tobacco Protest. Edward Browne, *The Persian Revolution of 1905–1909* (Cambridge: Cambridge University Press, 1910); Nikki Keddie, *Religion and Rebellion in Iran: The Tobacco Protest of 1891–1892* (London: F. Cass, 1966); and A. K. Lambton, "The Tobacco Regie: Prelude to Revolution,". *Studia Islamica* Vol. XXII (1965): 118–155 and Vol. XXIII (1965): 71–90.

73 The best account of the Revolution in English is presented by Browne. See note 72.

74 Shaykh Fazlullah Nuri was born in 1843. He studied with Mirza Shirazi in Najaf, Iraq, until 1882, when he returned to Tehran. He was very active in politics from his early youth. He took part in the Tobacco Protest. He participated in leading the Constitutional Revolution; he later opposed it, which led to his execution by the revolutionaries in 1909.

75 Na'ini was born in 1860. He studied in Isfahan under a powerful *'ālim* (pl. *'ulamā*), Aqa Najafi (d. 1913), who was at times very oppressive. Some scholars suggest that this early influence may be responsible for Na'ini's hatred of tyranny. (Hairi. *Shī'ism,* p. 111). He later left to study in Iraq. During the Constitutional Revolution, along with the major *'ulamā* in Najaf, he supported the movement. Later in his life he supported the Iraqi Uprising against the British in 1923. By then, however, he was losing his enthusiasm for revolutions. The hanging of Nuri and other distasteful consequences of the

ı influenced his decision of collecting and destroying the book. He ısappointed by the Revolution that he favored the governments in d Iraq "no matter how un-Islamic and tyrannical the government may oeen." (Hairi. *Shī'ism,* p. 148). The change in his views does not nish the importance of his work because the book represents a wave of ıking among the *fuqahā* rather than the exclusive views of the author.

hmad Kasravi, *Tārīkh Mashrūṭe-ye Iran,* 13th imp. (Tehran: Amir Kabir, 1356/1977) (hereafter cited as Kasravi. *Tārīkh*), p. 286.

Ibid., p. 287.

/8 Some of these can be found in Kasravi. *Tārīkh,* pp. 410, 414–423, 433–438 and 459; and M. E. Rezvani, "Ruznameh Shaykh Fazl-Allah Nuri," *Tārīkh* Vol. I no. 2 (1977): 159–209. An English translation of one of them can be found in Abdul Hadi Hairi, "Shaykh Fazl Allah Nuri's Refutation of the Idea of Constitutionalism," *Middle Eastern Studies* Vol. 13 no. 3 (October, 1977) (hereafter cited as Hairi. "Nuri"): 327–339.

79 Nuri, loc. cit.; Hairi. "Nuri," p. 331,

80 *Ibid.*

81 Nuri, loc. cit.; Kasravi. *Tārīkh,* p. 417.

82 Nuri, loc. cit.; Hairi. "Nuri," p. 336.

83 *Ibid.,* p. 337.

84 Na'ini. *Tanbīh,* p. 8

85 *Ibid.,* pp. 8–10.

86 *Ibid.,* pp. 11–12.

87 *Ibid.,* pp. 51–52.

88 *Ibid.,* p. 4.

89 *Ibid.,* pp. 86–87.

90 *Ibid.,* p. 46.

91 *Ibid.,* pp. 139–41.

92 For a good detailed analysis of the relations of the Pahlavis with the *'ulamā* see Shahrough Akhavi, *Religion and Politics in Contemporary Iran: Clergy-State Relation in Pahlavi Period* (Albany: State University of New York, 1980) (hereafter cited as Akhavi. *Religion*).

93 For Kashani's role in Iranian politics see Muhammad Hassan Faghfoory, "The role of the 'ulamā in twentieth century Iran with particular reference to Ayatullah Haj Sayyid Abul-Qasim Kashani," Ph.D. dissertation, Madison: University of Wisconsin, 1978; and Akhavi. *Religion,* pp. 60–71.

94 For Burujerdi's death and 1963 uprising see chapter III and the sources cited therein.

95 The first book was originally written in the form of an open letter to the major *'ulamā* before the 1963 political uprising. Not getting the proper response, the author published it in the form of a book; Nasir al-Din Amir-Sadeqi, *Rohānīyat dar Shī'a,* (Tehran: n.p., 1349S/1970) (hereafter cited as Amir-Sadeqi. *Rohānīyat*). He later added a second volume to it entitled *Hayāhū,* (Tehran: n.p., 1351S/1972–73) (hereafter cited as Amir-Sadeqi. *Hayāhū*). The second book is a collection of articles by important religious as well as political leaders; *Baḥsi dar Bāreye Marja'īyat va Rohānīyat,* Qum: Enteshar, 1341S/1962) (hereafter cited as Baḥsi).

96 See Ann Lambton, "A Reconstruction of the position of the *marja' al-Taqlid* and the religious institution," *Studia Islamica* Vol. XX (1964) (hereafter cited as Lambton, "A Reconstruction"): 115–135.
97 Amir-Sadeqi. *Roḥānīyat,* pp. 43–44.
98 *Ibid.,* pp. 119–21.
99 *Ibid.,* p. 121.
100 *Ibid.,* p. 118.
101 Amir-Sadeqi. *Hayāhū,* p. 172.
102 Amir-Sadeqi. *Roḥānīyat,* p. 48.
103 Amir-Sadeqi, *Hayāhū,* pp. 14–40.
104 *Baḥs̱i,* p. 2, and 36.
105 Lambton, "A Reconstruction," p. 122.
106 Murtaza Mutahari, in *Baḥs̱i,* p. 175.
107 *Ibid.,* p. 176.
108 *Ibid.,* pp. 184–89.
109 *Ibid.,* pp. 189–94.
110 Mahdi Bazargan, in *Baḥs̱i,* p. 125.
111 *Ibid.,* p. 114.
112 *Ibid.,* p. 117.
113 For the views of different thinkers on this subject see *Baḥs̱i,* pp. 30, 86, 119 and 197.
114 Bazargan, in *Ibid.,* 119.
115 On the influence of Marxism and neo-Marxism see Enayat. *Modern,* pp. 139–159
116 See *inter alia,* Ali Shari'ati, *Majmū'e Asar,* (Tehran: Ershad, n.d.) 8 vols. and Taleqani, *Islam.*
117 This organization began in the summer of 1965 and carried out some political assassinations until they came into the open in the fall of 1978. Later, its leaders opposed Ayat-Allah Khomeyni's interpretation of Shī'ī political thought and led an open opposition against his regime, which resulted in the exile of Mas'ud Rajavi, the chief leader of the organization's leader, in France. For a detailed analysis of the formation of the organization see *History of Formation and Activities of PMOI from 1965–1971* (Tehran: Mojahedin Press, 1358/1978). For the philosophy and views of the organization, see Bahman Bakhtiari, "A Comparison of the Ideologies of 'Ali Shari'ati and the people's Mojahedin in Iran," Masters Thesis at the University of Virginia, May 1981; and Shahram Chubin "Leftist Forces in Iran," *Problem of Communism* (July-August 1980): 1–25.
118 Author's interview with Ali Davani, a member of the *'ulamā* and a historian, in June of 1982 in Tehran, Iran.
119 Sermon delivered on June 25, 1980. See *Eṭṭelā'āt* (June 26, 198): 10.
120 *Islam and Revolution,* p. 126–134.
121 See for example, Mangol Bayat "The Iranian Revolution of 1978–79: Fundamentalist or Modern?" *The Middle East Journal* Vol 37 no. 1 (winter 1983): 30–42.

Chapter III

1 Seyyed Ruhollah Mustasfavi is Ayat-Allah Khomeyni's official name, that is on his birth certificate, passport and etc. He is better known by his place of origin that is Khomeyn.

2 The biographical account of Khomeyni is based on the following works: *Biyogrāfī-ye Pishvā* (n.p.: Panzdah Khordad, n.d.); Ali Davani *Nehẕat Roḥānīyūn-e Iran,* 11 Vols. (Tehran: Bonyad Imam Reza, 1360/1981) (hereafter cited as Davani. *Nehẕat*); Muhammad S. Razi, *Ganjīne-ye Dāneshmandān*, vol. 8 (Qum: Piruz, n.d.); S. H. Rouhani, *Taḥlīlī az Nehẕat-e Imām Khomeynī* (Qum: Dar-al-fekr, 1356/1977) (hereafter cited as Rouhani. *Taḥlīlī*), pp. 19- 113; and *Zendegīnāmeh*, 2 Vols. (n.p.: Fadak 1394/1974).

3 The formal religious studies in a traditional Islamic school consist of three levels: *Doure Moqadamātī* (preliminary level); *Doure saṭḥ* (middle or level of textual analysis); and *Doure Khārej* (open seminar). For more information on this discussion see Akhavi. *Religion*, pp. 32–55; 'Agigi Bakhshayeshi, *Yek Ṣad Sal Mobāreze-ye Rohānīyat-e Motaraqī,* vol. 3, (Qum: Navid, 1359/1980) (hereafter cited as Bakhshayeshi. *Ṣad Sāl*), pp. 73–81; and Mehdi Zavabeti, *Pazhūheshī dar Neẓām Ṭalabegī* (Tehran: Nashr Ketab 1359/1980) (hereafter cited as Zavabeti. *Pazhūheshī*), pp. 133–175.

4 Rouhani. *Taḥlīlī,* p. 27.

5 Akhavi. *Religion*. p. 101.

6 Ruhollah Khomeyni, *Meṣbāḥ al-Hedāya*, trans from Arabic into Persian by Seyyed Ahmad Fahri (Tehran: Payam Azadi, 360/1981) (hereafter cited as Khomeyni. *Meṣbāh*). According to a biographer, Khomeyni wrote this book in 1929. See Rouhani. *Taḥlīlī,* pp. 56–57.

7 Khomeyni. *Meṣbāh*, p. 119.

8 *Ibid.*, p. 152.

9 For Mulla Sadra's views see Seyyd Hossein Nasr, *Islamic Life and Thought* (Albany: The State University of New York, 1981), pp. 145–187; Fazlur Rahman, *The Philosophy of Mulla Sadra* (Albany: The State University of New York, 1975); and Abdulkarim Sourush, *Nahād Nā-Ārām Jahān* (n.p.: Anjoman Daneshjuyan, 1398/1977).

10 Khomeyni, loc. cit.; Ahmad Fahri's introduction to the latter's translation of Khomeyni's *Do'ā-ye Saḥar*, (Tehran: Nizhat-e Zanan Iran, 1359/1980) from Arabic into Persian, (hereafter cited as Khomeyni. *Do'āye Saḥar*), p. x.

11 *Ibid*., p. ix.

12 Khomeyni, "Leqā Allāh," *Keyhān* (July 27, 1982): 16.

13 Rouhani. *Taḥlīlī,* p. 40.

14 *Ibid*., p. 41.

15 For a long list of Khomeyni's students see *Ibid*., pp. 43–50.

16 For a bibliography of Khomeyni's work see the bibliography of the present works and *Ibid*., pp. 55–61.

17 Ruhollah Khomeyni, *Kashf Asrār* (Tehran: Islamiya, 1363 Q/1943) (hereafter cited as *Kashf Asrār*).

18 See Ahmad Kasravi, *Shī'igarī* (n.p., n.d.).

19 See the supplement to number 12 of *Parcham*. The full bibliographical information is as follows: Ali-Akbar Hakami-Zadeh *Asrār-e Hezār Saleh* (Tehran: Parcham, 1322/1943).

20 See for example Akhavi, *Religion*, pp. 60–91; Richard Cottom, *Nationalism in Iran: Updated Through 1978* (Pittsburgh: The University of Pittsburgh Press, 1979), pp. 206–242; and Rouhollah K. Ramazani, *Iran's Foreign Policy: 1941–1973* (Charlottesville: The University of Virginia Press, 1975) (hereafter cited as Ramazani, *Iran: 1941–73*), pp. 181–250.
21 Rouhani. *Taḥlīlī*, p. 99.
22 The author's interview with Ali Davani in Tehran in June, 1982.
23 See Akhavi. *Religion*, p. 63.
24 Hamid Algar, "The Oppositional Role of the Ulama in Twentieth-Century Iran." In *Scholars, Saints, and Sufis*, edited by Nikki Keddie (Berkeley: University of California, 1972), p. 244; and also Bakhshayeshi. *Ṣad Sāl*, vol. 2, pp. 70–71.
25 For land reform and economic reforms of the 1960s see, among other works, Eric Hooglund, *Land and Revolution in Iran: 1960–1980* (Austin, University of Texas, 1982); and Ann Lambton, *The Persian Land Reform, 1962–1966* (Oxford: Clarendon Press, 1969).
26 For the text of the Bill see *Eṭṭelā'āt* (October 8, 1962): 17–18 and (October 9, 1962): lff.
27 Davani. *Nehẕat*, vol. 3, p. 31.
28 For the text of the telegrams by various religious leaders see *Ibid.*, pp. 32–48.
29 The text could be found in Ali Davani, *Nehẕat Do Māhe-ye Roḥānīyat-e Irān* (Qum: Hekmat, 1341/1963), p. 52.
30 See *Eṭṭelā'āt* (January 19, 1963): 1.
31 For Khomeyni's, as well as other religious leaders' declarations to this effect, see Davani. *Nehẕat*, vol. 3, pp. 204–219.
32 Moharram is one of the most important months in Shī'ī Islam. It is the first month of the lunar calendar. During the 9th and 10th days of this month in 680 the third Shī'ī Imām and his family were murdered by the Ummayyad Caliph, Yazid. Every year during the first ten days of this month the devout Shī'is everywhere anguish over the martyrdom of this Imām. The passion during this month is so high that during the Revolution of 1977–79 many people believed that if the Shah's regime survived this month (it coincided with December 1978) it would survive but it did not.
33 For a detailed account of the incident see Davani. *Nehẕat*, vol. 3, pp. 254–360.
34 *Ibid.*, vol. 4, pp. 5–6.
35 Attack against Israel is a constant theme in Khomeyni's thought. He does it both on religious and political ground. Note the following excerpt from his book on Islamis government: "From the very beginning, the historical movement of Islam has had to contend with the Jews, for it was they who first established anti-Islamic propaganda and engaged in various stratagems, and as you can see, this continues down to the present." (*Islam and Revolution*, p. 27).

Politically, it began when Iran implicitly recognized Israel. Apparently Iran *de facto* recognized the State of Israel following the latter's formation in 1948. The Shah implied such a recognition in a press conference on July 23, 1960. In his answer to a question regarding Israel he said: "Recognition (of Israel) is not a new issue. It was decided in the past. Because of some problems and perhaps to cut government spending we recalled our representative from Israel." *Eṭṭelā'āt* (July 24, 1960): 19.

36 See a collection of Khomeyni's speeches entitled, *Majmū'e-'i az Maktūbāt, Sokhanrānīhā, Payāmhā va Fatvāhā-ye Imām Khomeynī*, compiled by M. Dehnavi (Tehran: Chapaksh 1360/1981) (hereafter cited as *Majmū'e*), p. 55.
37 Sermon delivered on June 3, 1963. See *Islam and Revolution*, p. 179–180.
38 See Hassan Pakravan's press conference in *Eṭṭelā'āt* (June 5, 1963): 16.
39 For a detailed, hour by hour, account of the incident see M. Dehnavi, *Qīyām Khūnīn-e Pānzdah-e Khordād-e 1342*, (Tehran: Rasa, 1361/1982), pp. 40–110.
40 Cited in Marvin Zonis, *The Political Elite of Iran*, (Princeton: The Princeton University Press, 1971) (hereafter cited as Zonis. *Political Elite*), p. 45.
41 Sermon delivered April 10, 1964. See *Majmū'e*, p. 64.
42 For a detailed analysis of this episode see Richard Pfau, "The Legal Status of American Forces in Iran," *The Middle East Journal* vol. 28 no. 2 (spring 1974): 141-153; and Ramazani. *Iran: 1941–73*, pp. 362–366.
43 For the views of the important religious leaders on this issue see Davani, *Nehẕat*, vol. 4, pp. 303–334.
44 *Islam and Revolution*, p. 182.
45 For the Persian text of the leaflet see Rouhani. *Taḥlīlī*, pp. 729–735. An English translation of it can be found in Floor, "'ulamā," pp. 521–524.
46 For the text of the government's statement see Zonis. *Political Elite*, p. 44.
47 One of his students, Jalal al-Din Farsi, the presidential candidate of the Islamic Republican Party in 1979 and an important person in the Staff of Cultural Revolution, transcribed the lectures and published them. (Ruhollah Khomeyni, *Ḥokūmat-e Islāmi yā Velāyat-e Faqīh* 6 vols. (Najaf: Adab, 1390/ 1971). It should be pointed out that each volume was compromised of only two lectures. All six volumes were edited and later published under different titles in one volume. *Ḥokūmat-e Islāmi* and or *Velāyat-e Faqīh* are the two most famous titles.
48 Ruhollah Khomeyni, *Kitāb al-Bay'* 5 vols. (Najaf: n.p., 1390–91/1970–71). For a review of this work see Calder. "Accommodation."
49 *Islam and Revolution*, p. 57.
50 *Ibid*., p. 126.
51 In his messages to Iranian students abroad or in other messages Khomeyni urged his audience to propogate the viability of Islam as a political alternative to the monarchy. See *Majmū'e*, pp. 159–188.
52 Ahmad Rashidi-ye Motlaq "Iran va Este'mār-e Sorkh va Siya'," *Eṭṭelā'āt* (January 7, 1978): 7. Some editorials later revealed that the letter was written by the Shah himself. See Ahmad Ahrar "Ahmad Rashidi-ye Motlaq Shakhs-e Shah būd," *Eṭṭelā'āt* (March 18, 1979): 8.
53 For a detailed account of the incident see Davani. *Nehẕat*, vol. 7, pp. 20–73.
54 See *Majūm'e*, pp. 284–297.
55 *Ibid*., pp. 296–297.
56 Ibid., pp. 364–65.
57 See A. H. H. Abidi "The Iranian Revolution: Its Origins and Dimensions." *International Studies* vol. 18, no. 2 (April/June 1979): 129–161.
58 See Davani, *Nehẕat*. vol. 8, pp. 125–126.
59 *Ibid*., p. 134.
60 For a detailed analyses of the whole episode see Abidi's article in note 57.

Chapter IV

1 Reinhold Niebuhr, *The Nature and Destiny of Man: A Christian Interpretation*, 2 vols. (New York: Charles Scribner's Sons, 1943), vol. 2, p. 1.
2 Sermon delivered on June 26, 1979. See a collection of his speeches, *Rūḥ Khodā Dar Velāyat Faqīh* (Tehran: Vezarat Ershad, 1980), (hereafter cited as *Rūḥ Khodā*), p. 138.
3 See Khomeyni, *Do'āye Saḥar*, pp. 101–102.
4 *Ibid.*, p. 103.
5 Sermon delivered on September 20, 1979. See *Rahnemūdha: Tābestān*, p. 204.
6 R. Khomeyni, *Resāleh Novvīn*, vol 4. (Tehran: Anjam Ketab, 1360/1981), (hereafter cited as *Resāleh*), p. 52.
7 Sermon delivered on September 9, 1982. See *Keyhān* (September 10, 1982): 18.
8 Sermon delivered on October 31, 1971. See *Khomeyni va Jonbesh* (n.p.: Panzdah Khordad, 1352/1973), (hereafter cited as *Khomeyni va Jonbesh*), p. 36.
9 According to the Islamic world view, beginning with Adam as the first, God has periodically sent prophets to guide man to the straight path. Based on this verse of the Qur'ān, "He [Muhammad] is the messenger of Allah and the Seal of the prophets," (XXXIII:40), Muslims believe that the prophethood ended with Muhammad in 610 A.D. when he was appointed as the last prophet.
10 See, *Rahnemūdhā: Tābestān*, p. 204.
11 Sermon delivered July 1, 1979. See *Rūḥ Khodā*, p. 189.
12 Bruce Mazlish, "The Hidden Khomeyni," *The New York* (December 24, 1979): 49–54.
13 Calder, "Accommodation."
14 The story of the origin of the force of evil in Islam conforms to the general message of Islam. According to Islam nothing is evil by nature; failure to live up to the set standard causes evil acts. The same is true about Satan. He is not evil by nature, rather he did not measure up to the standard set by God. The story is reported in the Qur'ān XV: 26–43 and XXXVIII: 72–84.
15 Khomeyni, "Lecture on *Surat al-fatiha,*" in *Islam and Revolution*, pp. 409–410.
16 This summary is based on Plato's *The Republic*, in particular Book VII and general review of the literature on Plato.
17 I am not suggesting that both Plato and Khomeyni are striving for the same end. I am aware that Plato's philosopher-king needs to experience the good (the *agathon*), whereas Khomeyni's perfect man is the active embodiment of the revealed law. The similarities are mostly in their view of man before he reaches perfection and in that both see the necessity of conversion to a higher state.
18 Sermon delivered on September 28, 1977. See *Majmū'e*, p. 252.
19 Sermon to student from Shiraz. See *Eṭṭelā'āt* (September 7, 1979): 15.
20 Algar's interview with Khomeyni. For the transcript see a collection of Khomeyni's sermons entitled *Rahnemūdhāye Imām: Ābān 1358 tā Ābān 1359* (Tehran: Nas, 1356/1980), (hereafter cited as *Rahnemūdhā: Ābān*), p. 46.

21 *The Shorter Encyclopedia of Islam*, s.v. "Nafs," by E. E. Calverley.
22 The example of the first meaning that is the self is "We will summon . . . ourselves and yourselves," (III:61). And the examples for the second meaning that is the soul is "Deliver up your souls," (VI:93).
23 Khomeyni in passing refers to the three parts of the individual's soul in a sermon he delivered on August 31, 1980. See *Rahnemūdhā: Ābān*, p. 268.
24 *Islam and Revolution*, p. 383.
25 *Ibid.*, p. 375.
26 See Khomeyni "Lecture on Supreme Jihad" in *Nāme'ī az Imām* p. 251.
27 *Ibid.*, p. 212.
28 Khomeyni restates this tradition quite often in his commentaries, tracts and speeches. See *inter alia* his *Asrār al-Ṣalāt*, vol. 1, trans from Arabic by Syyed Ahmad Fahri, (Tehran: Nehzat Zanan, 1359/1979), (hereafter cited as *Asrār al-Ṣalāt*), p. 116; *Ibid.*, p. 251; and his sermon on April 3, 1982, in *Keyhān* (April 4, 1982): 14.
29 *Islam and Revolution*, p. 388. Algar has translated *nafs* in this passage as "aspirations." I think appetite is closer to Khomeyni's view. Although I have quoted Algar's translation here, I have changed this one word.
30 See *Asrār al-Ṣalāt*, vol. 2, p. 116.
31 *Islam and Revolution*, p. 356.
32 *Ibid.*
33 Sermon on April 3, 1982. See *Keyhān* (April 4, 1982): 14.
34 *Resāleh*, vol. IV, p. 76.
35 Sermon delivered on May 28, 1981. See a collection of his sayings entitled, *Rahnemūd: Bahār 1360* (Tehran: Masjed Ali, 1981), (hereafter cited as *Rahnemūd*), p. 133.
36 Sermon delivered on March 19, 1981. See *Payām Imām*, No. 8 (Farvardin 1360/March-April 1981): 3.
37 Sermon delivered on February 8, 1982. See *Keyhān* (February 9, 1982): 30.
38 Kenneth W. Thompson, *Ethics, Functionalism and Power in International Politics* (Baton Rouge: Louisiana State University Press, 1979), p. 15.
39 See for example Hans Morgenthau, *Politics Among Nations*, 5th ed. (New York: Alfred A. Knopf, 1978) (hereafter cited as Morgenthau. *Politics*), pp. 3–4.
40 See for example Khomeyni, *Asrār al-Ṣalāt*, vol. 2, pp. 172–173 or sermon he delivered on May 27, 1981 in *Rahnemūd*, p. 119.
41 See *Tafsīr Sūrah Ḥamd* (Tehran: Komeyl, n.d.), p. 23. He is using the following verse in this dichotomy: "What is with you will perish, and what is with God will remain." (XVI:96).
42 Sermon delivered on March 19, 1981. See *Payām Imām* no. 8 (Fervardin 1360/March-April, 1981): 4.
43 See *inter alia, Islam and Revolution*, p. 419.
44 See note 42.
45 See Isaiah Berlin, *Four Essays on Liberty* (New York: Oxford University Press, 1960), pp. 121–122.
46 *Islam and Revolution*, p. 371.
47 Sermon on September 29, 1979. See *Eṭṭelā'āt* (September 30, 1979): 12.
48 *Islam and Revolution*, p. 375.
49 Sermon on August 2, 1981. See *Payām Imām* no. 20 (n.d.): 18.

50 See for example Abu Hayyan al Tawhihi, *loc. cit.,* Franz Rosenthal, *The Muslim Concept of Freedom: Prior to 19th Century* (Leiden: Brill, 1960) (hereafter cited as Rosenthal, *The Muslim*), p. 17. My discussion of the Islamic view of liberty is basically based on this informative and well researched work.
51 Loc. cit., *Ibid.*, p. 24.
52 Note for example Al-Tahanawi's definition, loc. cit., *Ibid.*, p. 27.
53 Ibn-Arabi, *loc. cit.*, *Ibid.*, p. 115.
54 *Islam and Revolution*, p. 415.
55 Sermon on August 2, 1981. See *Payām Imām* no. 18 (n.d.): 20.
56 The interested readers can consult W. M. Watt, *Free Will and Predestination in Early Islam* (London: Luzac, 1948), and the same author's *The Formative Period of Islamic Thought* (Edinburgh: The Edinburgh University Press, 1973), pp. 82–118. I should thank Mr. Ramazani for bringing the aforementioned Shī'ī tradition to my attention.
57 Rosenthal, *The Muslim*, p. 118.
58 *Ibid.*, p. 5.
59 The term in this derivation and meaning are found in The Qur'ān, II: 256–257; IV: 51, 54 and 76; V: 60; XVI: 36 and XXXIX: 17.
60 See Shorter *Encyclopedia of Islam*, s.v. "Shaitan," by A. S. Tritton.
61 *Resaleh*, vol. I, p. 98.
62 Khomeyni, *Asrār al-Ṣalāt*, vol. II, p. 173.
63 Sermon delivered July 19, 1979. See *Rūḥ Khodā*, p. 169.
64 Sermon August 31, 1980. See *Rahnemūdhā: Ābān*, p. 208.
65 See *Do'āye Saḥar*, pp. 101–103.
66 Sermon delivered on March 18, 1981. See *Payām Imām* No. 8 (Farvardin 1350/March-April, 1981): 3.
67 Sermon delivered on October 27, 1980. See *Rahnemūdhā: Ābān*, p. 288.
68 *Islam and Revolution*, p. 385.
69 Sermon on July 7, 1979. See *Rūḥ Khodā*, p. 268.
70 See *Asrār al-Ṣalāt*, vol. 1, p. 4.
71 See *Kashf Asrār*, p. 312.
72 *Ibid.*, p. 233.
73 One of the basic tenets of Shī'ī Islam is '*Adl* meaning god's justice. According to Shī'ism the five pillars of Islam are as follows: The first is *Tawhīd*, the oneness of God as the source of all existence. Second is '*Adl*, the notion that God is just. The third is *Nabovvat*, the prophecy. The fourth is *Imāmate*, the leadership. And the fifth is *Ma'ād*, the day of judgment. A very short interpretation is as follows. Everything begins with God (*Tawhīd*) and ends with God (*Ma'ād*). Being just ('*adil*), God sends prophets (*Nabovvat*) to guide people. The leadership (*Imāmate*) is necessary to perpetuate the message.
74 Sermon on July 7, 1979. See *Rūḥ Khodā*, p. 269.
75 Sermon delivered June 1, 1980. See *Rahnemūd*. p. 135.
76 *Islam and Revolution*, p. 386.
77 Sermon delivered October 14, 1978. See *Nedāye Ḥaq* (Tehran: Qalam, 1978), (hereafter cited as *Nedāye Ḥaq*), p. 163.
78 Sermon delivered on December 23, 1979. See *Rahnemūdhā: Ābān*, p. 3.
79 Plato, *The Republic*, translated by W. H. D. Rouse (New York: New American Library, 1956), Book VII, p. 313.

80 *Islam and Revolution*, p. 385.
81 Alfarabi "The Political Regime," trans. by Fauzi M. Najjar in *Medieval Political Philosophy: A Sourcebook*, edited by Ralph Lerner and Muhsin Mahdi, (New York: Cornell University Press, 1972), pp. 35–36.

Chapter V

1 Max Weber, "Politics as a Vocation," in *From Max Weber: Essays in Sociology*, trans. H. H. Gerth and C. Wright Mills, (New York: Oxford University Press, 1946) (hereafter cited as Weber. "Politics,"), p. 79.
2 Morgenthau. *Politics*, p. 42.
3 David Easton, *The Political System: An Inquiry into the State of Political Science* (New York: Alfred A. Knopf, 1965), pp. 136–137.
4 Harold Lasswell, *Politics: Who Gets What, When, How* (New York: Maridian Books, 1958).
5 Aristotle, *Politics*, trans. by Ernest Barker (New York: Oxford University Press, 1979), Book III, 1287a.
6 Khomeyni is referring to Hassan Pakravan, head of the Iranian secret police (SAVAK) between 1961 and 1965 who visited him in his detention on July 2, 1963. Pakravan told him "Politics involves lying, deception and viciousness; why don't you leave it to us?" See Rouhani. *Taḥlīlī*, p. 575.
7 Khomeyni, *Resāleh* vol. IV, p. 46.
8 *Ibid*.
9 *Ibid*., p. 47.
10 Sermon delivered on September 9, 1979. See *Rahnemūdhā: Tābestān*, p. 194.
11 Leonard Binder "Al-Ghazali's Theory of Islamic Government," *The Muslim World* vol. XLV No. 3 (July 1955): 229.
12 For the text of the request and the answer in Persian see *Keyhān* (May 30, 1982): 2.
13 This important feature of Islamic thought has been reiterated time and again in the works of most scholars in the field. See for example: Leonard Binder, cited in note 10; Ann Lambton, *State and Government in Medieval Islam* (New York: Oxford University Press, 1981) (hereafter cited as Lambton. *State*); Muhsin Mahdi "Alfarabi," in *History of Political Philosophy* 2nd ed., ed. by Leo Strauss and Joseph Cropsey (Chicago: University of Chicago Press, 1981), pp. 182–202; Erwin Rosenthal *Political Thought in Medieval Islam*, (Cambridge: Cambridge University Press, 1968) particularly chapter 2; and Henry Siegman "The State and the Individual in Sunni Islam," *The Muslim World*, vol. LIV no. 1 (January 1964) (hereafter cited as Siegman. "The State,"): 14–26.
14 *Islam and Revolution*, p. 38.
15 See note 17 of chapter III.
16 The entire book is a response to a series of questions proposed by Al Akbar Hakami-zadeh in a pamphlet he published in 1943 entitled *Asrār Hezār Sāleh*. This question is part of question number nine on page 38 of the pamphlet.
17 *Kashf Asrār*, p. 289.
18 *Ibid*., p. 291.

19 *Ibid.*, p. 312.
20 *Ibid.*
21 *The Shorter Encyclopedia of Islam*. s.v. "Shari'a," by Joseph Schacht.
22 H. A. R. Gibb, *Mohammedanism*, second, edition, (New York: Oxford University Press, 1979), p. 68.
23 The Council of Guardians is a council consisting of six theologian jurisconsults (*faqih*) and six lawyers who supervise the laws passed by the parliament (*majles*). The nature and function of the Council is laid down in Articles 91 to 99 of the Constitution. See "The Constitution of the Islamic Republic of Islam," with an introduction by Professor R. K. Ramazani, *The Middle East Journal*, vol. 34 No. 2, (spring 1980), (hereafter cited as "The Constitution."): 181–204. It should be pointed out that the idea of the council of Guardians is not new. The previous constitution (1905) provided a committee of five *mujtahids* invested with the power to reject any legislative proposal if it were contrary to the *Sharī'a*.
24 Sermon to the Council of Guardians delivered on July 21, 1980. See a collection of his sayings entitled *Payāmhā va Sokhan-rānīhā-ye Imām Khomeynī dar shesh Māhe-ye Avval 1359* (Tehran: Nur, n.d.) (hereafter cited as *Avval 1359*), p. 289.
25 See *Kashf Asrār*, p. 274.
26 *Ibid.*, p. 222.
27 *E.I.*, 2nd ed. s.v. "Hukuma," by H. J. Benda.
28 Sermon to the prime minister and his cabinet given on September 11, 1980. See *Avval 1359*, p. 376.
29 Khomeyni, *Jāme'e-ye Toḥīdī* (Tehran: Nas n.d.) (hereafter cited as *Jāme'e-ye Toḥīdī*), p. 5.
30 *Shorter Encyclopedia of Islam*, s. v. "Wali," by B. Carra de Vaux.
31 Sermon delivered on August 16, 1980. See *Rahnemūdhā; Ābān*, p. 233.
32 *Nāme'ī az Imām*, pp. 45–46; Algar's translation *Islam and Revolution*, p. 55.
33 *Kashf Asrār*, pp. 186–187.
34 *Ibid.*, p. 223.
35 Sermon delivered on October 31, 1971. See *Khomeyni va Jonbesh*, pp. 36–53.
36 See chapter III in particular note 47.
37 Sermon delivered on March 10, 1979. See *Eṭṭelā'āt*, (March 11, 1979): 8.
38 Interview with a reporter of *Le Monde* on November 13, 1978. For the text see *Nedāye Ḥaq*, p. 95.
39 The distinction between the sovereignty of God and the sovereignty of man is not Khomeyni's alone. This distinction, in the thinking of one leading Shī'ī scholar, Na'ini, has been discussed in chapter two. The Sunni philosopher Ibn-Khaldun makes a similar distinction; he distinguishes between *Khilafa* (viceregency of God) and *mulk* (rulership of kings).
40 *Kashf Arsrār*, pp. 289–90.
41 *Ibid.*, pp. 221–22. Most of the translation in this passage is taken from Algar's *Islam and Revolution*, pp. 169–70.
42 Sermon of August 28, 1977. See *Majmū'e*, p. 253.
43 Sermon of December 29, 1979. See *Rahnemūdhā; Ābān*, p. 46.
44 Sermon of August 28, 1977. See *Majmū'e*, p. 253.
45 *Nedā-ye Ḥaq*, p. 342.

46 *Ibid.*, p. 343.
47 For a study of totalitarianism, see, among others, Carl J. Frederich and Zbigniew Brzezinski *Totalitarian Dictatorship and Autocracy*, (Cambridge Mass.: Harvard University Press, 1956).
48 *Nāme'ī az Imām*, p. 35.
49 Sermon delivered on September 11, 1980. See *Avval 1359*, p. 376.
50 Sermon delivered in December 1981. See *Payām Imām* (no. 26, n.d.): 2.
51 *Islam and Revolution*, p. 63.
52 Sermon delivered on October 10, 1980. See *Imām va Jang*, (Tehran: Hezb Jomhuriye Eslami, n.d.) (hereafter cited as *Imām va Jang*), p. 19.
53 See *Nāme'ī az Imām*, pp. 151–164.
54 *Ibid.*, p. 56.
55 *Islam and Revolution*, p. 53.
56 Algar has translated *velāyat* as "government" in this passage. I have preserved his translation but added the Persian word in brackets.
57 *Nāme'ī az Imām*, p. 56.
58 *Ibid.*
59 For the text of the interview see *Enqelāb Eslāmi*, (December 1, 1979): 3.
60 Sermon delivered on June 21, 1982. See *Keyhān* (June 22, 1982): 3.
61 *Mollā* is a general name for religious leaders in Iran. It should be noted, however, that the term has acquired a pejorative connotation. Khomeyni here uses it in this pejorative sense.
62 *Ākhond* is also a general name for the religious leaders. At one time it was a very important title among religious groups. Nowadays it is also used by many people in a pejorative sense.
63 See note 60.
64 This is a tradition ascribed to the eight Shī'ī Imām, reported by Shaykh Saduq in his *'elal āl-sharaye'*, vol. 1, 182:9.
65 A tradition ascribed to the Prophet reported by Kulayni in his *al-kafi*, 13:5.
66 *Nāme'ī az Imām*, p. 82.
67 *Ibid.*
68 This tradition is ascribed to the third Shī'ī Imām, reported by Kulayni in his *al-kāfī*, 1:23.
69 *Nāme'ī az Imām*, p. 117.
70 *Ibid.*, pp. 88–92.
71 Tradition is reported from al-Hurr al-'Āmoli *Vasā'il al-shī'a*, a loc. cit., Ibid., p. 89. The translation of the tradition is Algar's. See *Islam and Revolution*, p. 84.
72 *Nāme'ī az Imām*, p. 89.
73 The tradition is reported in 'Amoli, *Vasā'il al-shī'a*, vol. XVIII:II,1.
74 Persian and Arabic text of the tradition is provided in *Nāme'ī az Imām*, pp. 100–102. The English translation is taken from Algar's translation. See *Islam and Revolution*, pp. 92–93.
75 For a discussion on this issue see Enayat, *Modern,* pp. 171–172. and the thinkers referred to therein.
76 For a scholarly and well-researched work on the structure and function of religious sciences in Islam, see Zavabeti. *Pazhuheshī.*
77 *Nāme'ī az Imām*, pp. 50–51. Hamid Algar has translated *'edālat* as "justice." I prefer "righteousness" because its meaning is much closer to Khomeyni's as

well as to the Islamic notion of *'edālat*. The *Oxford English Dictionary* provides this definition for righteousness: "conformity of life or conduct to the requirements of the divine or moral law." This is precisely what Khomeyni has in mind when he uses the term *'edālat*. An absolutely righteous person in Khomeyni's view, is a living manifestation of the *Sharī'a*.

78 *Islam and Revolution*, p. 62.

79 Siegman. "The State," pp. 15–16.

80 Sermon delivered on September 20, 1979. See *Rahnemūdhā:Tābestān*, p. 207.

81 This is a fundamental concept, although systematic treatment has not been given to it by the jurists in their books of jurisprudence. Within the Sunni political thought it has been always one of the qualifications for the office of attorney general (*hākim al-shar'*). In Shī'ī political thought, it has been applied to the Imām as well as to the theologian jurisconsult. For example, the Imām should have had a free hand, or his command should have carried weight, if he was to assume political leadership. This was expressed by the term *basṭ al-yad*, literally meaning "free hands," but in its technical sense meant absolute authority.

82 *Nāme'ī az Imām*, p. 57.

83 See "The Constitution," Principle V.

84 See *E.I.* second edition, s.v. "Dawla," by Franz Rosenthal.

85 Weber. "Politics," p. 78.

86 Morgenthau. *Politics*, p. 497.

87 Robert M. MacIver, *The Modern State*, (New York: Oxford University Press, 1966), p. 22.

88 Frederick Meinecke, *Machiavelism: The Doctrine of Raison d'Etat and its Place in Modern History*, (New York: Praeger, 1957), p. 1.

89 *Ibid.*, p. 2–3.

90 *Loghat Nāme' Dehkhodā*, s.v. "*Ummat*."

91 *Shorter Encyclopedia of Islam*, s.v. "Umma," by R. Paret.

92 Sermon given in December 1981. See *Payām Imām*, No. 26 (December 1981): 4.

93 He is referring to Shahpur Bakhtiyar, the last Prime Minister of the Palavi's regime. Ayat-Allah Khomeyni has incorrectly stated his place of residence. Bakhtiyar has resided, for the most part, in France, and from there he continues his political campaigns against the Islamic Republic of Khomeyni.

94 Sermon delivered on November 8, 1979. See *Rahnemūdhā: Ābān*, pp. 15–16.

95 Lambton. *State*, p. 13.

96 See *Majmū'e*, p. 101–102.

97 Sermon delivered on September 29, 1979. See *Eṭṭelā'āt* (September 30, 1979): 10.

98 Since the establishment of the Islamic Republic the Christians, the Jews, and Zoroastrians have had political rights. However, some members of the Jewish nation have been put to death under the accusation of spying for Israel. From among those groups who did not have any political rights in Islam, the Tudeh communist party, who had supported the regime was given political rights until the early summer of 1983 when that party was also banned and its leaders arrested. Ironically, the Mojahedin—who claim to be Muslim—have been outlawed and suppressed ruthlessly by the government because of their violent opposition to the theory of guardianship.

99 See *Payām Imām*, No. 23, (n.d.): 5.
100 The Imām of Age is one of the titles given to the twelfth Imām in Shī'ism. For justification and elaboration see Sachedina, *Islamic*, pp. 60–77.
101 Sermon delivered in December 1981. See *Payām Imām*, No. 26 (December 1981): 3.
102 See *Payām Imām*, No. 18 (July, 1981): 11.
103 Sermon delivered on September 18, 1982. See *Keyhān* (September 19, 1982): 14.
104 *Ibid.*
105 Sermon delivered on October 11, 1978. See *Nedāy-e Ḥaq*, p. 189.
106 Sermon delivered on September 19, 1979. See *Rahnemūdhā; Tābestān*, p. 197.
107 Sermon delivered on December 31, 1981. See *Keyhān*, (January 1, 1982): 14.
108 Sermon delivered on May 5, 1980. See *Rahnemūdhā; Ābān*, p. 95.
109 Cf. His sermon in 1964 in *Majūm'e* (p. 101) and his sermon on September 19, 1979 in *Rahnemūdhā; Tābestān*, (p. 197).
110 Sermon delivered on September 12, 1980. See *Imām va Jang*, p. 71.
111 See for example *inter alia*, the transcript of his sermon on June 12, 1979 in *Rūḥ Khodā*, p. 40.

Chapter VI

1 For the role of Khomeyni's view on the foreign policy of the Islamic Republic of Iran see William Millward, "The Principles of Foreign Policy and the Vision of World Order Expounded by Imam Khomeyni and the Islamic Republic of Iran" in *The Iranian Revolution and the Islamic Republic; Proceedings of a Conference*, eds. Nikki R. Keddie and Eric Hoogland (Washington: Middle East Institute, 1982), pp. 189–209; R. K. Ramazani, "Iran's Foreign Policy: Perspective and Projection," in *Economic Consequences of the Revolution in Iran*. Joint Economic Committee, Congress of the United States (Washington, D.C.: U.S. Government Printing Office, 1980), pp. 65–97; and R. K. Ramazani "Khomeyni's Islam in Iran's Foreign Policy," a paper presented in Royal Institute of International Affairs in London on July 13, 1982. I thank Professor Ramazani for showing me a copy of this paper.
2 Loc. cit.; Martin Wight, *Systems of State*, ed. Hedley Bull (London: Leicester University Press, 1977) (hereafter cited as Wight. *Systems*), p. 21.
3 Morgenthau. *Politics*, p. 237.
4 Hedley Bull, *The Anarchical Society*, (New York: Columbia University Press, 1977), pp. 5–10.
5 Wight, *Systems*, pp. 23–29.
6 *Ibid.*, pp. 23–24.
7 See *Rahnemūdhā; Ābān*, p. 116.
8 Sermon delivered on August 18, 1980. See *Ibid.*, p. 241.
9 Sermon delivered on November 5, 1982. See *Keyhān* (November 6, 1982): 22.
10 On this occasion he is referring to the Israeli invasion of Lebanon and the bombardment of Beirut beginning in June 1982. According to Khomeyni, Israelis do not do anything without Washington's authorization.

11 He is referring to the Russian occupation of Afghanistan.
12 Sermon delivered on August 31, 1982. See *Keyhān* (September 1, 1982): 18.
13 *Kashf Asrār*, p. 221. The translation of this passage into English is that of Algar. See *Islam and Revolution*, p. 169.
14 See for example the sermon he delivered on October 1978 in *Nedāye Ḥaq*, p. 267.
15 Sermon delivered on July 25, 1982. See *Keyhān* (July 26, 1982): 14.
16 The word *Jahān-khārān* literally means "the world eaters," and it is used to mean "the world imperialists."
17 Sermon delivered on March 21, 1980. See *Enqelāb Eslāmī* (March 29, 1980): 3.
18 Note for example the sermon delivered on November 5, 1979. See *Eṭṭelā'āt* (November 6, 1979): 10.
19 Note for example the sermon delivered on November 7, 1979. See *Eṭṭelā'āt* (November 9, 1979): 12.
20 For the United States relations with Iran during the Pahlavi's era see, among others, R. K. Ramazani, *United States and Iran: The Patterns of Influence* (New York: Praeger, 1982) (hereafter cited as Ramazani. *U.S. and Iran*); and Barry Rubin, *Paved with Good Intention: The American Experience in Iran* (New York: Oxford University Press, 1980).
21 See chapter III.
22 Sermon delivered on October 27, 1964. See *Majmū'e*, p. 125. This translation is from Algar. See *Islam and Revolution*, pp. 181–188.
23 Sermon delivered on June 13, 1979. See *Rūḥ Khodā*, p. 45.
24 *Kashf Asrār*, p. 167.
25 Sermon delivered on January 20, 1982. See *Keyhān* (January 21, 1982): 14.
26 Cf. Majid Khadduri's introduction to *Siyar* by Muhammed b. al-Hasan Shaybani (Baltimore: The Johns Hopkins Press, 1966), p. 11; or *E.I.* second ed. s.v. "Dar al-Islam."
27 Cf. Majid Khadduri *Ibid.*; or *E.I.* second ed. s.v. "Dar al-Harb."
28 See Abulfazl Shakuri, *Feqh Sīyāsī Islām*, vol. I (Qum: Nashr Hor, 1361/1982) part 1.
29 See *The Shorter Encyclopedia of Islam*, s.v. "Dar al-Sulh," by D. B. MacDonald.
30 See Ibn Ishaq *The Life of Muhammad*, trans. A. Guillamume (New York: Oxford University Press, 1978), pp. 740–755.
31 *Ibid.*, pp. 341–346.
32 He is referring to the following verse of the Qur'ān: "And we desired to show favor unto those who were oppressed in the earth, and to make them examples, and to make them the inheritors," XXVIII:5.
33 Sermon delivered on March 21, 1980. See *Avval 1359*, p. 8.
34 During the last two days of March 1979 the Iranians went to the polls to vote on a referendum which decided the future regime of Iran. The vote was one of "yes" or "no" for instituting the "Islamic Republic" as the future regime. On April 1, 1979, Ayat-Allah Khomeyni declared Iran an Islamic Republic or, as he put it, the "first day of the government of God."
35 Sermon delivered on April 1, 1980. See *Avval 1359*, p. 24.
36 Sermon delivered on November 21, 1980. See *Rahnemūdhā; Ābān*, p. 304.
37 See note 32.

38 Sermon delivered on February 9, 1980. See *Sobḥ-e Āzādegān* (February 10, 1980): 2.
39 Sermon delivered on June 22, 1979. See *Rūḥ Khodā*, p. 120.
40 Interview with Japanese news reporter. See *Enqelāb Eslāmī* (November 28, 1979): 10.
41 Sermon delivered on December 3, 1962. See *Majmū'e* p. 17.
42 Sermon delivered on August 17, 1979. See *Eṭṭelā'āt* (August 18, 1979): 2.
43 Sermon delivered on December 19, 1982. See *Keyhān* (December 20, 1982): 14.
44 *Ibid.*
45 *Ibid.*
46 See *Resāleh*, vol. IV, p. 76.
47 See note 33.
48 Crane Brinton *The Anatomy of Revolution*, revised ed. (New York: Vintage Books, 1965), p. 196.
49 Sermon delivered on November 2, 1979. See *Eṭṭelā'āt* (November 3, 1979): 12.
50 Algerian ambassador's interview with him on October 19, 1979. See *Eṭṭelā'āt* (October 20, 1979): 2.
51 See *Resāleh*, vol. IV, p. 140.
52 Sermon delivered on February 11, 1980. See *Rahnemūdhā; Ābān*, p. 379.
53 Sermon delivered on June 27, 1979. See *Rūḥ Khodā*, p. 158–159.
54 Sermon delivered on August 12, 1979. See *Rahnemūdhā; Ābān*, p. 219.
55 *Resāleh*, vol. IV, p. 346.
56 See note 54.
57 Sermon delivered on May 4, 1979. See *Eṭṭelā'āt* (May 5, 1979): 16.
58 See *Khat-e Imām Kalām Imām*, vol. I. (Tehran: Nur, 1360/1981), p. 31.
59 *Islam and Revolution*, p. 48.
60 *Ibid.*, 127.
61 *Ibid.*, p. 49.
62 The text of Fatemeh's sermon can be found in Al-Tabarsi, *al-' Eḥtejāj*, vol. 1, p. 134.
63 *Islam and Revolution*, p. 49.
64 Sermon delivered on October 20, 1980. See *Imām va Jang*, p. 37.
65 Khomeyni. *Dar Bāre-ye Felestīn*, (Tehran: Seyyed Jaml, n.d.) (hereafter cited as *Felestin*), p. 67.
66 Al-Afghani. "Eteḥād Islāmī," in a collection of his essays entitled, *Gozide 'Urvat al-vusqā*, (Tehran: Molla, n.d.), pp. 97–105.
67 He is referring to the different schools of jurisprudence in Islam. The Sunni Muslims recognize the following four schools of jurisprudence: (1) The Hanafi, formed by Abu-Hanifa (d 767) and his followers. (2) The Hanbali, formed by Ibn Hanbal (d. 855). (3) The Maleki, formed by Malik Ibn Anas (715–795). (4) The Shafe'i, formed by al-Shafe'i (d. 820). The Shī'ī school follows the Imami school of jurisprudence founded by the sixth Shī'ī Imām, Ja'far al-Sadeq (702–765).
68 Sermon delivered on July 21, 1980. See *Rahnemūdhā; Ābān*, p. 206.
69 See for example *Kashf Asrār*, pp. 105–166.
70 This is a recurrent theme in Khomeyni's thought. See for example *Majūm'e*, p. 183.
71 He repeatedly refers to Israel by this epithet. See for example his message concerning the October war of 1973 in Davani, *Neḥzat*, vol. 6, p. 126.

72 *Islam and Revolution*, p. 49.
73 Sermon delivered on September 10, 1964. See *Majmū'e*, p. 99.
74 *Islam and Revolution*, p. 210.
75 See the text of his message in Davani, *Nehẕat*, vol. 6, p. 120.
76 Sermon delivered on July 25, 1982. See *Keyhān* (July 26, 1982): 14.
77 *Ibid.*
78 See "The Constitution." This translation is generally good but has many mistranslations and inadequacies. For example, the translation of the principle quoted here required, for clarity, my adding some corrections.
79 See *Resāleh*, vol. IV, p. 172.
80 *Islam and Revolution*, p. 419.
81 *Ibid.*, p. 384.
82 Sermon delivered on October 3, 1982. See *Keyhān* (October 4, 1982): 14.
83 *Ibid.*
84 *Kashf Asrār*, pp. 229–30, cf. sermon delivered on April 18, 1980 in *Enqelāb-e Eslāmī* (April 19, 1980): 3.
85 For an excellent account of the development of the doctrine of *Jihād* in Shī'ī Islam see E. Kohlberg "The Development of the Imami Shī'ī Doctrine of *Jihād*," *Zeitschrift der Deutschen Morgenlandischen Gesellschaft* 126, (1976): 64–86.
86 Al-Tusi, *Al-Nihāya*, pp. 290–291, Loc. cit., *Ibid.*, p. 80.
87 Sermon delivered on April 2, 1982. See *Keyhān* (April 3, 1982): 12.
88 Sermon of October 20, 1980. See *Rahnemūdhā: Ābān*, pp. 276–277.
89 Sermon delivered on April 9, 1981. See *Rahnemūd*, p. 46.
90 *Ibid.*
91 Sermon delivered on August 6, 1980. See *Avval 1359*, p. 302. One passage is especially worth noting: "I think America has fooled the Soviet Union. The Russians are helping the Iraqis, while the Iraqis are the stooges of the Americans and not the Russians."
92 Sermon delivered on March 14, 1982. See *Keyhān* (March 15, 1982): 14.
93 Sermon delivered on October 28, 1980. See *Rahnemūdhā; Ābān*, p. 294.

Chapter VII

1 Weber. "Politics," p. 120.
2 *Ibid.*
3 A very famous Prophetic tradition.
4 Sermon delivered on October 28, 1980. See *Rahnemūdhā; Ābān*, pp. 284–285.
5 Sermon delivered on December 27, 1982. See *Keyhān* (December 28, 1982): 18.
6 See *Ibid.*, (November 3, 1979).
7 See "America Held Hostage: The Secret Negotiations," transcript of an ABC program shown on January 28, 1981, p. 52.
8 Ayat-Allah Khomeyni first talked about this theory in 1943. In *Kashf Asrār*, one of Khomeyni's earliest works, he deals with the issue but not in great detail. Reference to the guardianship of the theologian jurisconsult can be found in that work on pp. 185–190, 195, 197–198, 222, 223 and 295. He treated the topic in early 1970s, both in Arabic and Persian. For an English

translation of the Persian work see *Islam and Revolution*, pp. 25–166. In his Arabic treatment of the topic, he has followed the traditional methodology in Islamic jurisprudence. See *Kitāb al-Bay‘* 5 vols. (Najaf, 1971?).

9 See *New York Times Magazine*, (October 28, 1979): 67.

10 See *Keyhān* (December 23, 1982): 18.

11 Khomeyni's message given on October 8, 1978. See Davani. *Nehzat* vol. 8, pp. 132–138.

12 Message to the Iranian people on November 5, 1978. See *Nedāye Ḥaq*, p. 15.

13 See message on November 10, 1978 in *Nedāye Haq*, p. 20; interview with *Monday Morning*, an English language magazine in Beirut, on December 31, 1978; and Davani. *Nehzat*, vol 8, p. 243.

14 See *Eṭṭelā‘āt* (October 17, 1978).

15 See *Khabar Nāmeh* No. 23 (Aban 18, 1357). A copy of this issue is found in the journal of *Komīteh Barāy-e Defā‘ az Ḥoqūq-e Bashar va Pishraft-e Ān dar Irān* No. 16 (Day 10, 1357): 98.

16 The most notable attack on Khomeyni in this regard can be found in *Enqelāb Eslāmī dar Hejrat*. See for example the following article "vafāye be 'ahd va paymān," in its following issue: No. 10 (July 14, 1982): 5–6.

17 The text of the interview is found in *Nedāye Ḥaq*, pp. 105–108.

18 The nationalist elements did not notice because they proved to be ignorant of Islamic political thought in general and Ayat-Allah Khomeyni's understanding of it in particular. In the 1977–79 Islamic Revolution, the educated Iranians showed the same ignorance about the nature and the character of the Islamic government as did the religious leaders during the 1905–11 Revolution about the nature and character of Western democracy and constitutionalism.

19 The leaflet concerning the formation of the Revolutionary Council. For the text see Davani. *Nehzat*, vol. 9 pp. 179–181.

20 See *Keyhān*, (February 9, 1979).

21 For example, he appointed Hasan Nazih, who had openly called for the establishment of a Republic for Iran as the head of Iranian Oil Company. See *Keyhān* (February 21, 1979).

22 The party was founded on February 19, 1979 by a group of prominent religious leaders including Muhammad Beheshti, Ayat-Allah Murtaza Mutahari, Dr. Muhammad Mofateh and Hojat al-Islam Al-Akbar Hashemi Rafsanjani. The first three have been assassinated. Only Rafsanjani escaped assassination and is now the head of the Parliament.

23 See *Eṭṭelā‘āt*, (March 3, 1978): 8.

24 Sermon delivered on March 9, 1979. See *Eṭṭelā‘āt* (March 10, 1979): 8.

25 In an interview before his return to Iran Ayat-Allah Khomeyni said, "We are sure that Islam encompasses all groups and satisfy all their needs. Our ideology will undermine all other ideologies." See *Majmū‘e*, p. 325.

26 Sermon delivered on June 28, 1979. See *Rūḥ Khodā*, p. 165.

27 For the views of the Iranian politician on this issue see "The Seminar of Iranian Bar Association," in *Keyhān* (June 18, 1979).

28 Sermon delivered on June 17, 1979. See *Rūh Khodā*, p. 82.

29 See *Rahnemūdhā: Tābestān*, pp. 102–103.

30 See the leaflet of the Revolutionary Council in *Keyhān* (November 7, 1979).

31 See *New York Times* (December 11, 1979): A-19.

32 Sermon delivered on December 14, 1979. See *Enqelāb Eslāmī* (December 15, 1979): 3.
33 See *Ibid*. (January 2, 1980): 2.
34 See *Eṭṭelā'āt* (January 20, 1980): 1.
35 Message to a symposium on the Islamic Revolution. See *Sobḥ Āzādegān* (February 18, 1980): 2.
36 Message delivered on the opening of the Parliament on May 28, 1980. See *Avval 1359*, p. 141–145.
37 See *Ibid*., p. 206.
38 Sermon delivered on June 20, 1980. See *Ibid*., pp. 221–233.
39 Sermon delivered on June 22, 1980. See *Ibid*., pp. 233–236.
40 See *Eṭṭelā'āt* (July 8, 1980).
41 Sermon delivered on July 20, 1982. See *Avval 1359*, p. 284.
42 See *Enqelāb Eslāmī* (March 7, 1981): 1.
43 Message delivered on March 16, 1981. See *Payām Imām* no. 6 (Esfand 1359/Feb.-March, 1981): 1.
44 See *Rahnemūd*, p. 121.
45 For the text of the dismissal see *Rahnemūd*, p. 159.
46 See *The New York Times*, (June 14, 1981): 14.
47 See Mojahedin's Leaflet no. 25, June 21, 1981.
48 Sermon delivered on June 29, 1981. See *Payām Imām* no. 18 (Tir 1360/June-July 1981): 4.
49 Sermon delivered on January 13, 1982. See *Keyhān* (January 14, 1982): 14.
50 Sermon delivered on March 15, 1982. See *Keyhān* (March 16, 1982): 15.
51 Sermon delivered on (November 18, 1982). See *Keyhān* (November 20, 1982): 3.
52 For the text of this important message see *Keyhān* (December 16, 1982): 1ff.
53 Sermon delivered on December 25, 1982. See *Keyhān* (December 26, 1982): 18.
54 The head of the Qurayshi tribe in Mecca during the Prophet's youth and before the birth of Islam.
55 See *Keyhān* (December 27, 1982): 3.

SELECTED BIBLIOGRAPHY

The following bibliography contains works of Ayat-Allah Khomeyni as well as both those sources which have been used in this dissertation and some additional works which have direct bearing on the study of general Islamic and Shīʿī political thought.

Ayat-Allah Khomeyni's works basically fall into two categories: books and collections of speeches. Only those books which are republished recently and are most readily available are listed; his biographers claim that he has authored more than forty titles (see chapter III). The collections of Khomeyni's sermons and speeches are the most fruitful source for his political views because they are merely transcribed without any editorial addition or correction. These collections present a comprehensive source of Khomeyni's personality, style, mode of thinking and his views on different topics. Furthermore, a number of Khomeyni's recent speeches, declarations and messages are published in major Iranian daily newspapers for which, although no preference, I have used *Keyhān*, one of Tehran's major evening newspapers.

The other sources are mostly in Persian and Arabic as well as important Western sources in European languages. A number of important Persian Articles have also been listed. The most substantial Persian sources consist of a large number of relevant books which are easily found in major university libraries as well as the Library of Congress.

Ayat-Allah Khomeyni's Works

Books

Khomeyni, Ruhollah. *Asrār al-Ṣlāt* [The Secrets of Praying]. 2 Vols., Trans. Seyyed Ahmad Fahri. Tehran: Nehzat Zanan, 1359/1980.

________. *Ḥokūmat-e Islāmi ya Velāyat-e Faqīh* [Islamic Government or the Guardianship of the *Faqīh*]. 6 vols., Najaf: chap-e Adab, 1390Q/1970.

________. *Islam and Revolution: Writings and Declarations of Imam Khomeyni.* Translated and Annotated by Hamid Algar. Berkeley: Mizan Press, 1981.

_______ . *Islamic Government*. Trans. by Joint Publications Research Service, New York: Manor Books Inc., 1979.

_______ . *Jahād Akbar* [The Greater Struggle]. Tehran: Nas, n.d.

_______ . *Kashf Asrār* [Revealing the Secrets]. 2nd printing, Tehran: Islamiya, 1363Q/1943.

_______ . *Kitāb al-Bay'* [The Book of Transaction]. 5 Vols., Najaf: n.p., 1390-91Q/1970-71.

_______ . *Manāsek Ḥaj* [Haj Rituals]. Tehran: Mohammad Pub., n.d.

_______ . *Masā'el-e Qeẓavat* [The Question of Adjudication]. Trans. from Arabic into Persian Mohammad Amin, Tehran: Nehẓat Zanan, 1360/1981.

_______ . *Miṣbāḥ al-Hidāya ala al-khilāfa wa al-wilāya* [The Light of Guidance toward Rulership and Guardianship]. Trans. from Arabic into Persian Seyyed Ahmad Fahri. Tehran: Payam Azadi, 1360/1981.

_______ . *Nāme'ī az Emām Mosavī Kāshef al-ghetā'* [A Letter from Imam Musavi the Revealer of the Concealed]. [Tehran]: n.p., 1356/1977.

This is Ayat-Allah Khomeyni's famous tract on Islamic government. It has been published with different titles such as Islamic Government (*Ḥokūmat-e Islāmi*) or the Guardianship of a Theologian Jurisconsult (*velāyat-e faqīh*) and the title mentioned above.

_______ . *Reṣāleh Novvīn* [The New Treatise]. Vol. I [Devotional Act and Self Perfection], Trans. and annoted by Abd al-Karim Biazar Shirazi. Tehran: Anjam Ketab, 1360/1981.

_______ . *Reṣāleh Novvīn* [The New Treatise]. Vol II [Economic Matters]. Trans. and annoted by Abd al-Karim Biazar Shirazi. Tehran: Anjam Ketab, 1359/1980.

_______ . *Reṣāleh Novvīn* [The New Treatise]. Vo. IV [Political and legal matters], Trans. and annoted by Abd al-Karim Biazar Shirazi. Tehran: Anjam Ketab, 1360/1982.

_______ . *Reṣāleh Toẕīḥ al-Masā'el* [The Treatise of Explicating the Issues]. Qum: Islami, [1360/1981].

_______ . *Tafṣir Do'āye Saḥar* [An Interpretation the Dawn Prayer]. Trans. from Arabic into Persian by Seyyed Ahmad Fahri. Tehran: Nehzat Zanan, 1359/1980.

_______ . *Tafṣīr Sureh Ḥamd* [An Interpretation of the First Chapter of the Qur'an]. Tehran: Komeyl, n.d.

Collections of Declarations, Messages and Sermons

_______ . *Dar bāre Felesṭīn* [About Palestine]. Tehran: Seyyed Jamal, n.d.

_______ . *Imām va Jang* [Imam and the War]. Tehran: Hezb Jomhuriye Eslami, n.d.

_______ . *Jāme'e-ye Toḥīdī* [The Monotheistic Community]. Tehran: Nas, n.d.

_______ . *Khaṭ Emām, Kalām Emām* [Imam's Line and Imam's Words]. 2 vols., Tehran: Nur, 1360/1981.

_______ . *Khomeyni va Jonbesh* [Khomeyni and the Movement] n.p.: Panzdah Khordad, 1352/1973-74.

_______ . *Majmū'e'i az Maktūbāt, Sokhanrānīha, Payāmhā Va Fatvāhāye Imām Khomeyni* [A Collection of Khomeyni's Lectures, Messages and Legal Rulings]. Tehran: Chapakhsh, 1360/1981.

_______ . *Nedāye Ḥaq.* [The Voice of the Truth]. Tehran: Qalam, 1357/1978.

_______ . *Payāmhā va Sokhan rānīhāye Imām Khomeynī dar Shesh Māhe-ye Avval 1359* [Imam Khomeyni's Messages and Lectures in the First Six Months of 1359/1980]. Tehran: Nur, n.d.

_______ . *Rahnemūd: Bahār 1360* [Guidance: Spring of 1360/1981]. Tehran: Masjed Ali, n.d.

_______ . *Rahnemūdhāye Emām: Ābān 1358 tā Ābān 1359* [Imam's Guidances: From October/November 1979 to October/November 1980]. Tehran: Nas, n.d.

_______ . *Rahnemūdhāye Emām: Tābestān 1358* [Imam's Guidances: Summer of 1979]. Tehran: Nas, n.d.

_______ . *Rohānīyat, Ṭalāye-dār-e Islam Feqāhat* [Ayat-Allah Khomeyni's Sermons Pertaining to the 'ulamā]. Tehran: Miqat, 1361/1982.

_______ . *Rūḥ Khodā dar Velāyat-e Faqīh* [A Collection of Ayat-Allah Khomeyni's Messages during May/June 1979]. Tehran: Vezarat Ershad, 1359/1980.

_______ . *Rūz Quds* [Ayat-Allah Khomeyni's Lectures about Jerusalem]. Tehran: Hezb Jomhuriye Eslami, n.d.

_______ . *Shahīdī Dīgar az Rohānīyat* [Ayat-Allah Khomeyni's Messages Pertaining to his son's death in 1977]. Najaf: Rohaniyun Kharej az Keshvar, n.d.

_______ . *Yom Allāh* [The Day of God]. Tehran: Nas, n.d.

Other Sources

Books

Abrahamian, Ervand, *Iran: Between Two Revolutions*. Princeton: Princeton University Press, 1982.

Adamiyyat, Fereydun. *Ide'olozhī-ye Nehẕat-e Mashruṭīyyat-e Irān* [The Ideology of the Constitutional Movement of Iran]. Tehran: Payam, 1355/1976.

Akhavi, Shahrough. *Religion and Politics in Contemporary Iran: Clergy-State Relations in the Pahlavi Period.* Albany: State University of New York, 1980.

Al-Ahmad, Jallal. *Dar Khedmat va Khīyānat-e Roshanfekrān* [On Loyalty and Betrayal of the Intellectuals]. 2 vols., Tehran: Kharazmi, 1357/1978.

_______ . *Gharb-zadegī* [Weststruckness]. n.p.: The Muslim Student Association in America and Canada, n.d.

Algar, Hamid. *The Islamic Revolution in Iran*. London: Open Press, 1980.

_______ . *Religion and State In Iran: 1785–1906.* Berkeley: University of California Press, 1969.

Amir-Sadeqi, Nasir al-Din. *Hayāhū: Jeld Dovvom-e Rohānīyat dar Shī'a* [Uproar: Second Volume of Religious Leaders in Shī'īsm]. Tehran: n.p., 1351/1972.

_______ . *Roḥānīyat dar Shī'a* [Religious Leaders in Shī'īsm]. Tehran: n.p., 1349/1970.

Ansari, Shaykh Murtaza. *Al-Makāsib* [The Profit]. Tabriz: n.p., 1375Q/1955.

'Araqi, Mahmud. *Dār-al-Eslām* [The Abode of Islam]. Tehran: Ketabforushi-ye Eslami-ye, 1352/1973-4.

Baḥṡī Darbāre-ye Marja'īyat va Roḥānīyat [A Discussion on the Source of Following and the Religious Leaders]. Qum: Sherkat-e Enteshar, 1341/1962.

Bakhshāyeshī, 'Aqiqi. *Yek Ṣad Sāl Mobāreze-ye Rohānīyat-e Motaraqi* [A Hundred Years of Struggle by the Progressive 'ulamā]. 3 vols., Qum: Nashr Navid, 1359/1980.

Banisadar, Abolhassan. *The Fundamental Principles and Precepts of Islamic Government*. Translated from the Persian by Mohammad R. Ghanoonparvar, Lexington, Ky.: Mazda Publishers 1981.

_______ . *Moqe'īyat-e Irān va Naqsh-e Modarres* [The Position of Iran and Modarres' role]. n.p.: Entesharat-e Modarres, 1356/1977.

Bayat, Mongol. *Mysticism and Dissent: Socioreligious Thought in Qajar Iran*. Syracuse: Syracuse University Press, 1982.

Bayne, Edward A. *Persian Kingship in Transition: Conversations with a Monarch whose Office is Traditional and whose Goal is Modernization*. New York: American Universities Field Staff, 1968.

Bazargan, Mahdi. *Modāfe'āt dar Dādgāh-e Gheyr-ṣāleh-e Tajdid Naẓar-e Nezami.* [Defences in the Incompetent Military Court of Appeals]. n.p.: The Freedom Front outside of Iran, 1356/1977.

Behbahani, Muhammad Baqir. *Al-fawā'id* [The Gains]. Hand written manuscript, Mar'ashi library, Qum, Iran.

Bill, James A. *The Politics of Iran.* Columbus, Ohio: Charles E. Merrill Publishing Co., 1972.

Binder, Leonard. ed., *The Study of Middle East: Research and Scholarship in the Humanities and the Social Sciences.* New York: John Wiley and Sons, 1976.

Biyogrāfī-ye Pishvā [The Biography of the Leader]. 2 vols., n.p.: Panzdah Khordad, n.d.

Bonine, Michael E. and Nikki Keddi, eds., *Modern Iran: The Dialectics of Continuity and Change*. Albany: State University of New York Press, 1981.

Bozeman, Adda B. *The Future of Law in a Multi Cultural World*. Princeton: Princeton University Press, 1971.

_______ . *Politics and Culture in International History.* Princeton: The Princeton University Press, 1960.

Browne, Edward G. *The Persian Revolution of 1905–1909.* Cambridge: The University Press, 1910.

Bull, Hedley. *The Anarchical Society*. New York: Columbia University Press, 1977.

Carlesen, Robin W. *The Imam and His Islamic Revolution*. Victoria, ca.: The Snow Man Press, 1982.

Chardin, Jean. *Voyages du Chevalier Chardin en Perse et autres lieux de l'Orient*. 10 volumes et un atlas, Paris, 1811.

Chelkowski, Peter J. ed. *Iran: Continuity and Variety*. New York: New York University, 1971.

Corbin, Henry. *En Islam Iranien: Aspects Spirituels et Philosophiques*. 4 vols. Paris: Gallimar, 1971.

Cottam, Richard W. *Nationalism in Iran: Updated Through 1978*. Pittsburgh, Pa.: University of Pittsburgh Press, 1979.

Cudsi, Alexander S. and Ali E. H. Dessouki. eds., *Islam and Power*. Baltimore: The Johns Hopkins University Press, 1981.

Davani, Ali. *Nehẕat-e Do Māhe-ye Rohānīyat-e Iran* [The two Months' Movement of the Iranian *'ulamā* (in 1963)]. Qum: Chap Hekmat, 1341/1963.

________ . *Nehẕat-e Roḥānīyun-e Iran* [The Movement of the *'ulamā* in Iran]. 11 vols., Tehran: Bonyad Imam Reza, 1360/1981.

________ . *Vahid Behbahāni*. Qum: Dar-al-'Elm, 1337/1958–59.

Davari, Reza. *Enqelāb-e Islāmī va Vaẕ' Konūnī-ye 'ālam* [Islamic Revolution and the Present Situation of the World]. Tehran: Markaz-e Farhangi 'Allamah Tabataba'i, 1361/1983.

Dehnavi, M. *Qīyām Khūnīn-e Pānzdah-e Khordād-e 1342* [The Bloody Uprising of June 1963]. Tehran: Rasa, 1361/1982.

Donaldson, Dwight M. *The Shi'ite Religion: A History of Islam in Persia and Irak*. London: Luzac and Co., 1933.

Donhue John J. and John L. Esposito. eds., *Islam in Transition: Religion and Socio-Political Change*. Oxford: Oxford University Press, 1982.

Effendi, Abbas. *A Traveller's Narrative*. Trans. E. G. Browne, reprint, Amsterdam: Philo Press 1975.

Enayat, Hamid. *Modern Islamic Political Thought*. Austin: The University of Texas Press, 1982.

________ . *Shesh Goftār Dar Bārey-e Dīn va Jāme'-e*. [Six Lectures on Religion and Society]. Tehran: Moj, 1352/1973.

________ . *Seyrī dar Andīshe-ye Sīyāsīye Arab* [An Overview of the Arab's Political Thought]. Tehran: Amir Kabir, 1358/1979.

Esposito, John. ed., *Islam and Development*. Syracuse: Syracuse University Press, 1980.

Fada'iyan-e Islam. *Rāhnamāy-e Haqāyeq* [Guide to the Truth]. Tehran: n.p., 1950.

Farsi, Jalal al-Din. *Hoqūq-e Beyn-ul-Melal-e Eslāmi* [The Islamic International Law]. [Tehran]: Kanun-e Mohaselin, n.d.

Fischer, Michael M. J. *Iran, from Religious Dispute to Revolution*. Cambridge, Ma.: Harvard University Press, 1980.

al-Ghunaimi, Mohammad Talaat. *The Muslim Conception of International Law and the Western Approach*. The Hague: Martinus Nighoff, 1968.

Gibb, H. A. R. *Modern Trend in Islam*. Chicago: The University of Chicago Press, 1947.

________ . *Mohammedanism*. 2nd ed., New York: Oxford University Press, 1979.

________ . *Studies on the Civilization of Islam*. Boston: Beacon Press, 1962.

Gobineau, Joseph Arthur. *Religions et Philosophie dans l'Asie Centrale*. Paris: Gallimard, 1957.

Gozashteh Cheragh-e Rah-e Ayandast [The Past is the Guide to the Future]. n.p.: Jami, 1355/1976.

Graham, Robert. *Iran: The Illusion of Power*. Revised ed., London: Groom Helen, 1979.

von Grunebaum, Gustave E. ed., *Unity and Variety in Muslim Civilization*. Chicago: The University of Chicago Press, 1955.

Haim, Sylvia and Elie Kedourie, eds., *Towards a Modern Iran*. London: Frank Cass, 1981.

Hairi, Abdul-Hadi. *Shi'ism and Constitutionalism in Iran*. Leiden: E. J. Brill, 1977.

Hakami-Zadeh, Ali-Akbar. *Asrar-e Hezar Saleh* [The Secrets of a Thousand Years]. Tehran: Parcham, 1322/1943.

Halliday, Fred. *Iran: Dictatorship and Development*. New York: Penguin, 1979.

Hamidullah, Muhammad. *Muslim Conduct of State*. Revised and enlarged ed., Lahore, Pakistan: Sh. Muhammad Ashraf, 1961.

Heikal, Mohamed. *Iran: The Untold Story*. New York: Pantheon Books, 1982.

al-Helli, Hasan ibn Yusuf ibn 'Ali ibn al-Mutahar. *Al-Bab al-Hadi 'Ashar*. trans. William McElwee Miller, London: The Royal Asiatic Society, 1928.

________ . *Saraye'e al-Islam* [The Islamic Laws]. Translated from Arabic into Persian by Abolqasem ebn-e Ahmad-e Yazdi. Tehran: The University of Tehran Press, 1346/1967.

Hodgson, Marshal G. S. *The Venture of Islam*. 3 vols., Chicago: The University of Chicago Press, 1974.

Hooglund, Eric J. *Land and Revolution in Iran*. Austin: The University of Texas Press, 1982.

Hosseini, Seyyed Jamal al-Din (Al-Afghani). *Gozide 'Urvat al-wosqa* [A Collection of Essays by Al-Afghani]. Translated from Arabic into Persian by Abdullah Samandar. Tehran: Molla, n.d.

Hourani, Albert. *Arabic Thought in the Liberal Age: 1798–1939*. New York: Oxford University Press, 1967.

________ . *Europe and the Middle East*. London: Macmillan and Co., 1980.

Hourani, George F. *Islamic Rationalism: The Ethics of 'Abd al-Jabbar*. Oxford: Clarendon Press, 1971.

Hoveyda, Fereydoun. *The Fall of the Shah*. Trans. from French by Roger Liddell. London: Weidenfeld and Nicolson, 1980.

Ibn, Ishaq. *The Life of Muhammad*. Trans. by A. Guillaume. Oxford: Oxford University Press, 1978.

Ibn, Khaldun. *The Muqaddima: An Introduction to History*. Trans. Franz Rosenthal, 3 vols., Princeton: Princeton University Press, 1967.

Iqbal, Abbas. *Khāndān Nobakhtī* [The Nobakhti Family]. Tehran: Nashr Ketab, 1345/1966.

Iqbal, Mohammad. *Reconstruction of Religious Thought in Islam*. London: Sh. Muhammad Ashraf, 1962.

Jafri, Husain M. *Origins and Early Development of Shī'a Islam*. New York: Longman, 1976.

Jansen, G. H. *Militant Islam*. New York: Harper and Row, Pub., 1979.

Jazani, Bizhan. *Tārīkh Sī-Sāleh Iran* [Thirty Years History of Iran]. Tehran: Abdin, 1357/1978.

Kashfi, Seyyed. *Toḥfat al-Mulūk* [Token to the Princes]. n.p.: 1276Q/1859.

Kasravi, Ahmad. *Shī'īgari* [Shī'īsm]. [Tehran]: n.p., n.d.

_______ . *Tārīkh-e Mashruṭe-ye Irān* [A History of Constitutional Revolution in Iran]. 13th printing. Tehran: Amir Kabir, 1356/1977.

Khalili, Ali. *Gām be Gām bā Enqelāb* [Step by Step with the Revolution]. Tehran: Sorush, 1360/1981.

Katouzian, Homa. *The Political Economy of Modern Iran, 1926–1979.* New York: New York University Press, 1981.

Kazemi, Farhad. *Poverty and Revolution in Iran: The Migrant Poor, Urban Marginality and Politics.* New York: New York University Press, 1981.

Keddie, Nikki R. ed. *Religion and Politics in Iran: Shi'ism from Quietism to Revolution*. New Haven: Yale University Press, 1983.

_______ . *Religion and Rebellion in Iran: The Tobacco Protest of 1891–1892.* [London]: F. Cass, 1966.

_______ . *Roots of Revolution: An Interpretive History of Modern Iran*. New Haven: Yale University Press, 1981.

_______ . ed., *Scholars Saints and Sufis: Muslim Religious Institutions in the Middle East Since 1500*. Berkeley: University of California, 1972.

_______ . and Eric Hoogland eds. *The Iranian Revolution and the Islamic Republic; Proceedings of a Conference*. Washington D.C.: The Middle East Institute, 1982.

Khadduri, Majid. *War and Peace in the Law of Islam*. Baltimore: The Johns Hopkins Press, 1955.

Lambton, Ann K. S. *The Persian Land Reform, 1962–1966.* Oxford: Clarendon Press, 1969.

_______ . *State and Government in Medieval Islam*. New York: Oxford University Press, 1981.

Laqueur, Walter Z. ed. *The Middle East in Transition*. New York: Frederick A. Praeger, 1958.

Lerner, Ralph and Muhsin Mahdi. eds., *Medieval Political Philosophy*. New York: Cornell University Press, 1972.

Lockhart, Laurence. *The Fall of the Safavi Dynasty and the Afghan Occupation of Persia*. Cambridge: The University Press, 1958.

Mahdi, Muhsin. *Ibn Khaldun's Philosophy of History*. Chicago: The University of Chicago Press, 1971.

Majlesi, Muhammad Baqer. *Mahdī Mo'ūd* (vol. XIII of *Bahar al-Anvar*). [The Promised Mahdi]. Translated from Arabic into Persian by Ali Davani, Qum: n.p., 1339/1960.

Makarem-Shirazi, Naser. *Ṭarḥ-e Hokūmat Islām* [A Plan for the Islamic Government]. Qum: Matbu'ati-ye Hadaf, 1399Q/1979.

Makdisi, George. ed., *Arabic and Islamic Studies in Honor of Hamilton A. R. Gibb*. Cambridge, Mass.: Harvard University Press, 1965.

Makki, Hossein. *Tārīkh-e Bīst Sāleh-e Irān* [The Twenty Years History of Iran]. 3 vols., Tehran: 'elmi, 1323–25/1944–46.

Malikzadeh, Mehdi. *Tārīkh-e Enqelāb-e Mashrūṭiyat-e Irān* [A History of the constitutional Revolution of Iran] 7 vols., Tehran: Soqrat, n.d.

Mamaqani, Shaykh As'ad-Allah. *Dīn va Sho'un* [Religion and the Affairs] 2nd printing, Tehran: n.p., 1335/1956–57.

Mashkur, Mohammad Javad. *Tārīkh-e Shī'a va Ferqehā-ye Eslām tā Qarn-e Chāhārom*. [The History of Shī'a and other Islamic Groups up to the Fourth/Tenth Century]. Tehran: Entesharat-e Eshraqi, 1355/1976.

Meinekke, Friedrich. *Machiavellism: The Doctrine of Raison d'Etat and its Place in Modern History*. tran. from the German by Douglas Scott. New York: Frederick A. Praeger, Pub., 1965.

Modarresi Chardahi, Murtaza. *Shaykhīgari/Babīgarī* [Shaykhism Babism]. Tehran: Forughi, 1345/1966–67.

________ . *Tarīkh-e Ravābeṭ-e Irān va 'Erāq* [A History of Relationship between Iran and Iraq.]. Tehran: Forughi, 1351/1972.

Monzer, Ali. *Velāyat-e Faqīh va Demokrāsī-ye Ershād Shodeh* [The Guardianship of the Theologian Jurisconsult and the Guided Democracy]. Shahr Rey: Sepah-e Pasdaran, 1357/1979.

Monshi, Eskandar Beg. *History of Shah 'Abbas the Great (Tārik-e 'Ālamārā-ye 'Abbāsi)*. Trans. by R. M. Savory, Persian Heritage Series, ed. Ehsan Yarshater, no. 28. 2 vols. Boulder, Col.: Westview Press, 1978.

Morgenthau, Hans J. *Politics Among Nations: The Struggle for Power and Peace*. 5th ed., New York: Alfred A. Knopf, 1978.

________ . *Scientific Man vs. Power Politics*. Chicago: University of Chicago Press, 1946.

Mottahedeh, Roy P. *Loyalty and Leadership in an Early Islamic Society*. Princeton: Princeton University Press, 1980.

al-Mufid, Shaykh. *Kitab al-Irshad*. Trans. I. K. A. Howard, London: Balagha Books, 1981.

Muir, William, Sir. *The Caliphate, Its Rise, Decline and Fall*. New York: AMS Press, 1975.

Mutahari, Murtaza. *Jahān Bīnī Islamī* [The Islamic World View]. 4 vols. n.p.: Muslim Student Association, 1359/1980–81.

Na'ini, Muhammad Hossein. *Tanbih al-Umma va Tanzih al-Mella* [The Admonition and Refinement of the People]. Annoted and edited by Mahmud Taleqani, Tehran: Ferdousi, 1374Q/1955.

Naraqi, Muhammad Mehdi. *'Awa'id al-Ayyām* [The Gains of the Era]. Tehran: n.p., 1321Q/1903–04.

Nasr, Seyyed Hossein. *Ideals and Realities of Islam*. Boston, Beacon Press, 1972.

________ . *Islamic Life and Thought*. Albany: State University of New York Press, 1981.

Nazem al-Eslam-e Kermani, Mohammad. *Tārīkh-e Bīdārī-ye Irānīān* [A History of the Iranian Awakening]. 2 vols., Tehran: Bonyad-e Farhang-e Iran, 1357/1978.

Niebuhr, Reinhold. *The Children of Light and the Children of Darkness*. New York: Scribner, 1972.

________ . *The Nature and Destiny of Man: A Christian Interpretation*. 2 vols., New York: Scribner, 1943.

Nobari, Ali-Reza. *Iran Erupts*. Stanford: Iran-America Documentation Group, 1978.

Piscatori, James. ed., *Islam in the Political Process*. New York: Cambridge University Press, 1983.

Proctor, Jesse Harris. ed., *Islam and International Relations*. New York: Frederick A. Praeger, 1965.

Rahman, Fazlur. *The Philosophy of Mulla Sadra*. Albany: State University of New York Press, 1975.

Ramazani, R. K. *The Foreign Policy of Iran: A Developing Nation in World Affairs, 1500–1941*. Charlottesville: University Press of Virginia, 1972.

________ . *Iran's Foreign Policy 1941–1973: A Study of Foreign Policy in Modernizing Nations*. Charlottesville: University Press of Virginia, 1975.

________ . *The United States and Iran: The Patterns of Influence*. New York: Praeger, 1982.

Razi, Haj Mohammad Sharif. *Ganjīne-ye Dāneshmandān*. [The Treasure of Islamic Scholars]. 8 vols., Tehran: Chap-e Eslamiya, 1973–74. (vol. 1–4); and Qom: Chapkhane-ye Piruz, 1974–75 (vol. 5–8).

Richard, Yann. *Le Shi'isme En Iran*. Paris: Librairie D'Amerique et O'Orient, 1980.

Rizvi, Saiyid Athar Abbas. *Iran: Royalty, Religion and Revolution*. Canberra, Australia: Ma'rifat Publishing House, 1980.

Rodinson, Maxime. *Islam and Capitalism*. London: Allen Lane, 1974.

Rose, Jeffrey and Michael Ignatieff. eds., *Religion and International Affairs*. Toronto: House of Anasi, 1968.

Rosenthal, Erwin Isak Jacob. *Islam in the Modern National State*. Cambridge: Cambridge University Press, 1965.

________ . *Political Thought in Medieval Islam*. Cambridge: Cambridge University Press, 1968.

Rosenthal, Franz. *The Muslim Concept of Freedom Prior to the Nineteenth Century*. Leiden: Brill, 1960.

Rouhani, Seyyed Hamid. *Tāḥlīlī az Nehẕat-e Imām Khomeynī* [An Interpretation of Imām Khomeyni's Movement]. Qum: Nashr Asar 1356/1977.

Rubin, Barry. *Paved with Good Intentions: The American Experience and Iran*. New York: Oxford University Press, 1980.

Sachedina, Abdulaziz A. *Islamic Messianism: The Idea of the Mahdi in Twelver Shi'ism*. Albany: the State University of New York Press, 1981.

Saikal, Amin. *The Rise and Fall of the Shah*. Princeton: Princeton University Press, 1980.

Savory, Roger. *Iran Under The Safavids*. New York: Cambridge University Press, 1980.

Shahabadi, Muhammad Ali. *Shaẕarāt al-Ma'āref* [Pieces of Knowledge] Tehran: Nehzat-e Zanan, 1360/1982.

Shahabi, Mahmud. *Taqrīrāt Usūl* [Articulations on the Principles (of Jurisprudence)]. Tehran: 'Elmi, 1344/1965.

Shakuri, Abulfazl. *Fiqh-e Siyāsī-e Islām* [The Islamic Political Jurisprudence]. 2 vols., Qum: Nashr Hor, 1361/1982.

Shari'ati, 'Ali. *Ensān va Eslām*. [Islam and Man]. Tehran: Sherkat-e Enteshar, n.d.

________ . *Majmū'-e-ye Āsār* [The Collection of Works]. 8 vols., Tehran: Hoseyni-ye Ershad, n.d.

Sharif, M. M., ed., *A History of Muslim Philosophy*. 2 vols. Germany: Allgauer Heimatrerlag, 1966.

Shaybani, Muhammad b. al-Hasan. *Siyar*. Trans. and introduction by Majid Khadduri. Baltimore: The Johns Hopkins Press, 1966.

Siddiqi, Amir Hasan. *Caliphate and Kinship in Medieval Persia*. Philadelphia: Porcupine Press, 1977.

Smith, W. C. *Islam in Modern History*. Princeton: Princeton University Press, 1957.

Sourush, Abdulkarim. *Nahād nā-Ārām Jahān* [The Philosophy of Mulla Sadra]. n.p.: Anjoman Daneshjayan dar America, 1397Q/1977.

Strauss, Leo and Joseph Cropsey. eds., *History of Political Philosophy*. 2nd ed., Chicago: The University of Chicago Press, 1981.

Tabari, Ehsan. *Ozā' Irān dar Dorān Mo'āṣer* [Iran in Contemporary History]. n.p.: n.p., 1356/1977.

Tabataba'i, 'Allamah M. H. *Shī'ite Islam*. Translated and edited with an introduction and notes by Seyyed Hossein Nasr. Albany: State University of New York Press, 1975.

_______ . *Zuhūr Shī'a* [The Emergence of Shi'ism]. Tehran: Bazar Ketab, n.d.

Taleqani, Mahmud. *Islam va Malekiat* [Islam and Ownership]. Tehran: Nashr Ketab, 1354/1975.

_______ . *Society and Economics in Islam*. Translated by R. Campbell, Berkeley: Mizan Press, 1982.

Tehrani, Ali. *Madīneye Fāẕelah dar Islām* [The Virtuous City in Islam]. Tehran: Hekmat, 1354/1975.

Thompson, Kenneth W. *Ethics, Functionalism and Power in International Politics: The Crisis in Values*. Baton Rouge: Louisiana State University Press, 1979.

_______ . *Morality and Foreign Policy*. Baton Rouge: Louisiana State University Press, 1980.

_______ . *Political Realism and the Crisis of World Politics*. New Printing, Washington, D.C.: University Press of America, Inc., 1982.

_______ . *Understanding World Politics*. Notre Dame: University of Notre Dame Press, 1975.

Tunekabuni, Mirza Muhammad. *Qeṣaṣ al-'ulamā* [The Story of the *'ulamā*]. Tehran: 'Elmiya, n.d.

Va'ez Khiyabani Tabrizi, Haj Molla Ali. *Ketāb 'Ulama-ye Mo'aṣerin* [The Book on Contemporary *'ulamā*]. Tehran: Ketabfurushi Eslami-ya, 1366Q/1946–47.

Watt, W. M. *The Faith and Practice of Al-Ghazali*. London: George Allen and Unwin LTD, 1970.

_______ . *Free Will and Predestination in Early Islam*. London: Luzac, 1948.

_______ . *The Formative Period of Islamic Thought*. Edinburgh: The Edinburgh University Press, 1973.

_______ . *Islamic Political Thought: Islamic Survey 6*. Edinburgh: The Edinburgh University Press, 1968.

_______ . *Muhammad at Mecca*. Oxford: The Clarendon Press, 1953.

_______ . *Muhammad at Medina*. Oxford: The Clarendon Press, 1977.

Wight, Martin. *Systems of States*. ed. by Hedley Bull. London: Leicester University Press, 1977.

Zabih, Sepehr. *Iran's Revolutionary Upheaval: An Interpretative Essay*. San Francisco: Alchemy Books, 1979.

Zavabeti, Mehdi. *Pazhūheshī dar Neẕām Ṭalabegī* [An Investigation on the System Islamic Schools]. Tehran: Tarjemeh va Nashr Ketab, 1359/1980.

Zenegīnāmeh [The Biography (of Khomeyni)]. 2 vols., n.p.: Nashr Fadak, 1394/1974.

Zonis, Marvin. *The Political Elite of Iran*. Princeton: Princeton University Press, 1971.

Articles

Abidi, A. H. H. "The Iranian Revolution: Its Origina and Dimension." *International Studies* vol. 18 no. 2 (April-June 1979): 130–161.

Afshar, [Mahmud]. "Dīn va Siyāsat." [Religion and Politics]. *Āyandeh* vol. III no. 13 (August 1945/1324): 601–608.

Akhavi, Shahrough. "The Ideology and Praxis of Shī'īsm in the Iranian Revolution." Paper presented in American Political Science Association. Panel 1–4, "Religion and the State," 3–6 September 1981.

Algar, Hamid. "The Oppositional Role of the Ulama in Twentieth-Century Iran," in *Scholars, Saints, and Sufis*, edited by Nikki R. Keddie, Berkeley: University of California Press, 1972.

_______ . "Some Observation on Religion in Safavid Persia." *Iranian Studies* 7 (1974): 287–293.

Alper, Joseph. "The Khomeini International." *The Washington Quarterly* vol. 3 no. 4 (Autumn 1980): 44–74.

Amir Arjomand, Said. "Religion, Political Action and Legitimate Domination in Shi'ite Iran: Fourteenth to Eighteenth Centuries A.D." *European Journal of Sociology* vol. 20 no. 1 (May 1979): 59–109.

_______ . "The State and Khomeini's Islamic Order." *Iranian Studies* vol. XIII nos. 1–4 (1980): 147–164.

_______ . "The Ulama's Traditionalist Opposition to Parliamentarianism: 1907–1909." *Middle Eastern Studies* vol. 17 no. 2 (April 1981): 174–190.

Arani, Sharif. "Iran: from the Shah's Dictatorship to Khomeini's Demogogic Theocracy." *Dissent* (winter 1980): 9–26.

_______ . "The Iranian Revolution: Year Zero." *Dissent* (spring 1980): 144–148.

Bayat, Mangol. "The Iranian Revolution of 1978–79: Fundamentalist or Modern?" *The Middle East Journal* vol. 37 no. 1 (winter 1983): 30–42.

_______ . "Shī'īsm in Contemporary Iranian Politics," in *Towards a Modern Iran*, edited by Sylvia Haim and Elie Kedourie, London: Frank Cass, 1981.

Bill, James A. "Cromwell, Napoleon, and the Iranian." *The Christian Science Monitor* (September 9, 1981): 23.

_______ . "The Politics of Extremism in Iran." *Current History* (January 1982): 9–13ff.

Binder, Leonard. "Al-Ghazali's Theory of Islamic Government." *The Muslim World* vol. XLV no. 3 (July 1955): 229–241.

_______ . "The Proofs of Islam: Religion and Politics in Iran," in *Arabic and Islamic Studies in Honor of Hamilton A. R. Gibb*, edited by George Makdisi. Cambridge, Mass.: Harvard University Press, 1965.

Bozeman, Adda B. "Iran: U.S. Foreign Policy and the Tradition of Persian Statecraft." *Orbis* vol. 23 no. 2 (summer 1979): 387–402.

Calder, Norman. "Accommodation and Revolution in Imami Shi'i Jurisprudence: Khumayni and the Classical Tradition." *Middle East Studies* vol. 18 no. 1 (January 1982): 1-20.

Carpozi, George Jr. "Islamic Government by Ayatallah Khomeini." in Khomeyni. *Islamic Government*. Trans. Joint Publication Research Service. New York: Manor Books, 1979.

Cockroft, Jim. "Iran's Khomeini: His Life, His Program, His Words." *Seven Days* vol. III no. 1 (February 23, 1979): 17–24.

"The Constitution of the Islamic Republic of Iran." Introductory note by R. K. Ramazani. *Middle East Journal* vol. 34 no. 2 (spring 1980): 181–204.

Cottam, Richard W. "Goodbye to America's Shah." *Foreign Policy* no. 34 (spring, 1979): 3–14.

_______ . "Nationalism and the Islamic Revolution in Iran." *Canadian Review of Studies in Nationalism* IX (Fall, 1982): 263–77.

_______ . "Revolutionary Iran and the War with Iraq." *Current History* (January 1981): 5–9 off.

Curtis, Michael. "Khomeini's Thoughts on Jews and Israel." *Middle East Review* vol. XI no. 3 (spring 1979): 57–58.

Dekmejian, R. H. "The Anatomy of Islamic Rivival." *Middle East Journal* vol. 34 no. 1 (winter 1980): 1–12.

Eliash, Joseph. "The *Ithna'ashari-shī'ī* Juristic Theory of Political and Legal Authority." *Studia Islamica* XXIX (1969): 17–30.

_______ . "Misconceptions Regarding the Juridical Status of the Iranian *'Ulamā*." International Journal of Middle East Studies vol. 10 no. 1 (February 1979): 9–25.

Enayat, Hamid. "Khumayni's Concept of the 'Guardianship of the Jurisconsult' within the Catholic Trends of Islamic Fundamentalism." A paper presented in the "Conference of Islam in the Political Process" held in the Royal Institute of International Affairs, 24–26 June, 1981.

_______ . "An Outline of the Political Philosophy of the Rasa'il of the Ikhwan al-Safa'," in *Isma'īlī Contributions to Islamic Culture*, ed. S. H. Nasr. Tehran: Imperial Academy of Philosophy of Iran, 1398/1977, pp. 25–49.

_______ . "The Resurgence of Islam." *History Today* (February 1980): 16–27.

Encyclopedia of Islam. 2nd ed., S. V. "Akhbariyya." By W. Madelung.

_______ . 2nd ed., S. V. "Ansari Shaykh Murtada." By Abdul Hadi Hairi.

_______ . 2nd ed., S. V. "Hisham b. al-Hakam." By W. Madelung.

_______ . 2nd ed., S. V. "Hukuma." By H. J. Benda.

Farhang, Mansour. "The Outlook Interview: Watching Your Revolution Go Down the Drain." *The Washington Post* (November 28, 1982): C3.

Faksh, Mahmud A. "Theories of State in Islamic Political Thought." *Journal of South Asian and Middle Eastern Studies*. vol. VI no. 3 (spring 1983): 62–79.

Farmanfarmayan, Hafez. "The Forces of Modernization in Nineteenth Century Iran: A Historical Survey." in *Beginning of Modernization in the Middle East*, edited by Williams Polk. Chicago: University of Chicago Press, 1968.

Fathi, Asghar. "Role of the Traditional Leader in Modernization of Iran: 1890–1910." *International Journal of Middle East Studies*. vol. 11 (February 1980): 87–98.

Ferdows Amir H. "Khomaini and Fadayan's Society and Politics." *International Journal of Middle Eastern Studies*. vol. 15 no. 2 (May 1983): 241–257.

Floor, Willem M. "The Revolutionary Character of the Iranian Ulama: Wishful Thinking or Reality?" *International Journal of the Middle Eastern Studies*, vol. 12 no. 4 (December 1980): 501–522.

Fozouni, Bahman. "Imām Khomeini: A Profile of a Charismatic Revolutionary Leader." A paper presented at the 15th Annual Meeting of MESA, Seattle, Washington, November, 4–7, 1981.

Griffith, William E. "The Revival of Islamic Fundamentalism: The Case of Iran." *Hamdard Islamicus* vol. III no. 1 (spring 1980): 47–59.

Habiby, Raymond N. and Fariborz Ghavidel. "Khumayni's Islamic Republic." *Middle East Review* (Summer 1979): 12–20.

Hairi, Abdul-Hadi. "Shaykh Fazl Allah Nuri's Refutation of the Idea of Constitutionalism." *Middle Eastern Studies* 13 (1977): 327–339.

Hodgson, Marshall G. S. "How did the Early Shi'a become Sectarian?" *Journal of American Oriental Society* 75 (1975): 1–13.

Hugh-Jones, Stephen. "We children of God." *Economist* (December 25, 1982): 31–41.

Iqbal Ahmad. "Iran and the West: A Century of Subjugation." *Christianity and Crisis* vol. 40 no. 3 (March 3, 1980): 37–44.

________ . "The Iranian Revolution: A Landmark for the Future." *Race and Class* 21 (1979): 3–11.

Ismael, I. S. and T. Y. Ismael. "Social Change in Islamic Society: The Political Thought of Ayatollah Khomeini." *Social Problems* vol. 27 no. 5 (June 1980): 601–619.

Jafri, Seyed Husain M. "The Conduct of Rule in Islam." *Hamdard Islamicus* vol II no. 1 (spring 1979): 3–34.

Kazemzadeh, F. "Ideological Crisis in Iran." in *The Middle East in Transition*. edited by Walter Laqueur, New York: Frederick A. Praeger, 1958.

Keddie Nikki R. "Iran: Change in Islam; Islam and Change." *International Journal of Middle East Studies* vol. 11 no. 4 (July 1980): 527–542.

________ . "The Origins of Religious-Radical Alliance in Iran." *Past and Present* 34 (July 1966): 70–80.

________ . "Religion and Irreligion in Early Iranian Nationalism." *Comparative Studies in Society and History* 4 (1962): 265–95.

________ . "The Roots of the Ulama's Power in Modern Iran." *Studia Islamica* XXIX (1969): 31–53.

Kedouri, Elie. "Khomeini's Political Heresy." *Policy Review* no. 12 (spring 1980): 133–146.

Kohlberg, E. "The Development of Imami Shī'ī Doctrine of Jihad." *Zeitschrift Der Deutchen Morgenlandischen Gesellschaft* 126 (1976): 64–86.

________ . "From Imamiyya to Ithna-'Ashariyya." *Bulletin of the School of Oriental and African Studies* 39 (1976): 521–34.

Kotobi, Morteza and Jean Leon, "The March Towards the Islamic Republic of

Iran; Society and Religion According to Imam Khomeini." *Le Monde Diplomalique* (April 1, 1979): 6–7.

Lambton, Ann K. S. "A Nineteenth Century View of Jihad." *Studia Islamica* XXXII (1970): 182–292.

_______ . "Persia Today." *The World Today* vol. XVII no. 2 (February 1961): 76–87.

_______ . "Quis Custodiet Custodes?" *Studia Islamica* V (1956): 125–148 and VI (1956): 125–146.

_______ . "A Reconsideration of the Position of Marja'al-Taqlid and the Religious Institution." *Studia Islamica* XX (1964): 115–136.

_______ . "Some New Trends in Islamic Political Thought in Late 18th and Early 19th Century Persia." *Studia Islamica* 39 (1974): 95–128.

_______ . "The Tobacco Regie: Prelude to Revolution." *Studia Islamica* XXII (1965): 119–57 and XXIII (1966): 71–90.

Lewis, Bernard. "The Return of Islam." *Commentary* vol. 61 no. 1 (January 1976): 39–51.

"Man of the Year; The Mystic Who Lit Fire of Hatred." *Time* (January 7, 1980): 9–32.

Matelski, Marilyn J. "Khomeini's Argument for International Justice: A Relationist Perspective." *Journal of the American Forensic Association*, vol XVII no. 4 (spring 1981): 227–233.

Mazlish, Bruce. "The Hidden Khomeini." *The New York* (December 24, 1979): 49–54.

Mazzaoui, Michael. "Shi'ism in the Medieval, Safavid, and Qajar Periods: A Study in Ithna'ashari Continuity," in *Iran: Continuity and Variety*, edited by Peter J. Chelkowski. New York: New York University, 1971.

Millward, W. G. "Aspects of Modernism in Shi'a Islam." *Studia Islamica* XXXVII (1973): 111–128.

_______ . "Ayat-Allah Khomeyni's Political Vocabulary." A paper presented at the 15th Annual Meeting of MESA, Seattle, Washington, November 4–7, 1981.

_______ . "Iranian Nationalism." *Canadian Review of Studies in Nationalism* vol. VIII (1981): 141–53.

_______ . "The Principles of Foreign Policy and the Vision of World Order Expounded by Imam Khomeyni and the Islamic Republic of Iran." in *The Iranian Revolution and the Islamic Republic: Proceedings of a Conference*, edited by Nikki Keddie and Eric Hoogland, Washington, D.C.: The Middle East Institute, 1982.

Minorsky, Vladimir. "Iran: Opposition, Martyrdom, and Revolt," in *Unity and Variety in Muslim Civilization*, edited by Gustave E. Von Grunebaum. Chicago: The University of Chicago Press, 1955.

Nasr, S. H. and M. Mutahari. "The Religious Sciences." in *The Cambridge History of Iran*, ed. by R. N. Frye. Cambridge: Cambridge University Press, 1975.

Pfau, Richard. "The Legal Status of American Forces in Iran." *The Middle East Journal* vol. 28 no. 2 (spring 1974): 141–153.

Piscatori, James P. "The Study of Islamic Politics." Conference on Islam in the Political Process, the Royal Institute of International Affairs, 24–26 June, 1981.

Ramazani, R. K. "Church and State in Modernizing Society: The Case of Iran." *The American Behavioral Scientist* vol. VII no. 5 (January 1964): 26–28.

_______. "Iran's Foreign Policy: Perspective and Projection," in *Economic Consequences of the Revolution in Iran*. Joint Economic Committee, Congress of the United States, Washington, D.C.: U.S. Government Printing Office, 1980.

_______. "Iran: 'The Islamic Cultural Revolution'." in *Change and the Muslim World*, edited by Philip H. Stoddard, David C. Cuthell, and Margaret W. Sullivan. Syracuse: Syracuse University Press, 1981.

_______. "Iran's Revolution: Patterns, Problems and Prospects." *International Affairs,* vol. 56 no. 3 (summer 1980): 443–457.

_______. "Islamic Studies: A Concept and Approach." *The Muslim World* vol. LVIII no. 4 (October, 1968): 279–283.

_______. "Khomeyni's Islam in Iran's Foreign Policy." A paper presented to the Royal Institute of International Affairs in London, July 13, 1982.

Rashīdī-Motlaq, Ahmad. "Iran va Este'mār Sorkh va Sīyāh." [Iran and Black and Red Colonialism]. *Eṭṭelā'āt* (January 7, 1978): 8.

Rezvani, M. E. "Ruznāmeh Shaykh Fazl-Allah Nuri." [Shaykh Fazl-Allah Nuri's Newsletters]. *Tarikh* vol. I no. 2 (1356/1977): 159–209.

Richard, Yann. "Contemporary Shi'i Thought." in Nikki Keddie. *Roots of Revolution*. New Haven: Yale University Press, 1981.

Rodinson, Maxime. "Reveil de l'integrisme musulman?" *Le Monde* (December 6, 7 and 8, 1978).

Ross, Lester. "Khomeini's Iran and Mao's China: Crises of Charismatic Authority." *Asian Thought and Society* vol. 5 no. 14 (September 1980): 150–159.

Rouleau, Eric. "Khomeyni's Iran." *Foreign Affairs* vol. 50 no. 1 (Fall, 1980): 1–20.

Rubin, Barry. "Iran's Year in Turmoil." *Current History* (January 1983): 28–31.

Sachedina, Abdulaziz. "Al-Khums: The Fifth in the Imami Shi'i Legal System." *Journal of Near Eastern Studies* vol. 39 no. 4 (October 1980): 275–289.

_______. "A Treatise on the Occultation of the Twelfth Imamate Imam." *Studia Islamica* vol. 48 (1978): 109–124.

Scarcia, G. "Intorno alle Controversie tra Ahbari e Usuli Persso gli Imamiti di Persid." *Rivista degli Studi Orientali* XXXIII (1958): 211–50.

Shari'ati, 'Ali. "Din va Siyasat." [Religion and Politics]. *Masā'el Jahān* vol. 6 nos. 9–10 (January 1979): 16–22.

Siegman, H. "The State and the Individual in Sunni Islam." *The Muslim World* vol. LIV no. 1 (January 1964): 14–26.

Steinbach, Udo. "Iran—Half Time in the Islamic Revolution?" *Aussen Politik* [English ed.], vol. 31 no. 1 (1980): 52–68.

Tabataba'i, Muhammad Mohit. "Chegūnegī-ye Peydāyesh-e Maktab-e Mashrūṭe dar Irān." [How the Notion of Constitutionalism came about in Iran]. *Tehrān Moṣavar*. no. 1350 (June 1969).

Taqi-zadeh, Seyyed Hassan. "Doure-ye Jadīd." [The New Era]. *Kāveh* vol. 5 no. 1 (January 22, 1920): 1-2.

Tehranian, Majid. "Iran: Communication, Alienation, Revolution." *Intermedia* (London edition), vol. 7 no. 2 (March 1979): 6–12.

Thompson, Kenneth W. "Dogmas and International Realities," in *Religion and International Affairs*, edited by Jeffrey Rose and Michael Ignatieff, Toronto: House of Anansi, 1968.

Watt, W. M. "The Conception of the Charismatic Community in Islam." *Numen* vol. VII (1960): 76–90.

_______ . "Condition of Membership of the Islamic Community." *Studia Islamica* vol. 21 (1964): 5–12.

Young, Cuyler T. "The Problem of Westernization in Modern Iran." *The Middle East Journal* vol. 2 no. 1 (1948): 47–59.

Zubaida, Sami. "The Ideological Conditions for Khomeini's Doctrine of Government." *Economy and Society* vol. 11 no. 2 (May 1982): 138–172.

Unpublished Sources

Abu-Sulayman, Abdul-Hamid Ahmad. *The Islamic Theory of International Relations: Its Relevance, Past and Present*. Ph.D. Dissertation, University of Pennsylvania 1973.

Bakhtiari, Bahman. *A Comparison of the Ideologies of 'Ali Shari'ati and the People's Mojahedin in Iran*. Masters Thesis, Charlottesville: University of Virginia, May 1981.

Cadler, Norman. *The Structure of Authority in Imami Shi'i Jurisprudence*. Ph.D. Dissertation, University of London, 1980.

Campbell, W. R. and Djamchid Darvich. "The Totalitarian Implication of Khomeyni's Conception of Islamic Consciousness." Unpublished paper. Copy in author's possession.

Faghfoory, Muhammad Hassan. *The Role of the Ulama in Twentieth Century Iran with Particular Reference to Ayatullah Haj Sayyid Abul-Qasim Kashani*. Ph.D. Dissertation, Madison: University of Wisconsin, 1978.

Ferdows, Adele K. *Religion in Iranian Nationalism: The Study of the Fadayan-i-Islam*. Ph.D. Dissertation, Indiana University, 1970.

Garaussian, Vida (Riazi-Davoudi). *The Ulama and Secularization in Contemporary Iran*. Ph.D. Dissertation, Southern Illinois University, August, 1974.

Keddie, Nikke R. *The Impact of the West on Iranian Social History*. Ph.D. Dissertation, University of California at Berkeley, 1955.

MacEoin, M. Denis. *From Shaykhism to Babism: A Study in Charismatic Renewal in Shi'i Islam*. Ph.D. Dissertation, King's College, Cambridge, July 1979.

Millward, M. G. "The Political System of Islam in the Writings of Ayatollah Khomeyni, 1943–1970." Unpublished paper, January 1981. Copy in author's possession.

Piscatori, James, *Islam and the International Legal Order*. Ph.D. Dissertation, University of Virginia, Charlottesville, Virginia, May 1976.